GUATEMALAN JOURNEY

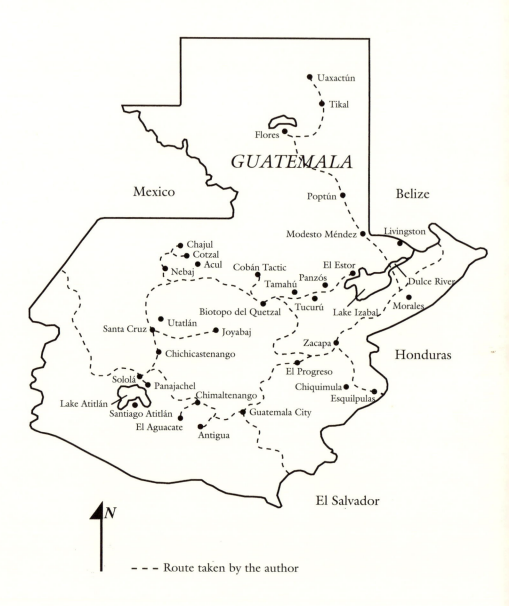

Uaxactún

Tikal

Flores

GUATEMALA

Mexico

Belize

Poptún

Modesto Méndez

Livingston

Chajul
Cotzal
Acul
Nebaj
Cobán Tactic
El Estor
Tamahú
Panzós
Dulce River
Biotopo del Quetzal
Tucurú
Morales
Utatlán
Lake Izabal
Santa Cruz
Joyabaj
Chichicastenango
Zacapa
Honduras
Sololá
El Progreso
Panajachel
Chiquimula
Lake Atitlán
Chimaltenango
Esquilpulas
Santiago Atitlán
Guatemala City
El Aguacate
Antigua

El Salvador

↑*N*

- - - Route taken by the author

GUATEMALAN JOURNEY

by Stephen Connely Benz

 UNIVERSITY OF TEXAS PRESS, AUSTIN

First edition, 1996

Requests for permission to reproduce material from this work should be sent to Permissions, University of Texas Press, Box 7819, Austin, TX 78713–7819.

The paper used in this publication meets the minimum requirements of American National Standard for Information Sciences—Permanence of Paper for Printed Library materials, ANZI Z39, 48-1984.

Library of Congress Cataloging-in-Publication Data

Benz, Stephen Connely, 1958–
    Guatemalan journey / by Stephen Connely Benz. — 1st ed.
        p.   cm.
    Includes bibliographical references (p.   ) and index.
    ISBN 0-292-70839-4 (alk. paper). — ISBN 0-292-70840-8 (pbk. : alk. paper)
    1. Guatemala—Description and travel.   2. Guatemala—History—1985–   3. Americans—Guatemala.   4. Benz, Stephen Connely, 1958–   . I. Title.
    F1464.3.B45   1996
    972.81—dc20   95-11138

To my mother, who taught me the value of poetry.
To my father, who taught me the value of reason.

Contents

Acknowledgments

I WOULD LIKE TO THANK the Fulbright Scholar Program, the Council for International Exchange of Scholars, the United States Information Agency, and the staff at the US embassy in Guatemala for providing the grant that allowed me to spend two years in Guatemala. The faculty and staff at the Universidad de San Carlos, especially those at CALUSAC, the Center for Language Study, merit special thanks for their kindness, their hospitality, and their conversation. Dean Hugh Ripley of the Barry University Library was most supportive in tracking down any odd book I requested. Theresa May, executive editor, and the rest of the staff at the University of Texas Press have been most enjoyable to work with as we have proceeded toward publication. Rachel Benz, Nathan Benz, and Stevie Benz shared the experience of Guatemala with me and made it the richer for their presence; furthermore, they helped keep me sane while I was writing the manuscript. Cheryl Benz provided valuable feedback and unflagging support when the work turned tedious. I love them very much. Finally, I thank Paul Caldwell-Jones, whose willingness to sink ever lower into the seedy side of the country provided me with anecdotes and information without which the text would be sorely lacking. His friendship was certainly one of the best parts of my sojourn.

GUATEMALAN JOURNEY

Los Encuentros

The phrase book tells me I'm at a crossroads,
I should expect encounters
in the vellum margins of this highway
where buses cough black clouds
and hanging men cry out destinations
I cannot find on the map.
I've heard rumors of what lies
ahead, the incidents hidden in hairpin
turns, dire straits for those who seek
passage through gullies, ravines, lava valleys.
The topography of this country
an explorer said, is like a crumpled page:
palimpsest mountains, parchment plains,
hieroglyphic highlands awaiting interpretation.
Lexicographers take notes on each twisting
nuance in the road, turns of phrase promise
arrival or departure, movement along this text
I'm traveling. I read ahead
through the codex of curves
and straightaways to the congested towns
where babblers hail strangers
in unrelated vocables.
I study the morphemes in a parrot's squawk,
signals sent up in volcano smoke,
stories revealed in aboriginal textile.
I skim long vistas of calligraphied macadam,
an endless panorama of road signs encoding
a traveler's tale, a new message.
But the phrase book's no help now,
it all translates the same—
I'm at a crossroads,
expecting encounters, still waiting.

STEPHEN CONNELY BENZ

Prologue

IN LATE NOVEMBER OF 1988—three months into my sojourn in Guatemala—two apparently unrelated events occurred on the same day. The coincidence helped me perceive the ambiguity inherent in Guatemala's social reality.

First, only a few blocks from my house, a new mall opened. This mall—Megacentro—featured more than seventy stores and that latest idea in US mall design, the food court. Megacentro imitated US malls in every aspect. It was anchored on either end by two giants in Guatemalan merchandising, the Paíz supermarket and the Cemaco home store. On the day I walked over for the grand opening, Christmas decorations were going up, and a huge crowd turned out to see the new marvel, the latest evidence of Guatemala's progress.

It was a festive day, and everyone was caught up in the excitement of Christmas shopping. Families looked over clothing and electronics while Christmas songs (a marimba version of "Chestnuts Roasting on an Open Fire") played over the sound system. I sat on the edge of a sparkling fountain and watched while window shoppers strolled the mall, dreaming of the day they could own the marvelous gadgets on display. According to some people, in the near future western liberal democratic capitalism might finally establish itself here, and Guatemala would become like Albuquerque or San Juan or Honolulu: just another neocolonized place with malls and freeways and suburban subdivisions. Megacentro seemed to signal the arrival of the future Guatemala, a Guatemala in which western-style consumerism would thrive and people would be happy because they could buy and sell and buy still more. When the US government or the Guatemalan elite said that Guatemala must be saved from communism, they located the country's salvation in places like Megacentro. Megacentro was a reification of their ideology, a tangible rejection of all the things that, according to this view, had debilitated Guatemala for so long—things like communist subversion and backward indigenes.

The next day the newspapers reported that a massacre had occurred in a little hamlet near Chimaltenango. At some time during the day of Megacentro's grand opening—perhaps even as the Christmas crowds milled about in front of the prettily decorated stores and sampled the treats at the food court—twenty-two men in the tiny *aldea* of El Aguacate were dragged from their homes and murdered.

In the days following the massacre, the newspapers were filled with accusations. The army's spokesman declared, "This massacre committed by terrorism is lamentable." The Christian Democratic government sided with the military and stated in no uncertain terms that the guerrillas were responsible. President Cerezo told the press, "It's enough to speak with the people of the hamlet for one to know that the guerrillas are responsible for the kidnapping and massacre."

The Unidad Revolucionaria Nacional Guatemalteca (URNG), "the voice of the guerrilla Left," offered a different version of events in its statement to the press: "The URNG accuses the army of being responsible for the massacre. It is totally and absolutely false that guerrilla forces of the URNG or the Organization of People in Arms (ORPA) would commit a massive kidnapping and murder of peasants." The URNG believed that the false accusation was part of "a carefully orchestrated plan" by the government and the army "to blame the revolutionary movement for the atrocities that are committed by them. This crafty action shows the degree of desperation of the high command of the army in light of the failure of their military offensives and their impotence to obtain victories against the guerrillas."

Cerezo and the government responded that the guerrilla claims had no basis, "since the government has the credibility of the population."

For several days, the newspapers carried scores of these denunciations and counter-denunciations. A typical article would lead off with a headline such as "PR Denounces Massacre." The column-length story would then tell how the organization's spokesman had issued a statement condemning the massacre (a safe enough position to take if no direct accusation was made). The spokesman then would go on to warn the public that "the continuation of a situation wherein elements operated outside of the law and disrupted society" was unacceptable and changes were necessary. Vague and contorted language typified these statements. Every politician, every party, every group—and they were legion—rushed to get a pronouncement in the newspaper.

It was clear that in Guatemala City there was little chance of learning anything about the massacre. To find out more, I decided to go to Chimaltenango and El Aguacate to see for myself. I went on the day of the funeral for the massacre victims.

Chimaltenango is thirty miles from Guatemala City out the Pan-American Highway, a bus ride of about an hour. There, I switched to a smaller, more decrepit bus for the dusty ride to San Andrés Itzapa. The bus was crowded. Feeling conspicuous, I stood in the rear and held onto a seat back. People were somber that day, and there was almost no talking. Some babies cried abruptly and then were hushed back to sleep. The driver and his assistant, ladinos, tried to keep up a jolly banter, but soon they too lapsed into silence, the driver's concentration drawn back to the road, which was obscured by the dust swirling in the wake of passing cars. The traffic to Itzapa was heavy that day; the press went to cover the funeral, and even some dignitaries put in an appearance.

Itzapa was the end of the bus line. From its tiny plaza, I had to walk to El Aguacate, a mile or so out of town. The day was warm. A high, bright sun beat down on the procession of people walking the rough road to El Aguacate. It was the dry season, and the corn stalks in the fields had withered. The paperlike husks drifted in the hard, hot wind, fell to the dusty road, and crackled under the feet of those who passed. Acotenango Volcano towered above, its peak just barely covered by a huge, hovering cloud. Little rectangular farms patchworked the volcano's lower slope. Somewhere in the rugged wilderness of the upper slopes, the ORPA guerrillas were thought to hide. All during the walk, I could hear the distant, monotonous chop of helicopters. The army routinely bombarded the volcano, a random bombing that reminded me of Marlow's description in *Heart of Darkness* of a French gunboat shelling the African coast.

In Aguacate, I followed the funeral procession to the cemetery. It was like a scene from a Latin American novel. Twenty coffins were carried up a hill of rocks. The wind whipped up dust and swirled it everywhere. It was still morning, but the sun felt intense, and the heat seemed to slow the march. The progress of the coffins was labored. The wails of the mourners, who were mostly women and mostly indigenous, their polychromatic garb covered by black shawls, echoed off canyon walls. About three thousand people made up the procession, many of them crying, inconsolable, bereft. The last three hundred meters up to the cemetery were very rough. The path became steep and rocks gave way under the feet of the mourners. Several people fell, and rocks tumbled down on those trailing behind. The dust caused people to cough. The wind and the heat contributed to an overdone and tedious symbolism.

At the cemetery, the mourners filled in every available space around the mounds and crosses. Some perched atop the larger adobe memorials. The surrounding trees—cedars, eucalyptus, and ceibas—bent and shimmied in the hot breeze, leaves coated with dust.

When the coffins were arranged on the ground alongside the twenty new holes, the widows rushed forward and threw themselves down, shouting "Rise! Rise!" and "Where are you?" Relatives tried to catch and hold the widows, and everywhere there were groups of weeping people kneeling in the dirt. A few women fainted by the coffins. They were taken up by friends, but no attempt was made to revive them.

Now the crowd turned its attention to three men who stood by the graves—the priest, the village mayor, and an evangelical minister. The priest prayed out loud: "Let it be known they were humble men, innocent men, ready to serve their community." He choked with sobs as he spoke, and the rush of the wind drowned his weakened voice. The coffins were blessed. Everyone, except the evangelicals, signed the cross on their breasts, and the tedious work of lowering the twenty coffins began. I stood at the edge of the crowd, able to see because I was taller than the natives. Behind me, where the road ended, were some luxury cars and four-wheel drive vehicles: the Guatemala City contingent. One man stood on the roof of a Chevy Blazer taking pictures. The word *PRENSA* (Press) was taped to the Blazer's door.

There were no clues as to why this massacre happened. No one suggested any direct motive for the unknown perpetrators other than deception. The army believed that the guerrillas did it in order to blame the army. The guerrillas argued that the army did it in order to blame the guerrillas. What either side hoped to gain by conducting a massacre only to blame the other side was unclear. The army's official announcement—though purposefully ambiguous—sounded obvious enough: "These acts were committed by groups acting outside the law."

From my perspective, newly arrived in the country, it was difficult to understand why such things seemed to happen so often in Guatemala. The president spoke of a "society frightened by *la violencia* (the violence)," a phrase used in Guatemala in the same ambiguous and ominous way that "the troubles" is used in Ireland. Violence in Guatemala seemed random and unattributable. A priest named Father Girón, leader of a peasant organization, noted that violence had been injected into the social system, like a virus: "The deteriorating social situation of Guatemala ends sooner or later in violence." I was reminded of what Graham Greene wrote about Mexico in *The Lawless Roads*. The ideals of the Mexican Revolution were gone by the

1930s, according to Greene, and the country's endemic violence, unattached to any cause and lacking in significance, just went on and on.

The only certain thing about this massacre in El Aguacate was that twenty-two people were dead. Maybe it didn't really matter who was ultimately responsible. The fact that someone or some group thought that there was something to be gained by murdering twenty-two peasants indicated how gravely amiss things were in contemporary Guatemala. The worst, as Yeats put it, were filled with a passionate intensity.

Caught in the middle of all the clamor were the bewildered peasants—the landless Indians, the widows wailing and fainting and crying for the dead to rise. They were the true *desconocidos*, unknown for nearly five hundred years as anything other than objects in the struggles between one cause or another—conquest, Christianity, capitalism, communism. For the rulers of Guatemala the massacre came at an inconvenient time. For three years they had been trying to forget *la violencia*. The president had called on the country to forget the past, to begin anew without looking back, without investigating, without making accusations or demanding justice. Unlike Argentina's leaders, Guatemala's rulers did not want closure. There was no one to cry out, "Nunca más (No more)." The staff of the US embassy certainly wanted to forget the past. During a decade of particularly brutal military regimes, the staff had sweated over the statistics and had tried to juggle the draconian numbers. With the election of a civilian president in 1986, all that was supposed to be past and forgotten. Guatemala had been declared a model of democracy for Central America. But suddenly, once again, all the denials, all the claims were negated. The trouble that always seemed to be boiling beneath the surface had bubbled up again. In foreign newspapers, Guatemala's name appeared one more time as it so often had before: in a brief article reporting random, senseless violence. To outsiders, the massacre at Aguacate was yet another sad moment in a long history in which violence, without the support of any particular ideals, just went on and on. For me, it was the beginning of a difficult struggle to better understand a place where malls and massacres could be so strangely juxtaposed.

PART ONE
GUATEMALA CITY

Arrival

GUATEMALA CITY WAS NOT at all as I remembered it. Ten years had passed since I last traveled through, a college student on a grand tour in search of some ambiguous combination of Shangri-La and the Heart of Darkness. But in my first few hours in Guatemala City this time around, I could see that it was not what I had remembered, not even close. For one thing, it was now September—cool and rainy and lush. Before, I had come in April, the driest, hottest month, when the hills were parched and brown and the city was engulfed in haze from burning cornfields. Now the hills were dense with rainy season verdure. Purple jacarandas and red bougainvillea flamed above the streets, and the cloying smell of tropical fecundity dominated the senses.

Back then, in the late 1970s, Guatemala was just beginning to earn its international reputation as a nightmarish place where politics was brutal and horrific. Those were the sanguinary days when General Lucas García was president: tanks and troops stood sentinel in the capital; there were informal curfews, frequent blackouts; and the downtown, where I was staying in a seedy hotel, was an eerie place after nightfall. The nights proved long, hot, and tortuous, and I lay awake thinking about Costa Rica and the quiet, cool nights there when I had caroused into the small hours and had never given a second glance at a national guardsman. But in Guatemala, my Central American jaunt turned ugly. The highlands were difficult to visit, the guerrillas were surging, and the police were suspicious of everyone. I rushed through the nearly vacant tourist sites—Antigua, Chichicastenango, Panajachel—and got out along the coastal route to Mexico just before the US embassy issued travelers' warnings for those areas.

In the intervening years, Guatemala had suffered through a long, dark, hellish night. Or so the reports issued by groups such as Amnesty International and Americas Watch led one to believe. The titles of these reports evoked the terror of the place: *Guatemala: A Nation of Prisoners; False Hope, False Freedom; Messengers of Death.* Over the years I had followed the desultory news and wondered at the horror that had befallen that picturesque country—one of the loveliest on earth according to even the most jaded travelers.

Throughout the 1980s, dramatic events in El Salvador, Nicaragua, and then Panama stole the headlines coming out of Central America. One heard less and less about Guatemala, as though it had been cast down to the deepest circle in the Inferno of nations, a benighted land of unspeakable horror, whose very name was now synonymous with tyranny, repression, death squads, and massacres.

When in 1988 I was offered the chance to go back to Guatemala as a Fulbright scholar, I was both excited and leery. I had waited a decade for this chance, but I wanted my family to go, too. Could I possibly even consider taking three small children to such a place? The Fulbright administrators in Washington assured us that things were fine, just fine, in Guatemala; what with a newly elected government and "lower levels" of violence, Guatemala had become a great place for a family. Now that the country had held an election and chosen a civilian president, the Reagan administration had even begun lauding Guatemala as a "model democracy," the region's great success story.

Well, we were not exactly talking about Orlando, and I remained dubious. In fact, a book called *Guatemala: Eternal Spring, Eternal Tyranny* (by Jean-Marie Simon) was just out, and I read it with increasing despair. Guatemala seemed as bad as or worse than ever. No one outside of the US government had anything good to say about the place. The Guatemala News and Information Bureau's report for January/February 1988 told of continued disappearances and deaths. Guatemala, it seemed, had not changed as significantly as the Washington administrators would have it. We arrived in Guatemala nervous, apprehensive, and prepared for a nightmare worthy of Orwell or the Third Reich.

But Guatemala, in those first few hours of my return, was neither the place I had remembered nor the place I had been reading about in the months previous. We had touched down in an entirely different Guatemala. Months later, I would look back on that arrival and appreciate the subtleties of its lessons; but at the time I felt nothing except relief—relief upon realizing, as the taxi took us out of the airport and along Avenida 7 of Zona 9 to our hotel, that we had arrived not in a land of terror but in what looked like a rather pleasant place of tree-lined avenues, expensive automobiles, and chic shops. We passed North American burger and chicken franchises fronted by large playgrounds swarming with happy children. We passed galleries of native art and fashionable boutiques, and as we drove around the Plazuela España and continued up Avenida 7, I could not believe the number of late-model luxury cars on the streets of Guatemala City. It was something of a shock to have made the long journey to a Third World country—one of the poorest in the hemisphere, according to the statistics I had seen—only to discover landscaped avenues and speeding BMWs.

That first weekend provided numerous surprises. From our hotel, the Villa Española, we walked down Avenida Reforma—a wide boulevard divided by a grassy, tree-shaded strip—to the American embassy. The embassy side of Reforma was located in exclusive Zona 10, a part of the city I did not visit on my first trip. Large estates and beautiful houses stood partially hidden behind high walls and huge eucalyptus trees.

Near the US embassy, we sat down to a brunch of pastries and coffee at a German-style pastry shop tucked away from the street in a large wooded enclosure. Classical music played on the radio. Children climbed on a swing set near the patio. A glass showcase held row after row of fine chocolates. The patrons read newspapers and chatted amicably. I found it hard to believe that this was the horrible place I had been reading about.

What I learned that first weekend, or rather what I began to learn, was one of the important lessons of my sojourn: you cannot anticipate a place like Guatemala; it defies facile definition. On arriving at the scene of turmoil, you often find, as Orwell did when he shot the elephant in Burma, that "a story always sounds clear enough at a distance, but the nearer you get to the scene of events the vaguer it becomes" ("Shooting an Elephant"). I began to realize, as I sipped espresso and ate a nut paste croissant, that Guatemala was much more complicated than I had thought. My black-and-white perception of the place would have to be revised to account for the all-too-obvious gray that I saw all around me. I would somehow have to account for the existence of pleasant pastry shops and wooded grounds where polite—extremely polite—Guatemalan families enjoyed a little conversation over espresso while Brahms played in the background.

These people were wealthy ladinos, the Hispanic minority who ruled Guatemala and were described in such disparaging terms in the publications of the human rights organizations. Yet here they appeared highly cultured and sophisticated, not bigoted killers at all. I remembered a college professor once telling the class how difficult it had been for him to adjust his thinking about South Africa after he had met white Dutch Reform Church ministers in Johannesburg.

They were good-hearted, devout Christian people who were meek, loving, and generous, and yet who supported apartheid. Something similar was going on in Guatemala, it seemed. The professor's conclusion was that good intentions, goodwill, even a "good heart" were not enough. The kindest people, he said, could support the cruelest policies. As I was to discover in the years to come, things would be much easier to understand if our black-and-white picture of a country like Guatemala held true once we got to know the place. But of course things are never so simple.

The Capital for Tourists

GUATEMALA CITY, the largest city in Central America (approximately two million people in 1990), has never been a favorite of travelers. Aldous Huxley, for example, called it a "rather ugly town" (*Beyond the Mexique Bay*) and more recently Paul Theroux (*The Old Patagonian Express*) dismissed it as commonplace, somber, and brutal. Tourists, more interested in the renowned sites of the highlands and the jungles, typically spend only a night or two in the capital, and then only if they cannot avoid it altogether. This slighting of the capital is understandable; anyone with only a short time to spend in Guatemala should naturally prefer to visit Antigua, Atitlán, and Tikal. The capital offers little of the exotica that travelers look for. Instead, it seems to present a tableau of pollution, overcrowding, car jams, homeless beggars, and street children—in short, all the problems besetting other sprawling Third World cities. In that sense, Guatemala City has much in common with Manila, Kingston, and Dakar. If you've been to one, you know all you need to know about Guatemala City. Better to head for the highlands. From expatriates, from tourists, and from embassy personnel, I heard endless denigration of the place. In my entire time there, I didn't hear one foreigner, not even one living in the capital, say that he or she actually liked Guatemala City.

I actually liked Guatemala City. Its problems and its ugliness in comparison with the rest of the country could not really be denied, but "Guate" (as everyone calls it) also had, for the person who lived there long enough to appreciate it, a certain character, not charm exactly, and certainly not sophistication, but a sort of nervous energy that was appealing only over a period of time.

To be sure, Guatemala City offers little to the tourist. Nineteenth-century travel writers, such as John Lloyd Stephens, Henry Dunn, and Helen Sanborn, considered the capital a modern oasis in a primitive wilderness. These travelers were relieved just to arrive in a place with some of the civilized amenities they were accustomed to. Before airplanes Guatemala City, surrounded by what seemed a vast wasteland, was the goal of a harsh and trying overland journey from the ports on either coast. But by the mid-twentieth century, airplanes had turned the capital into the starting point of a Guatemalan odyssey, and the surrounding "wasteland" was discovered to have remarkable attractions, such as ancient ruins, natural beauty, and aboriginal cultures. Meanwhile, the erstwhile oasis grew ugly, polluted, and overcrowded, to the point that tourists often spent no more than a night in the capital, and a disagreeable night at that.

One quick bus tour easily takes in what passes for tourist attractions in the capital. First, there is the map in Minerva Park, a very large relief map built in the early part of the twentieth century. Minerva Park, formerly the horse-racing track, is in Zona 2, an old section of the city built according to the familiar Spanish scheme of square streets and plazas. Minerva is Guatemala City's best park and just about the only public place in town where one can escape the congestion and ubiquitous filth of the capital. The map depicts the volcanoes of Guatemala in relief; but the vertical scale, for some odd reason, is much greater than the horizontal scale, making the volcanoes look more like elongated stalagmites. A tower gives the visitor an aerial view of the whole map, so that one can try to identify places one has visited. The tower also affords a pleasant panorama of the park's activities—families strolling, lovers lolling, children scurrying and gamboling. The more fortunate children entertain themselves by dropping sticks into the nation's rivers—represented by running water on the relief map. The unfortunate children, who know no holiday, try to sell candies and gum, or trail the well-to-do, offering to shine shoes.

After Minerva Park, the standard tour takes tourists downtown to Zona 1 for a colonial church crawl followed by a tedious inspection of the National Palace. The jaded, worldly traveler finds little of interest here. The churches are bulky and bland—particularly bland in the case of the metropolitan cathedral, a squat baroque structure with an almost bare interior, on the Plaza Central. The National Palace is an architectural monstrosity, horizontal and heavy, its concrete walls faced with imitation stone of an odd snot-green color. Enhancing it all is a patchwork of clashing ornamental styles. Inside, decorating the main stairways, there are some maudlin murals depicting Guatemalan history from Maya times to independence, with Don Quixote making an inexplicable cameo appearance.

Perhaps the Quixote theme is meant to reflect on the man who ordered the palace built, Jorge Ubico. Ubico was Guatemala's president and dictator from 1931 to 1944, and one of the more imaginative and capricious leaders that the country has had. Ubico came from a wealthy coffee family, but he built his power base during a military career and effectively used the army as a means to the presidency. Ubico fancied himself a Napoleon look-alike and did what he could to further the resemblance in his dress and habits. Despite a riding accident that left him impotent, Ubico affected the typical macho swagger necessary for political success in Central America.

Ubico timed things right. Guatemala was in a bad way in the late 1920s, when Ubico, then in his forties, formed his own political party. A succession of corrupt regimes had depleted the country of its wealth. By 1930, supposedly, no more than twenty-seven dollars remained in the national treasury. When yet another coup confused matters further, the United States, settling into its newfound role as international busybody, got tired of it all and stepped in, slapped some hands, then named an acting president to supervise a new election.

By 1931, Ubico had won favor with the gringos by touting a strong anticommunist line (so strong, in fact, he was a great admirer of Mussolini, Franco, and Hitler). In winning the election, Ubico set what must be a record for a free-world election: he won unanimously. If stability was what the US embassy wanted, it got it. Ubico remained president and dictator for thirteen years (he named himself president-for-life, but a popular revolution drove him out in 1944). The United States could be satisfied, too, with Ubico's record of public works. For the first time since Ubico's godfather, Justo Rufino Barrios, was president in the 1870s, the Guatemalan government was mobilized for the public good. In particular, Ubico concentrated on building a highway system. Cynics said that the president's fondness for motorcycling motivated his interest in the infrastructure, but the embassy was unconcerned about that kind of detail. Nor was the United States concerned about Ubico's heavy-handedness with opponents, nor bothered by a labor law that required Indians to work harvests on the haciendas owned by ladinos (including, of course, Ubico's own extensive plantations). These, in the US view, were trifling matters compared with the stability and the solidly pro-American stance that Ubico maintained while in the presidential palace. (He wavered a bit in the early days of World War II, unable to suppress his respect for Hitler and Mussolini; but he eventually came around, especially when it became apparent that the Allies would win the war.) Ubico said, "While I am president, I will not grant liberty of the press, nor of association, because the people of Guatemala are not prepared for democracy and need a strong hand." This attitude suited the Americans just fine.

The man had an ego a bit too big for the existing national palace. Thus, as part of his public works program, he ordered a grander palace built—the green monster that now sits on the Plaza Central. Unfortunately for Jorge Ubico, he was toppled from power only months after the palace's completion.

After the Plaza Central, one's tour of the city usually includes a dash through the central market, where tourists can shop for *típica*, a Spanish word that every visitor to Guatemala uses to refer to the various indigenous products—clothing, fabric, handbags—that have become fairly popular in the United States and Europe. Some of the goods are of high quality, but most of it—especially that sold at the central market—is tawdry and poorly made. Tourists seem to prefer getting a bargain to paying for good quality, and the Guatemalan merchants naturally give them what they want. As a consequence, the real art of native *típica* is being lost—driven out by the tourists' demand for cheap bargains. I had the impression that the *típica* sold at the central market in the capital was especially shoddy. The shopkeepers were mostly ladinos (no doubt the rent charged for a booth at the market was beyond the means of most Indians), and they bought in large volume from the craftspeople out in the highlands villages. To fill an order for a thousand blouses, the producers must surely cut corners. The traditional weaving method, using a backstrap loom, is slow, laborious, and dedicated to detail—undesirable qualities in the mass-production process. The ladino merchants, and some gringos as well, have introduced more rapid and efficient methods of garment production. As a result, the quality of the *típica* has diminished rapidly, and some collectors fear that the art of Guatemalan weaving might be lost because of it.

This decline in quality can best be seen if one goes to the Ixchel Museum in Zona 10. Guatemala's best museum, the Ixchel houses a collection of Indian textiles from all over the country. Many of the textiles are several generations old. Their sophistication, artistry, and craftsmanship are evident in the tight weave and intricate designs of the garments on display—a telling contrast to the poor quality of the goods for sale in the central market.

There are a few other museums in the capital, none quite so good as the Ixchel. Near the airport, in Aurora Park, stands the Museum of Archaeology, a pleasant museum with a small but intriguing display. An archaeologist friend told me that the collection was actually quite extensive but the building lacked the facility for displaying more of it. A visit to the museum was especially enlightening after a tour of Tikal, the Maya city.

Across the street from Archaeology stands the Museum of Natural History, which in our family became known as the museum of stuffed animals. Hundreds of stuffed birds, reptiles, and mammals were displayed under or behind glass. They looked decidedly dead, their death throes unerringly captured, as though the whole idea had been to display animal agonies. Some of the animals were placed in displays designed to replicate the natural habitat of the species in question. The phony scenery only heightened the macabre taxidermy, and one left the museum convinced that all aboriginal fauna had long ago disappeared from the country.

Aurora Park is also home to the zoo, a pleasant place where the animals are somewhat more lively than those in the Museum of Natural History. For a tourist, the zoo is the best place to see, albeit caged, some of Central America's unusual animals—peccaries, coatis, agoutis, jaguarundis, and (my favorite) tepezcuintles. The zoo, a popular Sunday attraction, also proved a good place for observing Guatemalans. The people of Guatemala, especially the poor, work very hard, often ten hours a day or more, six days a week. They reserve Sunday for diversion, dressing for the occasion in their best clothes. On Sundays, the zoo is crowded with thousands of immaculately dressed people enjoying a few brief hours away from their struggle to make ends meet.

For the tourist, Guatemala has ever been a deceptive land. For the most part you see pleasant pastry shops in the chic zones, quiet, musty museums, crowded parks full of happy people. It is so easy to forget or ignore the fact that many of the children around you, dressed in such handsome outfits, are malnourished; or that the men and women are spending two or three days' wages just to have a picnic in the park and buy some balloons, some colas, maybe go for a ride on the Ferris wheel. It is easy to forget that, if these same "happy" people ever thought to complain about their poverty, if they ever took some action like forming a union, they could well turn up dead, tossed into a ravine by a death squad. Most tourists during the late 1980s didn't know that a few hundred yards from the zoo was the entrance to an army post where, just behind the gate, there was a sign that read, "We will have peace in Guatemala only when the army imposes it."

Right at the entrance to the zoo, in fact, stands a huge monument to Guatemala's deceptiveness. This is the giant statue of Tecún Umán, Guatemala's Indian hero. Every Guatemalan knows the story of Tecún Umán, a Quiché chief who fought Central America's conquistador, Pedro de Alvarado, in a protracted hand-to-hand struggle. The fight set the paradigm for the future: Tecún Umán lost. His defeat was poetic and honorable, the stuff of tragedy; and it is the poetic, honorable, and tragic side of his story that is memorialized in statues, depicted on half-quetzal notes, and read about in textbooks. But Guatemalans have not failed to learn as well the concomitant message embedded in Tecún Umán's story: that the Indian was inferior; that no matter how nobly he fought, the Indian was doomed, the victory of the white conqueror inevitable. Every mestizo in Guatemala, every person of mixed Spanish-Indian descent, repeats in his or her soul the battle between Alvarado and Tecún Umán. And in each the result is inevitable: no matter how much pride the mestizo takes in the Indian's fierce final stand, it is in the end pride in something defeated and dead. Over and over again, the Spaniard wins, an ineluctable triumph of the stranger over the native. The Indian is suppressed; it is only in statues and other memorials that mestizos give voice to their Indian side (for example, the Misses Guatemala—always ladinas—often wear outfits of Indian design in the costume segment of the Miss Universe contest—and Guatemala once won the award for best costume; similarly, Guatemala's Olympic team sometimes attends the opening ceremonies in Indian-inspired garb). In all other aspects of life, they deny it, even despise it. It is thus ironic that a military government erected this statue of an Indian hero. The statue suggests that Guatemala regards its Indian heritage with pride, and that the ladinos, especially those in power, want to exalt that Indian heritage. Such is not the case. Pride and respect for the aboriginal culture is only an abstract concept for the ladino rulers. Statues might be erected for Tecún Umán as a symbolic gesture, but otherwise, Indian culture is rejected, demeaned, and brutalized. The honoring of Indian roots is a fiction.

Besides the statue of Tecún Umán, there is one other monument that all tourists are likely to see, if only because its location makes it unavoidable. Around town this monument—if such it is—is known as *"la torre,"* the tower. Guatemala City's tower, a smaller-sized replica of the Eiffel Tower, straddles a large intersection in a business district. There is nothing about the tower that would prove of interest to the tourist; it is not particularly photogenic; you cannot go to the top of it. It is just there, an amusing oddity, the kind of thing that would make you, upon first seeing it, scoff and say, "Just what in hell is that supposed to be?" And then, on second thought, you might decide to take a picture of it—just because it is odd and amusing and will provoke some laughs when shown to the folks back home.

The tower is dedicated to Justo Rufino Barrios, a president of Guatemala in the 1880s. Barrios was the great Liberal who, after seizing the presidency in a military coup, set about retooling the government according to Liberal principles. He reformed education, restricted the power of the Catholic Church, and built up the nation's infrastructure. It was also Barrios who promoted coffee as a cash crop and thus changed in a matter of a few years the face of the highlands. In order to support the fledgling coffee economy, Barrios created a transportation system where none had previously existed. Roads, railroads, and ports began to appear for the first time on maps of Guatemala. All together, this ambitious Liberal program constituted the period called La Reforma. This reform is memorialized in various places around town, most notably in the name of Guatemala City's handsomest boulevard and in the name of the city's largest funeral parlor (an irony not lost on pundits). The mock Eiffel tower is also dedicated to Barrios and his reforms.

This would appear to be only so much dead history, certainly not of interest to the casual tourist whose attention is attracted to the here and now. But history often has a double edge to it in Guatemala, and it is usually instructive to look beneath the surface of the story told in textbooks. The Reform and the Barrios presidency are good examples. The Liberal platform sounded quite laudable; it succeeded, however, as reforms often do, in improving the lot only of those already well off enough to take advantage of the changes. The winners under Barrios' program were elite landowners and foreigners, especially Germans. The losers, as ever, were the indigenous Guatemalans.

Before the development of coffee as a cash crop, Guatemala produced and exported cochineal, a dye made from a worm that inhabits a certain type of cactus. Cochineal was grown by small landowners, mostly ladinos, although a few Indians also profited from its production. Because a small plot was the most efficient means for producing cochineal, land remained in the hands of the peasantry and large plantations were not common in the highlands.

Coffee was a different story. Once the demand for cochineal dropped (synthetic dyes produced in Europe proved cheaper), Guatemalans looked for a new cash crop. For awhile, in the 1860s, they tried cotton. When he came to power in 1873, Barrios immediately began promoting the cultivation of coffee. His efforts to improve transportation were prompted by the need to move coffee from the rugged, isolated highlands to the newly constructed ports on the coasts (a port on the Atlantic side is named for him). Barrios also encouraged the immigration of German planters, who quickly came to dominate the production of coffee.

Barrios granted many advantages to these foreigners and to the landowning elite of Guatemala. Coffee, unlike cochineal, required vast plantations in order to turn a profit. Barrios thus ordered the seizure of Indian land by calling for, in effect, a privatization of lands worked communally in Indian villages. When the Indians could not afford to purchase their own plots, the government auctioned the land. The Barrios administration turned a tidy profit while the small holdings of the peasants gave way to large haciendas. Moreover, coffee, a notoriously labor-intensive crop, could be harvested only by large numbers of pickers, who must maneuver up and down steep slopes. But the most likely group from which to draw these workers, the Indians, was uninterested in the pittance paid by the landowners (only four cents a day in 1900). The Indians were quite content to work their own corn plots and exist self-sufficiently outside of the white man's economy. Barrios solved this problem by aggressively enforcing the old colonial institution of forced labor. His rural police force was charged with rounding up males from the Indian villages and delivering them to the haciendas. The landowners then kept the Indians in thrall through the practice of debt bondage. By lending Indians "advances" (to pay for their transportation, equipment, room, and board) at usurious interest rates, the landowners could ensure that the Indians would never work off their "debts." If they attempted to escape these debts, the landowners had the law on their side, and Barrios' police were ready to enforce it.

This, then, was the Liberal *reforma* of President Justo Rufino Barrios: he established a secret police; he professionalized the military and used it as his power base; he defrauded and enslaved the Indians in the name of the public good; and he won from all his dealings a tremendous fortune. The father of modern Guatemala was, in fact, the prototype of a Central American dictator. And this is what the gaudy tower in Zona 9 celebrates.

Walking around Town

TOURISTS CANNOT EASILY EXPERIENCE GUATEMALA CITY. In order to see the city as it really is , one has to go beyond mere tourism, to live in the capital awhile, negotiating its streets, making wrong turns, following blind alleys. One has to do business, buy, sell, barter. One has to pass time, walk around with no real purpose, loaf in parks and public places, talk with anyone who shows an inclination to talk. Above all else, to see the real Guatemala City one has to be willing to look beneath surfaces and to register not merely what a stranger sees in the city but what local people see as well; one has to discover the associations that enrich these places and make them meaningful in native eyes. It is not an easy task for the stranger. It is ever easier to remain distant and aloof, to remain a stranger estranged, to gaze upon foreign sites as a foreigner.

For me, immersion began with walking and bus riding. On the days when I had nothing to do at the university, I set off walking somewhere or I hopped a bus not knowing its destination. The most notable aspect of Guatemala City on these initial explorations was the extensiveness of the city's poverty. Everywhere I walked I passed from well-to-do colonies to downtrodden slums at the turn of a corner. Even in fashionable areas like Zona 10, hovels stood next to mansions. In poorer zones, the slums were vast and endless. Every bus route seemed to pass through one or more of the city's numerous barrios. Huge and labyrinthine, these slums went on and on, spreading into areas that even the most recent city maps left blank. The buses jounced along rutted roads and made turn after turn until I lost all sense of direction, and sometimes I would ride for more than an hour before the bus returned to familiar territory.

More often than not, familiar territory meant downtown in Zona 1, since almost all buses eventually wound up there. I liked to walk around downtown best of all. Not that it was a pleasant place, exactly—the narrow streets and the buildings trapped much of the automobile and bus exhaust, and one could feel the grime of it on the skin, taste it in the throat. I bought drink after drink on my walks downtown, to no avail; a burning throat and watery eyes were inevitable after even a brief walk. Still, there was more of interest downtown than out on the Americanized boulevards that had proliferated elsewhere in the city. Yes, downtown Guatemala was a city in its dotage, but that was what made it interesting. Like people in their dotage, the city center was quirky and inconsistent. What I saw and experienced there—trash wagons drawn by mules, a boy leading a herd of goats across a busy street—was never quite believable, not for the stranger anyway.

I think what impressed me the most about downtown was the intensification of the imagery. The streets were jammed and dizzying; incredible oppositions were juxtaposed. Every day, for example, a wizened man kneeled on the sidewalk of a busy intersection near the market, his shriveled black feet emerging from white Indian pants. A broken straw hat covered his head and he wore a soiled black sport jacket. Lyrical benedictions issued from his toothless mouth. And every day, without fail, he held in his dark leathery hand a single beautiful, fresh flower—the *monja blanca* (white nun), Guatemala's national flower. Contrasts like this were everywhere, boggling the imagination. On another corner sat a young man, strapping despite the loss of his arms. He manned the corner with his two small children, who crawled all over him like puppies, giggling constantly. He laughed and laughed with them, unable to hug them, but joyful just the same.

There were, in fact, beggars controlling almost every downtown corner, as if they had staked claims or begging rights to particular spots. No one considered chasing them off. I saw them so often I got to know their habits well, and I suppose they got to know mine, too. I was particularly attracted to one shoeless old woman who kneeled on a stone step outside a boot store. Somehow she maintained her upper body perfectly erect, the spine rigid, the face beatific. I couldn't see her eyes behind her shawl. I couldn't see her face at all, only the lizardlike skin of her hands as she held them out to me. She always called me *canche*—blonde one—and commended me to God, perhaps sensing that it was important for a fair-skinned man to receive that particular commendation.

For me, Guatemala's downtown was exciting because so much was happening right on the street, out in public. I grew up on quiet suburban streets deprived of imagery, and I've spent most of my life in cities like Spokane and Albuquerque, in which the streets were expressly designed to carry automobile traffic. Life in such places is lived isolated in the shell of one's own vehicle, at forty miles per hour. No one ever walks. The sidewalks are empty. Drivers stare with suspicion at lone pedestrians. But Guatemala was different. The sidewalks were jammed with life and possibility. I could shop on the sidewalks, eat on the sidewalks, exchange money on the sidewalks. Anything seemed possible as I bumped and squeezed my way through the crowds.

All of this excitement reached its poetic heights in a place called Plaza de la Concordia. This, more than the Plaza Central, was the center of downtown activity. Lottery ticket vendors, taxi drivers, and shoeshine boys lingered on the plaza's fringe, along with a whole row of people selling large cans of processed cheese. Some of the cheese came from Scandinavia; Guatemalans called it "Chernobyl cheese," since the European countries had begun donating it in the late 1980s. Other cans of cheese came from the United States. These cans were stamped with an image of two hands locked in a handshake and the words "Gift of the People of the United States of America: Not to Be Sold." Obviously, the warning did not worry the vendors.

Beyond the edges of the plaza, I found still more bizarre scenes. An electric band played while a man howled about Jesus, his microphone-distorted words and breathless delivery obscuring the content of his message. The driving bass guitar and the cheesy merengue organ heightened the hysteria communicated by the howler's single intelligible word—that potent name sung, shouted, screamed into the diesel thick air: Jesús, Jesús, Jesús. And over to the side a little bit, an old Indian man with a snake draped around his neck circled a blanket upon which were spread dried grasses and twigs and roots. Soft-voiced and without amplification, unable to compete with the Jesus-crier in volume, he nonetheless had gathered about him a substantial crowd, all straining to hear his words about the healing powers of the grasses he sold. Curious about the dangerous snake and more concerned with their immediate ills than with the impending apocalypse, dozens clamored about the old shaman and ignored the frothing evangelical minister.

Sometimes, seeking refuge from airborne contamination, I entered interesting-looking buildings, and in this way I discovered the Archivo General de Centro América. The archives quickly became a favorite place, a place to rest, to read, to breathe book dust instead of automobile exhaust. One room was stacked with tied-up bundles of newspapers and magazines. A card file, organized according to topics of interest in recent Central American history, directed me to periodicals with articles on that topic. Finding the putative periodicals, however, was a Herculean task, the researcher's equivalent of cleaning the Augean stables. For one thing, dozens of newspapers and magazines had sprung into operation (and failed) in Guatemala in the twentieth century. The articles that most interested me always seemed to be in those papers that had the briefest runs. The trouble was that the stacks of the archives were literally that: stacks. Bundles of newspapers tied up with hemp were piled in no particular order on dusty shelves. Even when I managed to find what appeared to be the appropriate bundle, the newspapers inside the bundle often bore no logical relation to one another. Still, the place was fascinating for the casual browser. Other than old newspapers, the archives held something I very much wanted to get a look at: a manuscript by Bernal Díaz del Castillo. But my scholarly credentials were not persuasive enough, and I had to be content with a clerk's description. It was "very old," he told me, and "hard to read."

Rainy Season in the Slums

WHILE AIMLESS WANDERING often led to worthy discoveries, I knew that I also needed some direction, some sense of purpose if I were ever going to learn what I ought to learn about Guatemala. The daily newspapers gave me some suggestions. I decided that whenever I read about events that seemed important, I would try to visit the sites of those events.

The first place I went, a few weeks after my arrival, was a slum in Zona 3. For several days I had been reading in the newspaper about landslides in these slums, avalanches of mud brought on by the tremendous September rains. September is the wettest month of the year, tropical storm season in the Caribbean. When the storms pass over the isthmus, mountainous Guatemala catches and holds the heavy clouds, and for days on end the rain does not stop—a continuous monotonous opening of the heavens that lends credence to the Noah story. The Guatemalans call it "*el temporal.*" During my first September in Guatemala, the *temporal* was especially heavy, for a tropical storm had roiled into a hurricane and pounded the Caribbean coast of Nicaragua.

At first I had difficulty finding a way into the slum. It was easy enough just to see it: the shantytown, a city landmark, adorned one side of a huge *barranca,* one of the numerous ravines that scarred the city. You could see it as you drove the main thoroughfare in and out of downtown. This thoroughfare, called the Anillo Periférico, crossed the great chasm by way of the Martín Prado Vélez Bridge. From the bridge, you could look across the *barranca* and down to where, about a kilometer away, hundreds and hundreds of shacks clung to the canyon wall. It was an impressive sight, so impressive that tourists would stop on the bridge and photograph it. I supposed they showed these photos to their friends back home so that everyone could admire the tenacity of the slum dwellers.

To actually go into the shantytown, to descend the *barranca,* I had to follow a road along the edge of the city cemetery and then through a lower-middle-class barrio where the houses and shops were small but in decent condition, the roads rough but paved. Wires carried electricity to the homes, the trash crews made their rounds, and a fire station watched over the neighborhood in the inflammable months. The municipality did not, however, bestow this kind of attention on those who lived behind and below this barrio. I came upon the last road and there it was: the vast and beautiful *barranca,* a long green ravine extending for several kilometers along the city's northwestern edge. In days past, before the Martín Prado Vélez Bridge and the Anillo Periférico were built, the *barranca* had served as the city's boundary and defense. It was necessary to cross the *barranca* down and up by mule to reach the city gates. Now the southern rim and wall of the ravine were home to thousands of people.

Footpaths descended from the main road and wound through shacks and hovels. The day I went down, a light drizzle fell, a brief respite from the downpours that had lately inundated the slum. Rivulets ribboned the paths, taking trash and mud down the slope. The footing was treacherous long before I reached the really steep parts. Two things immediately struck the senses—the sound of children screaming and the smell of burning rubbish. Children were everywhere—running after deflated plastic balls, squatting in the mud, picking through trash heaps. Children and trash. Two tiny boys, naked, poked a trash heap with sticks. Small fires burned here and there in the heap, smoking furiously, in spite of the drenching rain.

I descended farther. At one vantage point, a vast panorama of the shantytown presented itself. I could now see some of the details that could not be seen from the bridge. I was surprised to find that there were actually roads in the slum and that trucks somehow maneuvered up and down the slick ruts. Not without difficulty, however: just below my vantage point, a Toyota pickup was pitched nose first into a deep rut, mud up to its axles.

It started to rain a little harder, and then came the deluge. I had reached an intersection of paths where one of the shacks served as a small commissary, its handpainted sign announcing the sale of *artículos de primaria*—primary goods—which in Guatemala means things like eggs, tortillas, milk, and perhaps soap. I dashed for the store and pressed myself against its rough planks, newly painted turquoise and red. There was just enough of an overhang to keep me out of the rain, although the runoff from the tin roof splattered my shoes and pants with mud. Dense, roiling clouds rolled up the *barranca*, energetically swallowing the spurs of land to which the shanties clung. Then these tongues of cloud passed on, briefly revealing again the blue and green and turquoise shacks before new tongues surged up and swallowed the hovels in whiteness.

The roar of the rain on the galvanized roofs was terrific. Even the cries of the children were drowned. A mother pig and her piglets, unfazed by the storm, snorted past, their snouts investigating the mud, my legs, the puddles. On the paths, rivulets of filth had become channels of rushing water. There were swells and eddies in the current. Trash tumbled on the flow, and I stared in amazement at a branch channel that cut a passage close to me, carrying downstream the pink plastic torso of a doll followed by a flailing scorpion. It was hard to believe that water, a blessing from God, the symbol of life, restoration, and renewal, could suddenly turn so destructive.

A young man splashed down the road-become-river, carrying his shoes in his hand. As he passed he caught sight of me and shouted above the roar, "How does it look, gringo, just like the United States, right?" And then he vanished into the mass of clouds.

Below me, somewhere in those boiling clouds, it was worse. Down there, where the *barranca* walls were steeper and where the poorest of the poor lived—the squatter who had only lately arrived in the barrio, having emigrated from the highlands most likely, and who had no alternative but to try to make a go of it on land that was not land but cliff—down there, the mud was surging and pressuring and collapsing the weak shanty walls, the rain was pounding through the patchwork roofs, and the humans were howling to their God, who had forsaken them. Some of those newly arrived immigrants were dying, their corpses pitched into the *barranca* along with scorpions and rats and other vermin. I shivered.

But it was not long before I was home, safe and dry. In the evening I drove in the rain to the university and taught my classes. At the break, over coffee, rain still falling outside in the black, bleak night, I told a colleague about my visit to the Zona 3 slum. She smiled. Yes, she said, yes it happens every year with the *temporal.* People die in the landslides. But you see, some people never learn. Every year they build their shacks in the same places. And then the rain comes . . . very stupid. Very sad, yes, but also very stupid.

The City Dump

IT WAS EASY ENOUGH TO FIND THE DUMP. From the *trébol,* the clover-leaf interchange where the capital's main roads met, you simply looked up in the sky for the circling vultures. As you drew nearer, of course, the smell directed you. On the day I visited the dump, a hard rain had just fallen, and this added a special pungency to the air. The dirt roads, lined by little houses and stores, had turned muddy, making the walk difficult. Scores of frothy-mouthed dogs sulked through the puddles, the bitches dragging distended teats. I had never seen so many mangy and wretched animals moving together. The curs sniffed as I passed, and my main fear turned out to be not the people (this was supposed to be a rough neighborhood) but a sudden attack from one of these rabid pariahs. But this day they let me pass, and I advanced toward the pit.

The people, contrary to the warnings I had received, were friendly. A few nodded and said *adiós.* Children interrupted their soccer games to watch me pass, the bold ones shouting, "How are jew, meester?" while the rest laughed themselves silly. There were even a few store-front churches, loud with prayers and ecstatic singing.

The road ended abruptly at a ledge about thirty feet above the trash heaps. Guatemala's dump had become a neighborhood. It was one of the busiest places I had ever seen. From my vantage point, looking down, I saw a column of people advancing along paths through the debris and up the steep walls of the ravine, which were notched with stairsteps. Every back was burdened with a load, a sack full of tin or cardboard or some other precious commodity won from the smoking mounds below. A few people stumbled up the path toward me, and I watched their progress on the slippery, muddy slope. After maybe fifteen minutes of climbing, they gained the ledge and set off at a trot with their haul. I asked a boy where he was taking his load.

"Por allá." Over there, he waved. "They buy the things over there." "What things?" Glass, wire, wood, cardboard, burlap, metal—everything, even rags. "What was the best thing to find?" I asked. That was an easy one—copper wire, which paid a lot and was easy to carry. The hardest thing to get out of the dump was a tire—very heavy and clumsy. His two brothers had to help him get one up the path. His whole family, including his grandmother, worked the dump. It was hard work, he said, but not too bad. He liked it better than guarding cars downtown, which he sometimes did. That was boring and didn't pay too well. The boy—his name was Alex—said that he went to school "sometimes" and went to church "always." His family went to an evangelical church, an *iglesia bautista* (Baptist church).

Alex asked me if I wanted a guide to go down into the dump. I thought about it, but declined. "I think I'll just look from above," I said.

"Yes," he agreed, "it's not so good for you to go down."

Alex left to sell his treasure, and I went back to my observations. The view from the top of the ravine was, well, almost scenic. On the mountain highways in Guatemala, there are scenic overlooks called *miradores*, which are marked by signs put up by the Guatemalan tourist bureau. It seemed to me that this site also deserved such a sign, for it was as good a *mirador* as one could find in Guatemala City. The main action was taking place across the ravine about five hundred feet from my vantage point, where a steep road led into the pit. The garbage trucks, mostly old yellow stake bodies, descended by this road to dump their dross. Actually, since most were not dump trucks, the trash had to be shoveled off the truck beds. Crowds of people waited for the shovelfuls to come flying off. They attacked the new piles and jostled with each other like pigeons in a park when the popcorn lady has arrived. Some mongrels tried to get in on the action but they were beaten back by the humans. Vultures were everywhere. Huge, cocksure, and patient, they hovered overhead, brooded atop smoking heaps, tore at carcasses, and aired their wings on nearby rooftops. They were not pretty, but they were efficient and diligent; the place would have been far fouler without their scavenging.

An acrid, nauseating haze detracted from the scenery. Guatemala City was producing fifteen hundred tons of trash a day. Since there was no treatment facility, it all had to be burned, and it was smoke from these burning heaps, combined with escaping methane gas, that produced the haze. I noticed that a few people wore bandannas over their faces, but most did not. Perhaps after a lifetime in such a place, one simply became inured to the smell and the smoke, but I couldn't imagine how. After a half hour, I had a headache and burning, tear-filled eyes.

Of course, my first reaction upon seeing the Guatemala City dump was outrage. How can the world be so unjust that people live this way? The sad thing was that the work of these dump people was probably necessary if Guatemala's plunge toward ecological disaster were to be slowed. Like the vultures, they kept things cleaner with their scavenging. Of the fifteen hundred tons of garbage produced each day in the city, a good percentage was recycled—a far greater percentage than ever got recycled in the United States, I was sure. The people down in the pit were hauling up everything with the slightest value, even cardboard. One thing I had noticed about poor countries—they were not as trashy as we in the First World thought. Most of the trash—paper, food, cans, bottles, rags—did not lie on the ground very long before it was picked up and put to use. Waste, it seemed, was a luxury of the wealthy nations.

Along the Railroad Tracks

A FEW MONTHS LATER, the newspaper ran several stories about protests among the squatters who lived along the railroad tracks. Apparently, the National Railways of Guatemala—FERGUA—had begun evicting the squatters and destroying their shacks. The squatters were fighting back by attacking the evictors and the wreckers. This I had to see.

I had been meaning to walk the tracks in Guatemala City anyway. Every day I had to drive under the bridge that carried the tracks over Boulevard de Liberación. Concrete steps led up to the tracks, and the sight of people going up and down this stairway made me curious to see where they were going. The map showed the tracks slicing right through the middle of the city, so I decided that a walk across town on the tracks might be an interesting way to see the capital.

Dense foliage—smelling of rot and human urine—guarded the bridge. The tracks emerged from this foliage into a small shanty-town, with the tracks serving as the main street. In following the tracks, I was walking the border between Zonas 8 and 9, a distinctive border in that Zona 8 was mostly shabby and run-down, while Zona 9 was mostly chic and expensive. As I walked, I could see Zona 8, slightly above me to the left, its hills crammed with the small box bungalows of the lower middle class. To my right, Zona 9 bloomed green with trees and shrubs, above which towered the glass and steel high-rises of the business district.

The railroad track that separated these two zones was in fact a zone unto itself, a numberless zone, a frontier for the lost. Those who lived along the tracks were poor and abandoned, and they had little hope of ever reaching even the shabby heights of Zona 8, which they could gaze at from their shacks. The railroad tracks were a sociological fault line every bit as volatile as the geological fault lines that crisscrossed the city.

The tracks themselves were in poor condition. Many ties were missing, the bed was unstable, and the rails were frequently gapped. In fact, the entire railway system in the country had deteriorated to the point that few trains operated now—passenger service had been terminated altogether, and the few freight trains still in operation had to go very slowly in order to negotiate these inconsistent rails. Since so few trains passed, people paid little attention to the railroad. Children played soccer along the tracks with a ball made from newspaper-stuffed chicken wire. Dogs slept curled against the rails. Chickens hunted and pecked for seed in the eroded railbed. Women carrying baskets of tortillas and jugs of water on their heads walked down the middle of the tracks—and so did I, feeling fairly conspicuous.

Although I had walked through several slums and barrios, I was more aware of my strangeness on this occasion. I didn't like the rabid look of the dogs, and there was something meaner in the countenances of the people—probably because of the evictions and the protests. After all, the only stability they had was now threatened—and in appearance I was clearly a representative of the oppressor class, the enemy. The mood in the railroad barrio that day was hungry and angry. I knew I needed someone to help guide me through the vagaries of that mood.

My Vergil turned out to be a twelve-year-old boy named Julio, who wore a blue school uniform and carried a book bag. He came upon me as I was nervously attempting to negotiate my way past a foul, skeletal cur that had let loose with a furious yowling when I approached it.

"Don't worry about him," the boy said. "That dog does not bite. It is a coward." And to prove his point, he picked up a rock and cocked his arm. The dog scurried away.

After a few questions, I learned that Julio was on his way home from school, that he lived in Zona 4, near the bus terminal, and that he was the only person I had met in Guatemala who had actually heard of my hometown, Albuquerque.

"In Nuevo México, right?" he said.

I was impressed. "Very good. Where did you learn that?"

Geography, he said, was his favorite subject. He loved globes and maps, studied them all the time, memorizing names and borders and features. He dreamed of the day when he could visit all those beautiful names—La Florida, Irlanda, Moscú. This desire I could well understand and appreciate.

We stopped for drinks at a clapboard kiosk, and while we drank I took out my map of the city and spread it on the ground. Julio glanced at it and immediately fixed our position. "Right here are we," he pointed.

"Absolutely correct," I said. I told him that I was looking for the protests, and he nodded, slid his finger along the map, and tapped it. "More or less here."

"Well, then, Julio," I said, "I invite you to be my guide."

Julio grinned. We shook hands and walked on. As we walked, Julio told me that the evictions had been going on for some time, but only recently had the squatters begun to fight back. Although he did not live along the railroad tracks, he walked them twice every day to and from school. He clearly sided with the protesters. He explained: "The railroad is not a good railroad, so why not use the land for houses? People need houses. When the railroad tears down the houses, they don't make the improvements they say they will make. Then the houses are built again but always worse than before."

We heard the bulldozers first, and then the angry shouts of the crowd. As we drew near, I saw that the crowd was very large, but only a core group was actually participating in the protests. Most people hung back on the fringes, observing, craning their necks to see, chatting, even laughing. A few vendors worked the outer crowd, hawking gum and candies. One man with a pushcart of ice cream jangled some bells and shouted, "Helados, helados!" It resembled the crowds one saw at the weekend soccer games out at Campo Marte. Meanwhile, the core of the mob—maybe two hundred people, mostly women— raged and shrieked. They threw rocks and bottles, shouted curses, wept. The bulldozers stood still and snorted, the five drivers huddled in a group about fifty yards off, talking, pointing. One ate a banana and dropped the peel on the railbed.

Outside of several shacks, entire families—parents, children, grandparents—squatted on the dusty stoops before their condemned homes. The bulldozers would have to remove these people before the shacks could be leveled. Only once while I was there did a bulldozer attempt it. The driver brought his rig around and faced a hovel. The family, staring at the ground, did not move. The bulldozer halted and snorted loudly once, twice, a third time. Suddenly, a rain of rocks pelted down on the machine, and the driver was forced to cover his head. When the pelting became too vicious, he fled, and a cheer of triumph rose up from the crowd. For the time being, bulldozers and squatters were at an impasse.

Julio had to get home to eat his lunch, so we left the tracks and entered Zona 4. He led me to the bus terminal, where I could catch a bus home. When I offered Julio some money, he refused to take it. I pressed him, but he was adamant until I suggested that I buy him a small gift instead of giving him money. To this idea he was more amenable, and he led me into the market area of the bus terminal. Inside the maze of shops we came upon a small bookstore, where Julio found what he wanted most of all: a globe. To this day, I think it was the best purchase I made in Guatemala.

The railroad squatters incident ended strangely. After two days of protests, a riot squad accompanied the bulldozers to the site. While the US-trained riot squad—wearing helmets and carrying shields and clubs—held back the crowd, the bulldozers made short work of a row of shacks, and that was the end of it. Nothing more was done. The Railway Agency, as Julio had predicted, never followed up on its plans—if there had ever been any—to use the property. In fact, within a year the shacks were rebuilt. I was ever amazed in Guatemala at the many acts of random and pointless cruelty perpetrated by the government, but perhaps no act that I witnessed was more random or more pointless than this one in the railroad barrio.

A GAM Rally

I WITNESSED A GOOD NUMBER of strikes and protests while I was in Guatemala. It was the time of the *paquetazos*, a series of drastic measures undertaken by the government—under pressure from the International Monetary Fund—in an attempt to restructure the country's shaky economy. Nearly everyone was affected by these measures, none more so, of course, than the poor. The most drastic measure, in terms of its immediate effect on the lives of common people, was the move to float the quetzal. Until then, the quetzal had remained fixed at 2.7 to the dollar, but the freeing of the currency led to rapid devaluations. Soon 5 quetzals were needed to buy a dollar, and prices rose, especially the price of gasoline. (Ironically, for me the devaluation made life as an expatriate American paid in dollars much easier and, for a time anyway, much cheaper.) Transportation costs doubled and tripled. There were long lines at gas stations and no fuel available. Bus fares doubled, and people took to the streets. There were protests by the teachers, protests by the students, strikes at factories.

Nearly every day I could go downtown and observe a protest of some sort. But of all that I observed, the one protest that stands out for me was one not directly connected to the *paquetazos*. It was a downtown march by GAM, the Group for Mutual Support, an organization dedicated to demanding investigations into the thousands of disappearances and murders that had resulted from political violence. GAM was formed in 1984 by a woman named Nineth Montenegro de García, whose husband had been disappeared in 1983. It is impossible to fully appreciate the courage it took for a Guatemalan woman to organize such a group. For decades, the Guatemalan military did not hesitate to murder anyone who protested or even merely questioned the actions of the armed forces. But Señora Montenegro de García's persistence was remarkable, even miraculous, and GAM's membership grew from twenty-five in the initial meeting to several hundred by the late 1980s—an unprecedented grassroots movement in Guatemala. While it was encouraging to witness the success of this movement, it was also sobering to realize that these hundreds of people were all related to someone murdered or missing.

Two very large marches, one in 1984 and one in 1985, had attracted international attention. Members of the US House of Representatives had wanted to attend the latter one but were deterred by death threats. Given that Guatemala's paramilitary death squads felt no compunction at threatening members of the US Congress, the courage of GAM's members was all the more remarkable. They persisted in their protests even after the military stepped aside in 1986; like a gadfly, GAM pestered the new civilian government for investigations into unsolved disappearances.

The march I saw filled an entire city block. Despite the somber occasion, the scene was surprisingly beautiful. Bold colors dominated the street. A large banner, painted in vivid primaries, depicted Jesus leading a GAM march, the word *"Solidaridad"* in bright red above the scene. A poster of sharply drawn flowers, the colors glowing in the strange hazy air of downtown, demanded, "Where have they hidden these flowers?" And then there was the clothing: it seemed as though half the crowd or more was made up of Indian women, all dressed in their motley *huipiles*. I recalled the funeral march in El Aguacate, and I thought how even in mourning there was nothing so beautiful, so colorful as a Guatemalan crowd; their appearance was itself a statement, a rejection of that oppression, a determination to be beautiful, bold, and distinctive in spite of the overwhelming forces opposed to their existence—the forces, drab in comparison, that even now surrounded them. Soldiers and police were everywhere, and periodically an army helicopter circled over the crowd, hovered, and then darted off.

Virtually everyone in the march carried the image of another person, either enlarged photographs or drawings of a missing relative. Some images were turned into placards and attached to white sticks so that they could be raised above the crowd. Other images were made into posters and fitted with string so that the protesters could carry them by looping the string around their necks. Most of the posters were made from photographs taken for some special occasion—graduation, wedding, confirmation. The people in the pictures were dressed in their best clothes, but they were not smiling—almost as if they were thinking of the solemnity of this future occasion rather than the joy of the photographed moment. Along the borders of these posters the protesting relatives had scrawled laments: Where is my husband? Where do they have Oscar David, my son? Some people simply carried framed pictures, the kind one finds on the mantel of any home.

One old man, dressed in black, with a heavy, hoary beard, stood to the side of the march, head bowed, his hands cradling a framed photo of a girl in a school uniform. The anguish that gripped him was so keen that those who passed him were forced to lower their heads and cross themselves.

During the march, I studied the photos: boys and girls in graduation gowns; a man wearing a volunteer fireman's helmet; a groom cutting a wedding cake; a woman holding a sleeping newborn. Never had Guatemala's political violence seemed so senseless. Were these really the subversives the government feared?

Authority in Guatemala

ON OTHER OCCASIONS, the protests and marches came to more violent ends. As the strikes around the city intensified, the authorities were more and more disposed to respond aggressively. A huge teachers' strike, shutting down some ten thousand public schools, brought the middle class to the streets. For weeks in August, in the middle of the school year, downtown was jammed with protesting teachers (countrywide, forty thousand were on strike) and other public employees who joined them (some twenty thousand workers from Public Works, Finances, Civil Service, and the Postal Service). When the strikers' tactics turned somewhat militant—on one occasion they surrounded the national palace; on another they occupied the Organization of American States offices—the government responded harshly. Beatings by police were common, and near the end of the strike one teacher died as a result of a beating.

The government was especially harsh on unions, which had long been subject to state-sponsored violence in Guatemala. The most infamous case involved the union at the Coca-Cola bottling plant. In the late 1970s and early 1980s, most of the leaders of this union were murdered or driven into exile. The brutality of the murders—tongues cut out, throats slit—made the matter notorious worldwide. The walls of the union office to this day are decorated with photographs of the eight martyred leaders. By 1989, violence against union leadership and against striking workers was commonplace in Guatemala. I had been reading for several months about a few protracted strikes during which unionists had occupied some factories. The Christian Democrat government—which won union support in the 1985 election—was officially committed to a moderate stance in labor disputes and thus favored serious negotiations with the unions. But the constitutionally elected executive branch of the government was not completely in control of what all government agencies did, especially out in the streets. The police, the military, the *guardia de la hacienda* (a kind of Border Patrol), and customs—to name only a few agencies—often operated according to their own capricious agenda, even when that agenda conflicted with the official policy of the elected government. In a country like Guatemala, there was no single Authority, but many authorities, each operating more or less independently, unchecked by momentary changes in government or policy.

In democratic Guatemala, Authority was *less* beholden to the official government than it had been in the days of brutal dictatorships. During the repressive days of the Lucas García regime (1978–1982), everyone knew who was in charge, who was formulating policy, and who was enforcing it. But the democratic government elected in 1985 inherited from previous regimes a bulky bureaucracy of agencies whose function was to carry out the policies of the caudillo. With the caudillo gone, these agencies were like satellites on automatic pilot: they just continued hurtling through the darkness. They simply were not going to respond to a Christian Democrat, not even a wily politico like Cerezo who, like most politicians in Latin America, had a bit of the caudillo streak in him. Guatemala was thus a country with only a titular democracy; the huge framework of pre-democratic authoritarian government was still in place and still operating. But now it was out of control and functioning on its own, pursuing the age-old policies in Guatemala of repression, terror, and corruption. This framework was the de facto Authority in democratic Guatemala.

The response of this Authority to striking workers and factory takeovers was a good indication of just how little control the government had of its own agencies. Surely Cerezo and the Christian Democrats did not want direct confrontations with workers, a huge part of his coalition. And yet time and time again, a protest march or a factory occupation was ended with an attack by police, or soldiers, or even unidentifiable plainclothes "troops" carrying automatic weapons—institutionalized goons, as it were. For example, the striker-occupied CAVISA plant, where glass products were made, was attacked at four-thirty in the morning by a police force armed with high-caliber guns, tear gas, fragmentation bombs, and hand grenades. The Lunafil plant (cotton, thread, and yarn products) was attacked at six in the morning by machine gun–bearing men in civilian clothes. The newspaper accounts I read were vague, as newspaper accounts in Guatemala tended to be on any subject other than sports. The attackers could never be specifically identified, though they were often referred to, significantly, as *las autoridades*, the authorities: a plural form that nowhere was more apt than in Guatemala.

A good example of the way these nebulous authorities worked was the affair of the *panel blanco*, the white van. This van had reportedly been involved in several kidnappings and murders, including that of a pregnant twenty-five-year-old employee of the university. It was commonly believed that the police were behind these murders. A spokesman for the Ministry of the Interior denied that the government was involved and claimed that the so-called Death Van was merely a ploy by opposition groups "to discredit the government and make the citizenry believe that we have returned to repression." The national police was charged with the responsibility of investigating the alleged Death Van. It did. In fact, by an amazing coincidence, it was the chief of the national police himself who discovered the van on the highway to El Salvador. After surrounding the van, the chief and his men closed in and found inside six uniformed troops of the treasury police, armed with machine guns. The treasury police was a different force altogether, a special unit supposedly responsible for stopping contraband. The six were arrested and taken to the national police headquarters. When the treasury chief learned of the arrests, he promptly dispatched a squad of one hundred armed soldiers to surround the national police headquarters. Eventually, the treasury chief and the police chief reached an agreement that kept the treasury policemen in jail, charged with theft and abuse of power (but not charged, significantly, with any political crime). The treasury chief claimed that the agents were involved in a search for adulterated milk; he was subsequently fired by President Cerezo, who told the press that there had been "a problem of hierarchy."

The affair of the *panel blanco* (though it was never conclusively proven that the treasury van was the van involved in the kidnappings) was another indication that checks and balances did not exist in the government of Guatemala. Different agencies pursued their own political agenda regardless of official government policy, often, in fact, in direct contradiction of that policy. An understanding of terror in Guatemala must begin with the recognition that this lawlessness of *las autoridades* makes combating state-sponsored violence a difficult task, a battle, in essence, with a hydra-headed monster. One ironic side effect of democracy was the fragmentation of responsibility—no single person or branch of the government could oversee the actions of other agencies in that government.

Maquilas

READING THE ACCOUNTS of discontent at the factories got me interested in working conditions in Guatemala, especially in the factories owned by American corporations and investors, the so-called *maquilas*. A new kind of factory, the *maquilas* operated by a special arrangement with the government. They were allowed to import dutyfree the components of unfinished products; these components were then assembled in the Guatemalan factory and reexported to the "mother country," usually the United States or South Korea. This type of arrangement had become extremely popular in Third World countries because it seemed to offer benefits to everybody: the host country got jobs and wage money was pumped into its economy; the foreign corporations could benefit from the lower wages without having to worry about import-export duties; and back in the corporation's home country, consumers got to buy their products at bargain prices. A beautiful arrangement. Unfortunately, the arrangements were manipulated so that their principal achievement, as ever in human affairs, was the further oppression of those already oppressed.

The number of *maquilas* had grown rapidly. Before Cerezo's presidency, there were few *maquilas* and only a handful of workers employed in them. Near the end of his term in office, somewhere around fifty thousand Guatemalans were working in more than 250 factories, almost all in the garment industry. US and South Korean corporations were the principal investors, and the US Agency for International Development (USAID) had aggressively promoted the concept. For American businesspeople, the opportunity was too lucrative to pass up. Flying to Guatemala from Miami, one would find among other passengers several businesspeople going down to set up operations or check on factories already up and going. On one flight I sat next to a man in the towel business. For years he had operated out of Hialeah, Florida, employing illegal aliens and immigrants. But even though such practices had kept expenses relatively low, nothing could compare with the deal he got in Guatemala. "Two bucks a day," he told me over and over again, as though I should be impressed at the bargain he had found. "Two bucks a day, and they're glad to have the job. I can afford to throw in little benefits, you know, a yearly bonus or something that keeps the union happy and makes me look like a philanderpist!" The towel man spoke no Spanish ("I'm trying to learn it, but it's so damn hard. Anyway, I've got by without it in Miami, so I figure I'll make do all right") and knew nothing about Guatemala. He hadn't even visited the tourist sites, though he meant to make the time on one of his trips. For him, Guatemala meant nothing more than cheap labor, and I could imagine that this somewhat cavalier approach would lead to trouble someday.

For the most part, the *maquilas* employed women. Their jobs weren't easy. The *maquila* concept is based on the idea that certain labor-intensive aspects of production—such as the piecing together of garments—are most efficiently (read "cheaply") performed in countries where a large, unemployed, and unskilled labor force is available to do the worst work for the lowest pay. In other words, the operators of *maquilas* look for places where there is a certain group of people who have been traditionally exploited and who have no means for protesting that exploitation. Guatemala, where women (particularly indigenous women) could be expected to put up with the worst of conditions for the lowest pay, was perfect. Indeed, Guatemalan women fit the job profile perfectly. They had no voice— many did not even speak Spanish—thus any attempt to protest or organize would go unheeded. And because the country had gone through a long civil war in which many men had died, leaving widows to fend for themselves, there was an ample supply of women desperate for any kind of job. A job in a *maquila* meant working six days a week for anywhere from twelve to fourteen hours a day. The wage, as the towel man had delightedly discovered: between one and two dollars a day. And there were long lines of job seekers whenever there were openings.

This sounded bad enough, but I had no idea just how bad the work could be until I had the opportunity to visit a couple of factories. My first chance came as a result of a party at the international school where my wife taught, the school attended by the children of foreign families in Guatemala, that is, the children of diplomats, embassy personnel, and corporate executives. I happened to fall into conversation with the manager of operations for a well-known US shirt manufacturer. He was soft-spoken, thoughtful, and pretty well versed in the realities of life in Central America. He spoke Spanish well enough, and had previously been stationed in El Salvador. In other words, he did not fit the stereotypical description of a multinational corporate capitalist overseeing the exploitation of the local population. Moreover, he was quite proud of the work he and the US company were doing in Guatemala, and he was really eager for his compatriots to visit the factory and "see for themselves." When I expressed my interest in such a visit, he encouraged me warmly. "Please do. You must come by. It's not like you think it is, not as bad as you've heard." I thought it interesting that he simply assumed I had heard that the factories were bad—I had not said a word to indicate that I knew anything at all about the *maquilas.* Anyway, it was clear that the US shirt manufacturer was sensitive to criticism of its factories, and the invitation to visit the factory was extended with the idea that guided tours would help squelch such criticism.

It was an overcast day, blustery and dusty, when I arrived at the factory compound for my visit. A guard passed me through the gate; I had been expected. Like many of the guards in Guatemala, he had the habit of indicating directions with his weapon; the burnished barrel had become an extension of his hand. After you had been in Guatemala awhile, these things no longer surprised you. Why would a sentry at a shirt factory need to be armed as though he guarded the mint? Why was a guard necessary at all? Such questions elicited only shrugs.

I parked at the concrete block building that housed the offices. The secretary, a beautiful young woman, phoned word of my arrival to the manager. Several minutes passed before he appeared, and during that time I watched the secretary, demonstrating the unusual patience that Guatemalans have with their telephone system, dial and redial the same number at least a dozen times. At last, the manager appeared and ushered me into his office, a nicely appointed room—

nothing lavish, just a few pieces of handsome Spanish leather furniture, a computer, and some wall hangings made from indigenous textiles to give the room a pleasant native touch.

He seemed very glad to see me. I sensed the man was proud of his work and his company. He was eager for others to see its merits and confirm them. He apologized for the wait—it had been a hectic day of urgent communications with the home offices in the States. A major retailer was taking bids on a huge shirt order and "home base" had to have an accurate estimate of what "Guatemala" could produce on short notice. The company had factories in countries all around the Caribbean and in Asia, and it had become the habit of its managers to refer to these factories by the name of the country in which they were located, appropriating the country's name, as it were, and thus subordinating the identity of the larger entity to the smaller. This I gathered from my compatriot's frenzied phone conversations, which repeatedly interrupted our own: "Yeah, yeah, sure fifty thousand. But why can't Indonesia handle ten thou? . . . Oh? Malaysia will do it? Then can Dominican fill that short sleeve business? . . . What about Honduras? . . . If one of them can handle short sleeve, then Guatemala can deliver those striped oxfords . . ."

In between phone conversations, the manager recited for me the argument defending the *maquila* industry in Guatemala: it brought jobs to the country, good jobs that paid more than the norm. The benefits were better than workers could expect in other industries. Furthermore, the garment factories employed a segment of the population that had traditionally been excluded or marginalized from the labor force—women. He rattled off some statistics about wages and benefits, repeating each number twice, with emphasis, as though I were a reporter taking notes. At any rate, he had no doubt that the families of these workers, and the entire country for that matter, were far better off since the shirt manufacturer set up operations. As for working conditions, well they were quite simply not as bad as you imagined. Again, the manager's speech had adopted a defensive tone. The underlying concern of his presentation was that I disapproved of the *maquilas*—everything he said, anyway, implied or anticipated criticism. Since I had not said anything to reveal my disapproval, I could only assume that the manager generally expected criticism of and even hostility toward the presence of the shirt manufacturer in Guatemala.

The workers, he continued, were treated well. This was no sweatshop in the Orient, that was for sure. In fact, he would bet that he had one of the cleanest factories in the city. Go to any factory, especially one run by a Guatemalan, and you'd see a different story. The only companies paying attention to sanitation codes or safety regulations were the foreign plants. "Got to," he chuckled, "otherwise, the government bureaucrats—they're kind of slimy bastards, you know—would be here in two seconds flat fining and bribing us. Have to pay them off a bit as it is. These people are hungry for bribes, they live by 'em, see." The manager was willing to bet that not even OSHA could find fault with his factory.

The telephone had been quiet for ten minutes, and the manager took this as a sign that the little problem had been ironed out ("Sorry—an old shirt industry joke!"). That gave us a chance to have "a look-see" at the factory itself. We crossed over to a large warehouse-type building, all steel and concrete, no windows. Even from the outside I could hear the steady buzz of machinery, and above the buzz a male voice shouting angrily. Before he opened the door, the manager surreptitiously, perhaps subconsciously, patted his jacket and I noticed for the first time a bulge at his chest and the outline of a strap running up and over his shoulder. He was armed.

He opened the door. The angry male voice broke off mid-threat.

Inside, there were scores of tables fitted with sewing machines. Women, most dressed in native *huipiles,* sat on stools before these tables and worked the machines. One long wall was lined with metal shelves stacked with bolts of cloth. As we walked down the rows between the tables and the buzzing machines, I noticed that the room was very warm—probably because of the sewing machine motors. There was also a strong smell of new cloth and cloth dust. Little pieces of cloth and snips of thread lay in our path. The women did not look up at us; their stare did not waver from the needle as they jabbed the seams of the shirts. One man, a Guatemalan, stalked the rows, studying the operations. Now and then he stopped at a table to examine a finished shirt. While we were in the factory he was judiciously silent. But as he was the only man there, it was obvious that his was the angry voice I had heard from outside.

At the far end of the room, another group of women stood at tables folding, pinning, and bagging the finished shirts, which were then placed in boxes for shipment to the states. I thought of those tags that read "Inspected by #48," and I wondered if "48" was an indigenous woman making two dollars a day. It was something that had never occurred to me before, and no doubt most Americans likewise ignored the social implications of those tags.

The manager said nothing as we strolled. He had a wide grin on his face, a kind of beam or glow, as if he found the whole thing just too grand for words. I asked no questions. The buzz made it hard to think, and by the time we had finished the first row, I was feeling a bit dizzy and queasy. At first, I thought that the caffeine in the strong coffee I'd drunk in the manager's office was getting to me. But when we left the warehouse, the sensation passed.

Only later, when on a visit to another *maquila* I had the same lightheaded feeling, did I realize that something about the harsh glare of the fluorescent lighting in these factories made me feel put off balance. I had to blink often, and my eyes watered. I wondered how the young women working there could manage to concentrate on needle, thread, and seam in that eerie glow.

This second visit to a *maquila* was even stranger than the first. It came about when I met a young British man one evening in a nightclub. An Oxford graduate, he had set off after college to explore the world. For the time being, he had settled in Guatemala with a Nicaraguan girlfriend and was making a little money by giving occasional English lessons. One night in that same club, he happened to fall into conversation with the plant manager of a *maquila,* and the next thing he knew he was showing up in suit and tie for work. The pay, he said, was too good to pass up—he was making "a nice packet, a nice packet indeed." I told him about my visit to the *maquila,* and since I could tell he was a cynic, I mentioned that I was pretty sure that what I was shown in the *maquila* did not accurately reflect working conditions, the *real* working conditions in the factory. He had a laugh at this and said that if I really wanted to see the naked truth I should come out to his factory. He'd show me a pretty thing or two.

This particular *maquila* was a freelancer; that is, it belonged to no parent corporation. It contracted for work all over the globe—piecing together anything from shorts to bathing suits. They did a good business in children's clothes, especially for South Korea. The day I went out with my friend proved to be typically chaotic. A fax had come in from South Korea in vague, botched English, a common problem in doing business with Asians, he said. There was a mad scramble to interpret the order and get things set up for filling it—then when everything seemed ready, further communication proved that the order had in fact been misinterpreted, the "bloody Koreans" were mad that their postmodernist English had not been understood, and the offices of the company were in turmoil.

Presiding over all this frenzy was a very fat man: the American businessman who owned the factory. He waddled around the offices bellowing at anyone who came into his field of vision. "He's a real nutter," my British friend said, "a real bloody nutter." A "nutter" who, it turned out, was having enormous problems with his workers and even with the Guatemalan government. The workers had been trying to unionize for a couple of years, but the owner had fired the union's officers and had even, according to the workers, hired thugs to follow activists home and beat them up. Paychecks were frequently late, and the American was openly contemptuous of the workers' efforts to force changes. Things had gotten so bad that even the government, generally blind to abuses in the *maquilas,* had tried to fine the American owner. Court injunctions had required him to hire back the dismissed union officials. In the face of all this, the American was defiant. Perhaps he knew what was becoming more and more apparent to everyone else in the country—that the Christian Democrats would not win the next election, which meant that those now in power would, in the months remaining in their tenure, be concerned only with making their little piles before being turned out. They would be susceptible to bribery, and those with money, like the American, could thus act with impunity. No doubt he also knew that the government was divided and did not act with one voice. The vice-minister of labor might criticize the American and the *maquila* all he wanted, but when it came right down to it, the wily "nutter" knew he could count on the government—or at least on those who mattered most in the government, those with the force to support him. A case in point: after the union officers were fired, they built a shack outside the factory and occupied it for nearly a year, keeping their protest visible for the other workers. Then one day the police showed up, probably at the American's bidding. As my English friend explained, the police came in with riot gear—shields, clubs, helmets—"maybe fifty coppers in all against no more than a dozen workers. As you Americans say, they beat the living shit out of the workers—and in daytime in full view of the other workers. I'd say they got the message."

The point was, of course, that the owner would not hold anything back. If the workers wanted a union, well, that was tantamount to declaring war on the company, and the company was prepared to fight tooth and claw.

It was not hard to understand why the workers wanted a union. Working conditions at the factory were appalling. As the Englishman took me on a tour of the plant, he pointed out things that my untrained eyes had missed at the other *maquila*. For example, the women had to use stools instead of chairs because the owner had a theory that, unable to lean back, they would be forced to sit upright on the stools and would therefore get more done. The pressure to work faster and more proficiently was constant. The floor managers were essentially martinets who roamed the factory yelling and swearing at the women to do more and to do it faster and better. The factory was almost always behind schedule because the owner would constantly bid for contracts that tested the production limits of his small factory. This meant overtime. All workers were required to stay late if necessary—and it was necessary more often than not, sometimes for months on end. Those who couldn't meet this requirement were fired—there were plenty more desperate Guatemalans willing to take the job.

During these overnight sessions, abuse was especially harsh. Breaks for dinner were not allowed. Instead, the floor managers passed out amphetamines—the Englishman showed me an envelope of the pills, which he had in his pocket. I was reminded of the little brown pills that the banana company handed out to employees in *100 Years of Solitude*. In the *maquila*, the drugs were intended to take away hunger and keep the women awake. "It's a great time for rape, too," my friend said. I looked at him. "Sure. It's common enough anytime, of course. But at night when the women are wired, the floor managers take the ones they like to the storage rooms. Of course, the girlies do it anytime they have to—after all, their jobs are on the line. But they're especially pliant when they're wired. So I'm told. Not my cup of tea, actually." The most vulnerable were the younger workers. Many teenagers worked at the factory, some as young as fourteen, and these were the floor managers' favorites.

The Englishman told me all this, and more, as we walked around the factory. He explained that the constant operation of the motors made the foot pedals of the machines very hot, and the women, who could afford only very cheap shoes, often had blistered feet. Many complained of eye pain from the constant strain of staring at seams. The dizziness I had experienced at the other factory returned while we toured the place. He said it was a fairly common sensation under the harsh lights. In fact, all in all, the working conditions in the *maquila* reminded him of the factories in Dickens' novels.

So why, if he found it so terrible, did he continue to work there? Didn't he feel he was contributing to the perpetuation of an abusive situation?

He shrugged and smiled. "The money. I make a huge packet here. Easy, stupid money."

And it didn't bother him?

"Yeah, sure, a bit. But in Guatemala you get used to a lot of perfectly horrible things. You get so you don't even notice it anymore—like the beggars downtown or the soldiers with machine guns on street corners. That's part of being here, you become blind to the horror of it all."

El Churrasco

THE PROTESTS I SAW—the railroad protest, the GAM rallies, the strikes—all involved violence, though the violence was usually unspectacular: the bulldozing of shacks, the bombing of the GAM headquarters (a periodic event that usually occurred when the office was empty), riot squad attacks on workers. I say unspectacular and of course I mean *relatively* unspectacular; in Guatemala, where massacres of whole villages had become almost commonplace, violence of the order I witnessed was really quite mild, exciting little attention locally and none internationally, except among the ever-vigilant human rights watchdogs. For *spectacular* violence, nothing I saw or heard about in the capital could compare to the infamous Spanish embassy imbroglio of early 1980, which occurred during the time of Lucas García, when the brutality of the state reached such stunning proportions, even the outside world began to notice and to question the horror going on in Guatemala.

It happened like this. Some indigenous activists from the highlands, representing the newly formed Committee for Peasant Unity (CUC), had organized a march to the capital in late 1979. In the capital, they engaged in several actions intended to bring their concerns to the attention of the powerful. One of their final actions was to occupy foreign embassies, in the hopes of attracting international attention. The Indians "occupied" the Spanish embassy at the invitation of the Spanish ambassador. In the view of the Guatemalan government, however, the Indians ("delinquent subversives," according to the military) had seized the embassy and were holding the Spanish ambassador hostage. The government insisted on this interpretation of events despite the Spanish ambassador's call for negotiation and dialogue. The ambassador, Máximo Cajal, was in fact sympathetic to the Indians; several Spanish priests had been murdered by the army in the highlands, and Cajal had journeyed to the department of El Quiché to see for himself Guatemala's killing fields. He was therefore disposed to hear the Indians' list of grievances. A press conference was called; a former vice-president of Guatemala and a foreign minister arrived to talk with the peasants. But the national police arrived as well and surrounded the embassy compound. The ambassador shouted from an upstairs window that the police were not to enter—the embassy was technically foreign soil, a place outside Guatemalan jurisdiction. But before the negotiations could get under way, the police broke down the door and stormed the building. Somehow during the attack the embassy caught fire and the peasants were trapped inside, unable to escape in part because the police shot at anyone trying to leave the building. The ambassador survived by leaping from a window, but thirty-nine Guatemalans died—Indians, university students who were assisting in the negotiations, and the two government officials. Only one Indian survived; badly burned, he was taken to a private hospital, supposedly under police protection (at the insistence of the Spanish ambassador), but that same night he was abducted, tortured, and murdered. The body was dumped on the grounds of the university.

Spain immediately broke off diplomatic relations. There should be nothing surprising or unexpected in this response—Spain's territory was attacked, its property was burned and destroyed, its ambassador barely escaped with his life—all done without provocation. By any objective standard, the Guatemalan government had committed a grave offense, and I assumed that the whole affair was a source of extreme embarrassment to Guatemalans. I found out, however, that such was not entirely the case. Many Guatemalans felt that Guatemala was the wronged party in the affair. Spain, they felt, had overreacted and had insulted their country.

I first discerned this attitude at, of all places, the university. One morning, I decided to look for the former Spanish embassy, just to see what the site of the massacre looked like ten years later. I was unable to find it, though I knew it was somewhere in Zona 9, near the Torre de la Reformador and McDonald's. Later that day, over coffee, I told some colleagues about my search.

"Ah, *el churrasco*," one said, and they all giggled.

I was puzzled. *Churrasco* is a kind of barbecue, very popular in Guatemala; there were *churrasco* restaurants all over the capital.

"*Churrasco?*" I asked. "What do you mean?"

"That's what people call the Spanish embassy fire—*el churrasco*—because, well, because it was like a barbecue."

They all looked at me, smiling, to see if I had appreciated the humor of the little joke. They went on to tell me that people had been very angry at Spain for breaking off relations—it was an unjust thing for Spain to do, and showed a lack of respect. After Spain severed relations, anything Spanish became the object of opprobrium for many Guatemalans. Even Plazuela España—where mariachi musicians used to hang out in the evenings waiting for gigs (people would drive up and hire a band for a party, a wake, or any occasion that suddenly required music)—had fallen out of favor merely because it was named for Spain. The bands now awaited business in a far inferior and dirtier location. A decade had gone by, but the musicians still had not returned to the Plazuela. The fact that one of the cruelest events in a long history of cruelty had become the subject of sopho-moric humor helped explain much about the perpetuation of terror in Guatemala. It was perpetuated not just because there were de-monic generals who had turned the place into hell-on-earth; it was also perpetuated because ordinary, good people like my colleagues made jokes about it. This made the terror seem abstract and unreal.

My colleagues seemed convinced that those who died in the Span-ish embassy massacre were not peasants and students, but guerrillas engaged in a terrorist action. It was, of course, unfortunate that people lost their lives, they said, especially the foreign minister and the former vice-president—though they had been fools to try to ne-gotiate with subversives. Negotiation did not work with them; best to let the army do the negotiating. And surely it was not good that Spanish property was burned . . . but anyone who knew Guatemala, who *really* knew Guatemala, would understand the necessity of a "disciplined response" (it didn't take long in Guatemala to notice that military-style discourse had become part of everyday civilian speech; the military was very successful—through billboards, news-paper ads, and television spots—at coercing the general population, urban ladinos, that is, into accepting its construction of reality). You had to remember, they argued, the epoch in which all this took place: early 1980, when Carter was president and delivering Central Amer-ica to the communists. (No one was more reviled in Central Amer-ica, by the elites, the military, and the middle class anyway, than Jimmy Carter, or, as they liked to call him, "Jimmy Castro." He was blamed for every ill that Central America suffered, especially the Sandinista victory in Nicaragua and the guerrilla uprising in El Sal-vador. Despite ten years of equally ineffectual Reagan/Bush policies, it was still Carter who bore the brunt of the blame, in their eyes.) What if Guatemala had let these subversives get away with their ter-rorism, the way Somoza had when the Sandinistas invaded the con-gressional building in Managua and held the Nicaraguan congress hostage? Guatemala would be communist, just like Nicaragua, that's what. A strong response was necessary, and the army did what had to be done, Spain be damned.

I was surprised by the intensity of these statements, and by the anger that some of my colleagues still felt toward Spain. It seemed to defy the facts; indeed, they seemed unaware of the facts. The big problem, I believe, was the unavailability of reliable information. Much of what I heard in Guatemala was either blatant rumor or someone's revision of events carefully packaged to ensure that the news was understood "correctly." It was almost impossible to get a reasonably objective account of anything political, and in Guatemala everything was political. I understood, anyway, how intelligent, well-intentioned people could so thoroughly misinterpret events in their own country. Quite simply, they did not know enough, could not know enough, to make informed interpretations. The atmosphere of the place skewed your vision, and sometimes even blinded you, so that you were left groping for understanding.

For example, I didn't learn about many of the important events that happened in Guatemala while I was there until later, when I had left the country. I had been a dedicated newspaper reader and radio listener, but in Guatemala you could not gather much information about the country through the media. It seemed ironic that in the United States organizations interested in Central America complained about the lack of media coverage where countries like Guatemala were concerned. How could a civil war of such a bloody magnitude as Guatemala's be so often ignored in the US media, they asked—and they were right to do so. But if anything, the dearth of coverage was even greater in Guatemala itself. This was why the comfortable ladinos of the middle class could remain so aloof to the violence: like the German populace in 1941, they didn't know what was going on or they didn't understand it. Many people I talked to, for example, were certain that the violence in Guatemala was no longer primarily political, but criminal. Their preoccupation was not with the state-sponsored violence in the highlands but with the apparent increase in street crime and auto theft. Again and again, I was surprised at the conviction with which such opinions were advanced, and at how often those opinions were contradicted by basic facts, facts apparently unknown and probably unavailable to the opiner.

Ladino Attitudes

THERE WERE OTHER REASONS WHY some of the ladinos of the capital, even those who were educated, remained blind to the violent campaign against the indigenous Guatemalans (a campaign so brutal that many observers in the world considered it genocidal). One very powerful factor was the prevalent imagery of Indians as primitive, helpless, and brutish. This imagery was reinforced by advertising. Most commonly, it was reinforced simply by omitting Indians from the picture. Products were universally marketed with the images of light-skinned European people, thus making their appearance the ideal and suggesting, by negation, that Indian characteristics were undesirable. Sometimes, however, the racial depictions in Guatemalan advertising were more overt. One commercial, in particular, comes to mind.

I saw it one day at a movie theater. Commercials, usually the same as those aired on television, were frequently shown at the beginning of movies, though sometimes in a longer version. It was the usual stuff: colas, fashion wear, beers, cigarettes. The cigarette commercials always amused me, first because it was odd for a US citizen to see the product advertised at all, and second because the American brands like Marlboro still used the same commercials that were on American television decades ago, before cigarette advertising was banned from the air. Seeing them again as they crackled across the screen was almost nostalgic, a return to the scenes of childhood, especially when the Marlboro man rode across the chaparral to the theme of *The Magnificent Seven.*

It was not Marlboro, however, but a Guatemalan brand—Rubios— that produced the most memorable spots. Rubios commercials shared a general theme; the Rubios smoker was depicted as a strong, independent, accomplished man with rugged good looks, a man who got satisfaction from things other, more ordinary, people overlooked. Typically, the commercials developed a little plot in which the Rubios man did something macho yet altruistic, then smoked a Rubio for his reward. The best of these spots was shown in movie theaters in an extended version that drove home both a superficial and a subliminal message.

It went like this: Close-up of a muscular man smoking a cigarette. His eyes show him to be essentially a man of action who also recognizes the value of contemplation. He is white-skinned, with dark curly hair and a thick mustache. His appearance suggests someone who is at home both on the Mediterranean and in the Alps. He is busy at something just now—we see a hammer in his hands. A medium shot reveals he is on the roof of an uncompleted but fine-looking chalet. But something is wrong off-camera. Our man sees it, knits his brows in concern. The camera follows his preoccupied gaze. Not far away from the chalet there is a lakeshore, apparently Lake Atitlán, where some Indians, in complete native costume, are struggling to get from the shore to a bobbing launch. The Rubios man spots the problem: the old dock appears rotted, and the *inditos,* lacking resources, are forced to walk in the water to board the boat—even the poor old women, one of whom pathetically stumbles, helpless under the burden of her heavy sack. Our man, observing this, purses his lips, puffs his cigarette in cool contemplation, and nods to himself. He has made a decision, plotted some bold course of action, and he will put his plan into action anon. A series of scenes in quick succession shows him at work, alone, on the old dock. Forthwith, he replaces the old wood, redesigns the entire docking structure, and in no time has a smart new dock up and ready for the *inditos*. Boy will they be surprised! And sure enough, the *inditos* do not let us down: the commercial ends with the return of the Indians, surprised and pleased and more than a little baffled. Whence came this boon, they wonder, looking around—perhaps from the lake gods? Ever the lone eagle, back at work on the roof of his chalet, the Rubios man smokes his reward and nods in self-satisfaction. The voice-over announces the moral of the story: Rubios is the taste of winners.

The subtext to this little morality play was too blatant to need or merit explication. It was, simply, another in the constant series of images depicting whites as the possessors of knowledge, technology, and strength as opposed to the pervasive ignorance of the enfeebled Indians. Well, what could one say? No one in the audience, no ladino I ever spoke to about it, found such imagery in any way remarkable. In Guatemala, it sold cigarettes and other products. And in fact Rubios was the best-selling brand of cigarettes in the country.

It seemed that the best image of the Indians that one could find in Guatemala's media was this one used in the Rubios ad—the Indian as a poor, pitiful brute worthy of ladino sympathy and charity. More often they were represented as something far worse, and the representations were often remarkably contradictory. The Indian was cunning and full of guile. The Indian was dumb as an ox and easily duped. The Indian was a cruel and sanguinary savage. The Indian was meek and humble. The Indian was too lazy to care about anything. The Indian was a traditionalist devoted to an anachronistic way of life and opposed to progress. The Indian was a communist ideologue eager to overthrow the established order. And so on. It would be tedious to review all of the demeaning stereotypes presented daily in the Guatemalan media.

Soccer in Guatemala

GUATEMALA SUPPORTED a large professional soccer league, discussion of which occupied a good amount of time in restaurants, bars, and university hallways. Out of a score of teams, only four really mattered as the playoffs drew near; year after year one of these four captured the title, and inevitably the semifinals and finals came down to some pairing off of these four teams. Of the four, two were popular and two unpopular; like professional wrestling—or better, like the roller derby—Guatemalan soccer featured heroes and villains. If all went right, and it usually did, the heroes squared off for the championship. In the capital, the loyalty of the fans was divided between Municipal, or Los Rojos, and Comunicaciones, or Los Cremas. The nicknames referred to the colors of their jerseys. The villains were Aurora, sponsored by the military, and Del Monte, sponsored by the banana exporter.

Every year the country geared up for the championship match, which almost always featured Rojos versus Cremas. One year, to the surprise and horror of everyone, Aurora, the military's team, broke through to the final. The stadium that day was charged with passion—nobody but nobody could tolerate the thought of Aurora as champion. It was the unruliest crowd I saw in Guatemala: constantly hissing, booing, whistling, swearing, shooting off firecrackers. And it got worse as the game wore on and Aurora went ahead. By the time it was over, however, as *los militares* took their victory lap, the crowd's intensity was spent. Most fled quickly into the drunken afternoon. Those who stayed observed the on-field celebration in silence, already well inured to defeat by the military.

But most of the time, soccer matches were good entertainment in Guatemala, and I went often to Ciudad Olympica to take in a league match, or the occasional international match. The games were good, but the real fun was simply being part of the crowd. I always opted for the cheap seats, the *sol* side of the stadium (the side exposed to the sun), where the rowdies sat or, rather, stood, since the concrete benches were more conducive to standing than to prolonged sitting.

The matches began with a curious demonstration. While the opposing squads went through their warm-ups, a short man, barefoot and obviously Indian, suddenly darted onto the field. A mild cheer rose from the tribunes. Then some belligerent guard dogs dashed off in pursuit of the trespasser, and the crowd, now more interested, roared louder. Near midfield, the first of the dogs, a sleek German shepherd, snatched a leg and caught the prey. The shepherd's allies quickly closed in and pounced on the now-flailing man. The crowd, especially the rowdies, screamed approval. The first time I saw this, I dropped my bag of beer and thought, this can't be real. And of course it wasn't. After a moment of thrashing about in apparent anguish at midfield, the victim jumped up, the dogs backed off and wagged their tails, and the little man waved to the crowd amidst new cheers and general glee. The whole crew trotted off the pitch while a garbled announcement—a warning to stay in the stands—blared from the loudspeakers. After this Guatemalan addition to pregame ceremonies, it was time for soccer.

The stadium was a good place for drinking beer. Middle-aged women and young boys hauled Styrofoam coolers full of bottled beer around the stadium. They poured your beer into a plastic sandwich bag, and you drank it with a straw. Maybe it was a bit inconvenient that way, but after a while you ceased to notice. Anyway, the bags came in handy for the less decorous members of the crowd: rather than miss any of the action by repairing to the mossy wall outside the stadium, they simply voided themselves into the bags. Given the similarity in the color of product and byproduct, I had to wonder if anyone had ever accidentally confused the two. My British friend related an incident in which the urine-filled bags had in fact served a purpose: one in the endless succession of exploding firecrackers sent a spark onto a man's shirt and the shirt caught fire. His quick-thinking comrades doused the flames with their recycled baggies. I was surprised only that the bags weren't employed more often as projectiles; maybe even the most sophomoric rowdiness has its scatological limits.

The rowdies' tribune provided the setting for all manner of puerile fun: exploding firecrackers, wisecracking, taunting, swearing and swearing some more at anybody and everybody—referees, opponents, pork-rind vendors, and especially gringos in attendance. Some travel writers have described attending a Latin American soccer match as a hellish experience. I didn't see it that way; it was all in good fun, and God knew the lower-class people in the cheap seats needed some release, some diversion in their otherwise docile lives. And if that release was a momentary bout of lawlessness, so what? The guard dogs and the machine gun–bearing soldiers in riot gear were always close by, a reminder of how constricted their lives really were.

Street Children

GUATEMALA CITY DOES NOT FIT the stereotypical image of an exotic tropical city where any pleasure can be readily satisfied. It isn't Bangkok or the Havana of old; it doesn't even measure up to San José, Costa Rica—Central America's mild version of a sin city. The Guatemalan demeanor is too formal and, to some extent, too prim for openly displayed vice. Compared with other Central Americans, Guatemalans are almost prudish. Though appreciative of off-color jokes, especially those involving double-entendres, they dislike blunt vulgarity, and their strongest swearing is but common speech in, say, El Salvador and Mexico. Guatemalans, for example, deplore public use of the word *puta*—"whore"—a word so common in El Salvador it is practically a term of endearment. Even the excessive use of English vulgarities in American movies disturbs Guatemalans. In clothing, too, Guatemalans favor the conservative. American diplomats who have been stationed previously in other Central American countries are surprised at how often they need to dress up in Guatemala. Suits and ties are more common than the tropical guayabera favored in more relaxed countries. And wanton displays of exposed flesh are far less common than in the rest of the isthmus.

Likewise, the illicit sectors of Guatemala City are not too prominent. In Zona 10, well-to-do Guatemalans can find a relatively thriving nightlife of upscale restaurants, discotheques, and boutiques. The names of these places—Dash, Safari, and the like—indicate their spurious ambience, designed to imitate Europe or New York. There are brothels nearby as well, swank establishments where you are likely to share the barroom with a government official or a foreign minister.

Of course, these places hold little attraction for aficionados of truly illicit action. There are, for the desperate and damned, little pockets of vice here and there around town where the thrill seeker can bottom out. The cheap whores are found in hovels that line the railroad tracks near the Customs offices. And there is a thriving though officially unrecognized transvestite trade working the seediest downtown streets. For gambling, there are backroom sessions of a ludicrous card game called nines in some of the Chinese restaurants downtown, where you can see derelicts from the street wager hundreds of quetzals on complete chance. For betting on the cocks, there is the Palenque de Gallos "La Florida" out in Zona 7, where the fighting, the drinking, and the gambling are intense. And for marijuana, there is El Gran Comal, a jammed reggae club in Zona 4, where the bands come from Belize and sing about the hard lot of the black man in Guatemala. (The crowd favorite at El Gran Comal when I was there was a song in Spanish—"Con cédula o sin cédula, la policía te va a llevar" [With or without your ID card, the police haul you away].)

But if I went downtown after midnight, what ultimately caught my attention, what really impressed me, was not the prostitution or the gambling or the drug dealing or the evangelical street preachers ranting at it all; no, what impressed me the most were the roving gangs of street kids that seemed to occupy every corner of downtown. Around five thousand street children roamed the city's streets. Primarily indigenous, they came for the most part from families that had migrated to Guatemala City in the 1980s in order to escape the war in the highlands. But the poverty and the hopelessness proved too much for many of the families, especially the large ones with too many bodies to feed and too little space. All too often the children ended up out on their own, begging or stealing just to live.

If you were walking around downtown after midnight, after an evening of drinking at, say, the Europa Bar, where expatriates liked to hang out, you'd see these kids huddled in doorways, the smaller ones—as young as six, seven—curled like kittens in cast-off cardboard boxes. If you turned down Sixth Avenue and kicked your way through the windblown trash left behind by street vendors, you'd see some of them sniffing a kind of glue called Resistol, sniffing it from plastic bags to concentrate the fumes. The buzz helped put off hunger pangs, made it easier to ignore the chill of the high-altitude night, and gave the kids, known by the collective name *"los resistoleros,"* enough strength to endure their street battles. And sometimes a glue fix helped dull the pains of beatings inflicted by the police. If you bothered to talk with them, the kids would tell you this happened all the time—kicks, punches, pistol-whipping. Sometimes, at random, a gamin was picked up and hauled off to a police station or an alley and beaten still more severely. And there were rumors of a game, a hunting game, that the police and security forces played using these children as the prey.

Suppose you continued down Sixth Avenue, past the boot shops to Eighteenth Street, where there were some all-night kiosks serving up tortillas and grilled meat, corn on the cob, *café con leche,* and lukewarm Gallo beer. You sat on a stool and ordered a meal. You watched the out-of-town buses arrive, the passengers just waking from the stupor of travel. Before long, a police cruiser or two (Volkswagen Rabbits donated by the German government) happened by, three or four cops to a car. They got out, grinning and looking dumb. They joked with the matron of the kiosk, tilted their caps just so, and played with their holsters.

If you asked them about the street kids, the policemen told you that, yes, it was a big problem for the city, but not a very interesting one; they would rather talk about an upcoming match between the Cremas and the Rojos. If you pressed them on the issue, they ended up sounding like their leaders—ambiguous and noncommittal. And if you asked them directly whether it was true that some police beat and tortured the children, they thought that you were some foreign journalist, and they were reluctant to discuss the matter anymore with you, unless they had been drinking beer, in which case one might get angry, lose his cool, and denounce "interference from the outside." Guatemala could handle its problems in its own way, he would say. No damn foreigner should tell Guatemalans what to do in their own country. As for street children, discipline was necessary.

Most were just delinquents who had to be taught a lesson. When respect for the law was lost, the best response was a strong response. The others nodded while he spoke—this was a popular attitude in Guatemala City, not just among the police force, but in the general population as well: discipline, respect, order. The popularity of military candidates among the middle class was based on the belief that military discipline was what the country needed.

But in fact the city was doing nothing to deal with the problem. Guatemalans might have resented "interference from the outside," but the only agency doing anything for the kids was a place called Casa Alianza run by a British man, Bruce Harris. For years, Harris had kept a shelter for homeless kids, providing not only a place to stay and food to eat, but also programs for the mental well-being of the children. Casa Alianza's basic goal was to give the kids a future, something Guatemalan society was denying them. Harris was also investigating police brutality—including the recent death of a thirteen-year-old beaten by four policemen—and trying to present documented cases of abuse to the courts. It wasn't easy; the judicial system was slow at best and openly hostile at worst. Investigating the police was no easy matter, and Harris had been threatened many times. But he was a remarkably dedicated man who knew that "anytime you have an effective program in Guatemala you are going to be attacked." On occasion, the government had tried to shut down his operations, but protests from around the world had helped keep Casa Alianza open. There were few places in Guatemala City where you could find hope, where you could feel that there might yet be some chance that humanity would save itself, in spite of its boundless capacity for cruelty. Casa Alianza was one such place.

Despite its successes, despite the hope it extended, Casa Alianza was a sad place to visit. Scores of kids were getting food and care at the shelter, but the refuge was only temporary. Surrounding the Casa were the same mean streets, and the same mean society that had kept them poor, hungry, and doomed. One of the saddest things I have ever seen was a group of these gamins engaged in some small crafts activity. They were interested, observant, and willing as they watched the counselor lead them through the process, but after a few minutes, once they got the hang of it, their labors turned perfunctory, like workers on an assembly line. Most of the kids were around nine or ten years old, but they looked older. All the happy energy of childhood had been sapped from them, and they could not take a child's delight in things like arts and crafts. The world had dulled them to all that.

Buying a Scooter

MUCH OF MY DAILY LIFE in Guatemala was spent running errands that brought me face to face with Guatemalan bureaucracy. I have bitter-sweet memories of those long, complicated days. On the one hand, I have never done anything more exasperating or more trying. On the other hand, I learned a great deal about the people of the country, learned even more about the language, and came away with a re-newed appreciation for the realistic and comic genius of Kafka.

Bureaucracy was an immediate and pervasive fact of life in urban Guatemala, so pervasive that I was surprised how unprepared I was for it. I heard often enough about the inefficiency and disorder of Latin American societies, but I didn't realize the extent to which that inefficiency and disorder had been institutionalized.

Just where this predilection for mind-boggling bureaucracy came from was a mystery to me. I would have guessed that Latin Ameri-cans, of all people, would recoil from the structure and regimen-tation that bureaucracy required. And yet, there was no denying that bureaucracy was a far more prominent part of everyday life in Guatemala than it was in the United States. There are obvious contradictions in such a statement, despite its basic truth. For example, the United States is an overly regulated society, while Guatemala tends to be underregulated. Street vending best illustrates the point. Almost no rules govern the selling of items, even food items, from carts and kiosks out in the streets of Guatemala. Anyone can make some sandwiches and try to hawk them on the street cor-ner. In the United States, by way of contrast, such vending is care-fully controlled by licenses, fees, inspections, and so on. Yet the country with the more burdensome, unwieldy, and intrusive bureau-cracy is Guatemala.

How could such a situation come about? What were the system's origins? The more I realized the extent to which bureaucracy infil-trated Guatemalan life—and this was impressed upon me not only in my own affairs but in talking with Guatemalans, who always seemed to have some red tape errand to run—the more amazed I was at the paucity of information on this basic fact. Nothing prepared me for the entanglements, neither guidebooks nor travel accounts nor area handbooks nor scholarly studies. Why was urban Guatemala so bureaucratic?

Because Latin American bureaucracy differed in kind from the North American and European varieties, it clearly had different roots. The byzantine nature of Latin American bureaucracy might very well have nboriginated in the *patrón* system of the Spanish court. Each little official in Guatemala's many acronymic agencies regarded his little cubicle as a fiefdom over which he was lord. Anyone needing a stamp or a signature had to wait until the "lord" allowed him to make proper obeisance. Such scenes were played out every day in Guatemala.

It was also possible that machismo had contributed to bureaucratic bulk and excess. In the family, a man was esteemed for the number of his dependents—a large family proved his machismo. In a business or in a government office, a boss was esteemed for the number of his entourage. In any given office, there were many underemployed aides, people whose function, it seemed to me, was not to perform a particular duty or range of duties, but simply to occupy space, to *appear* necessary. They constituted a staff, whether a staff was needed or not, because the size of the staff indicated the importance, the sublime machismo, of the boss. Whenever one needed a document or a signature, one first had to confront this retinue of minions and underlings who understood implicitly that their principal task was to enhance the boss's importance by making access to him exceedingly difficult. Most of the time the boss was in his office doing absolutely nothing (or maybe playing with the telephone—with Guatel, the phone company, an entire morning could be spent making one or two calls); but the longer the suppliant was forced to wait, the more prestigious the boss appeared. A favorite trick was for the boss to leave for lunch, or better still for the day, so that the suppliant was forced to return later or the next day. There is a popular traditional drinking song in Spanish called "Little King of Nothing"; it sometimes seemed to me that the purpose in life of these mid-level bureaucrats was to construct little kingdoms of nothing.

I was often at the university until eight o'clock in the evening, when the last bus left the campus. It was always a mad scramble for these evening buses, and I would end up squashed among a dozen students in the narrow entrance to the minibus. To get off, I would have to shout the name of my stop, hope the driver heard me over the distorted disco beat of his sound system, and then fight my way through, over, and around the other passengers to the door. During the rainy season, there was frequently a downpour just as classes ended, and everyone on board was stinking, soaking wet.

I decided to seek another means of transportation. Many young Guatemalans rode around town on small 80cc motor scooters. These scooters could go about sixty kilometers an hour, and while they were not very safe, given Guatemala's capricious drivers, for short trips to the university a little scooter would do nicely. I resolved to buy one.

The main problem with owning a scooter in Guatemala, however, turned out to be not traffic dangers but the actual act of buying it. Guatemala is one of those rare places where the verb "to buy" has a present perfect progressive tense, as in "I have been buying a motor scooter for a year now."

I chose a used scooter from a reputable dealership whose founder had been kidnapped by the guerrillas, buried underground during the ransom negotiations, and eventually executed. I didn't buy it then; I *began* buying it. I paid for it. I was in possession of it. But I did not yet own it, not in the view of the Guatemalan government. Certain papers needed to be filed and a license plate obtained. Until then, I was only the de facto owner.

Getting the damned license plate was the most difficult thing I tried to do in Guatemala. A Guatemalan friend, a lawyer who had attended Georgetown University Law School, helped me figure out the procedure. The first move, logically enough, was to go to the license plate office in the Parque Industrial. The office occupied a huge metal shed that reminded me of the 4-H Club barn at state fairs. Inside the dim and dusty place, there were several long lines that led to flimsy card tables where the bureaucrats presided over the examination of papers, the collection of fees, and the dispensation of license plates. Behind the tables stood huge piles of old license plates that had been exchanged for new ones. When the old plates were turned in, the clerk who received them flung them over his shoulder into the pile. It looked like a decade's worth of discards had piled up.

There were no signs anywhere, no directions. The Guatemalan propensity for neglecting to provide appropriate directions and signs was difficult to understand. Guatemalans simply did not foresee the need for or recognize the benefit of a few simple signs to direct people, to give warning, or to clarify procedures. Wherever there was roadwork, for example, warning or detour signs—when they existed at all—were placed at the very spot of construction and not a couple hundred yards before. Once, I saw a sign indicating a particularly dangerous pothole placed just *behind* the danger.

What you have to do in such circumstances, of course, is to begin asking others what to do. What is this line for? What papers are necessary here? How much does this service cost? In other words, you have to interact, not only with officials, but also with other form filers. A certain camaraderie necessarily develops. In its way, the system—or nonsystem if you will—was brilliant precisely because you were forced to communicate with others, face to face. You had to leave your shell and enter into the community of human beings, a community that was confronted with a problem that had to be solved collectively. Put simply, the lack of signs gave Guatemalans the opportunity to talk with one another. I was always amazed at the number of conversations I entered into while standing in lines; even the fact that I was a foreigner did not inhibit Guatemalans. I was frequently asked questions about the procedure we had queued for—questions I could hardly answer. But the correct answer was not the point. It was all an excuse, I now think, to talk, to spend a little time in conversation. Topics for these conversations would include anything—family and soccer were two favorites. Rumors and jokes also circulated freely.

What really impressed me was that no one complained or got too upset about the red tape. Guatemalans readily agreed that it was pointless, frustrating, and unnecessary, but they agreed with a simple nod, maybe a smile ("Oh, yes, in Guate it is very bad"), and that was it. A typical Yankee, impatient with inefficiency, I was at first very much put out by the lines and the waiting; I had to bring a book with me to keep from dwelling on the time I was losing. But eventually I grew fond of the conversations and looked forward to them. I met many people that way. A few times I got invited out for drinks—to celebrate success in form filing, I guess—and once I even ended up agreeing to write a letter of recommendation for a young man who was hoping to get to the United States and earn some good money.

But that first time I encountered Guatemalan bureaucracy, in the license plate office, I had no idea what to do. I lost a lot of time standing in the wrong lines until I figured out that there was a line especially for motorcycles. Forty-five minutes later, I was presenting my documents to a clerk. He wanted my old plate. There was no old plate, I told him. He frowned, shook his head vigorously, and said, "No, no, no, no, no. Aquí no."

"Not here? What do you mean? What do I do then?"

"Fíjase, señor," he said. This was not the first time I had heard that word, *"fíjase."* In fact, I heard it quite often in Guatemala: it was practically the national motto. Translated literally, it means "fix yourself," but it was mostly used idiomatically to mean "take note" or "get this" or "it's like this." Its use almost always prefaced an excuse, a rejection, or an explanation of why what you wanted or needed to do was impossible. The tone could vary from demure to severe, though it was most often said with a sense of helplessness on the part of the speaker—a washing of the hands, if you will, an admission that all was beyond the speaker's control. When someone said *"fíjase,"* he was about to dodge the issue, pass the buck.

The clerk seemed almost thrilled to hand me back my packet of papers. "Fíjase, señor, this office is only for renewals. For *new* plates you must go to the Ministry of Finances."

Eventually, I learned that in my gringo naïveté I had bought an unlicensed scooter. Any Guatemalan would have noticed this in the showroom and walked away, or used the missing license plate as a serious bargaining chip. Certainly any Guatemalan could have predicted the bureaucratic nightmare awaiting the person who purchased an unlicensed vehicle. It was like buying a phantom.

I headed downtown to the Ministry of Finances building, not even beginning to comprehend the mess I'd gotten myself into. Inside, the ministry looked as if it had been built according to an M. C. Escher blueprint. Elevators went only to certain floors, but there was no way of telling which elevators went to which floors. Lines of hundreds of people led up to closed doors (so it seemed) or empty counters.

An armed guard, stationed by the nonfunctional escalator, told me that License Plates was on the twelfth floor. On the twelfth floor, I was directed by still another armed guard to a long line. Twenty minutes later, at the front of the line, I learned from a frowning clerk that I needed the seventeenth floor. At seventeen, I at last found the right line, but then learned that my file lacked the original owner's identification number. For that, I had to go to the first floor, to inquire at the computer terminal. The computer was out of order for more than an hour, but I endured and finally came away with the requisite number. Back at seventeen, I was told that I needed to fill out a certain form, which I could obtain only by standing in another line. I filled out the form as best I could, and then took it back to the line on the seventeenth floor. When I got to the front again, the clerk took one look and said, "*Fíjase*, it has to be typed."

Typed? But where could I find a typewriter?

"Outside on the plaza."

In disbelief, I went out to the plaza in front of the building, and sure enough there was a whole row of men sitting on stools behind rickety tables. And on the tables there were ancient Royals and Smith-Coronas, older than the men themselves. An entire cottage industry was at work, form filling for a quetzal. I began to see the grace of this clumsy bureaucracy. It was not designed for efficiency— a huge understatement—but it did manage to employ thousands of people that a more streamlined organization could not. These typists simply waited for people to bring forms out of the Ministry of Finances and then, with remarkable accuracy, considering the antiquity of their machines, they completed the forms. True professionals, they knew every form by rote. A pudgy man with a wide, disarming grin breezed through my form without making a mistake, and in no time I went back up to the seventeenth floor to present my credentials. This time I was accepted: the clerk took the form and piled it with hundreds of others. But I was still not done. I was required to pay a fine for the two years that the original owner had neglected to license the scooter. This involved another line, another form, and payment. I finished just before closing time. I had spent an entire day at the Ministry of Finances, making more than a dozen trips on the untrustworthy elevator and confronting at least ten suspicious clerks and bureaucrats, and still I did not have a license plate. I would have to come back the next day.

The next day, when my turn came, the clerk scrutinized my pile of papers, brought down an abrupt stamp on each of them, and then rather unceremoniously (given the work involved to reach this moment) took a license plate from under the counter and handed it to me. Never before—and I hope never again—had I felt such a surge of excitement and relief upon receiving a license plate.

But I was still not through. Every vehicle in Guatemala must have something called the *tarjeta de circulación*, a "circulation card," which certifies to whom it may concern that the vehicle is properly registered and bears a proper license plate. I had to go to another floor and another line to pick up mine. To my very great surprise, the *tarjeta* was there and waiting for me. Unfortunately, nothing ever goes that smoothly in the Ministry of Finances. The clerk's grim-faced scrutiny of the new document revealed a discrepancy: it seemed that someone had typed a wrong number on the *tarjeta*. This error was not so easily eradicated. Somehow, even though the error originated with the ministry, it became incumbent upon me to get it corrected. I was given the faulty form and told where I could buy a blank one, which then had to be filled in with the correct information.

Once again I had to go outside to have a form typed. My friendly typist was all too pleased to do the job. I asked him if he often retyped incorrect forms. Oh, yes, quite often. I was amazed at the system's genius. Somewhere in the giant ministry building was a salaried typist who had made a simple error. He or she, however, was not responsible for correcting it. Instead, the suppliant—for that is how I now thought of myself—had to buy a form and hire a typist to correct the official typist's error. I imagined that errors like this must be routine, as well they might be. Each error employed a few more people, pumped a few more quetzals into the economy. Society as a whole was better off when the bureaucracy was inefficient. It was an absolutely brilliant system.

Finally I had my *tarjeta de circulación*. But I still did not own the scooter. All the work I had done up to this point had succeeded only in obtaining a license plate and *tarjeta* in the original owner's name. Next I had to initiate the process of transferring ownership to *my* name. But at least I finally had what was needed to make the scooter street-legal.

Bureaucracy Revisited

HAVING PAID FOR MY LITTLE YAMAHA MOTOR SCOOTER and become the de facto owner of it, I now had to go about becoming the de jure owner as well. This meant getting a title for the scooter in my own name. Eventually, I learned that in Guatemala, if you had any money at all to spare, you hired a person called a *tramitador* who specialized in dealing with the various bureaucracies. The Spanish word is interesting and instructive, there being no English equivalent for the job title. A *tramitador* is a professional form filler/filer, someone who serves as your go-between whenever you need to do paperwork with the government—a sort of red-tape intermediary. The profession doesn't exist in the United States, but in Guatemala it is a fairly honorable occupation that requires some savvy and proficiency. The title comes from the word *trámite*, which is the generic term for the numerous forms that different government agencies require. Things were so complicated that some *tramitadores* specialized in dealing with certain agencies—Customs, for example, or Commerce. Most people required the services of a *tramitador* for even the most basic obligations, such as acquiring a driver's license or getting a title for a vehicle.

"Doña Hilda," a brusque woman who supposedly could help me with the papers that would transfer ownership of the scooter into my name, was recommended to me. Her office was downtown in the blocks surrounding the Plaza de la Concordia, the area where most *tramitadores* had set up their offices. Because of my many visits to Doña Hilda, I came to know this section of the city fairly well. The headquarters for the police, a strange building that was supposed to recall a Renaissance palace, but was much more reminiscent of the Inquisition, was located just off the plaza. Much of the *tramitadores'* business was conducted with the police, and with other nearby government offices.

Doña Hilda's office was a tiny cubicle barely large enough for two small desks. Though the office dealt specifically with documents, there were no filing cabinets. Doña Hilda kept her records in some boxes stashed under the desk, and as I was to learn again and again, she had absolutely no method for organizing those records. On the garish green walls of the vestibule were various representations of the Virgin and two calendars years out of date.

Doña Hilda was one of the few Guatemalans I had real difficulty understanding. Generally, Guatemalan Spanish is slow and clear, a little bit musical, and pretty to listen to. But Doña Hilda spoke rapidly in a sharp, blue jay–like voice, and she punctuated her explanations with frequent exclamations of "eh?" which elicited my agreement even when I had no idea what I was agreeing to. It is impossible to exaggerate the despair I felt whenever I approached her office. I imagined that the inscription above the gate of Dante's Inferno would serve equally well over her door: Abandon all hope ye who enter here. I certainly did.

Actually, I was full of hope the first time I visited Doña Hilda. Exhausted by the effort to get a title for the scooter, I was relieved to learn that I could hire someone to continue with the procedure. And Doña Hilda assured me there was no problem; in two weeks, no more, the whole matter would be settled. But of course in two weeks it was not settled. It was not, in fact, settled in two years' time. At first, the *tramitadora* had plausible excuses: the people in charge of title transferring at the Ministry of Finances were on vacation; there was a number typed incorrectly on the form and the whole thing had to be done all over again, and so on. After two months, I started dealing with people I had not seen at the cubicle before. Doña Hilda happened to be out whenever I came by. The assistants always frowned as I made my explanation, and then, obviously at a loss over what to do, retrieved one of the dusty boxes from beneath the desk and began flipping through hundreds of forms, their slow perusal of each one accompanied by much head-shaking and muttering.

By the third time that I was forced to watch this painful search, I knew that it was a hollow exercise. The boxes were, in fact, nothing but a dead-form file, the final resting place of hopeless cases. Their volume did not bode well for the fate of my own papers. Eventually, as the months became a year, the exasperated Doña Hilda concluded that my papers had been lost at the Ministry of Finances. But since there was no proof of this, the Ministry of Finances refused to admit any culpability on its part. Bereft of hope after a year and a half of trying, I gave up the paper chase.

The remarkable thing in all this was that for two years I operated the scooter on the streets of Guatemala City, and the government had no record anywhere to indicate that I was doing so. I didn't care. In fact, the whole mess gave me a sort of impunity to do as I wished with the scooter. Most traffic cops in Guatemala covered their beats on foot. Standing at busy intersections, they whistled down motorists, who then stopped and negotiated the amount of the "fine." If you didn't stop, the cops wrote down your license number and turned it in. Sure enough, somewhere, some time, these traffic violations would catch up with you and you would end up paying a much bigger fine—or bribe—than if you had stopped and negotiated. The license number on my scooter, however, could only be traced to the man who had first owned it, and he had no way of ever putting the police on the right trail. I could thumb my nose at the law. When the traffic cops whistled me, I darted away, grateful to the Ministry of Finances.

The whole scooter affair was not resolved until my last days in Guatemala. I put the thing up for sale, and a man looking to please his daughter bought it—even after my lengthy explanation of the legal complications involved with the purchase. I could tell that he really didn't understand the consequences. He gave me the cash, I gave him the keys and the papers and agreed to sign the contract for him the next day. Instead, as I feared, I got a call from his lawyer, who wanted an explanation.

It was my next-to-last day in Guatemala, and a fitting ending it was. The lawyer's office was downtown in an old Spanish-style building with a courtyard in the middle and offices surrounding the courtyard. The tiles were broken, the place smelled of dust and mold, and the walls were painted in dismal blues and greens that had dirtied with time. I had noticed before that professionals in Guatemala, including doctors and lawyers, showed little concern for the attractiveness of their offices, which tended to be strictly functional, with little or no adornment, and often very dirty. I was impressed with their lack of concern for professional appearances. The office of the lawyer I visited on that next-to-last day was particularly impressive. Everything in the office, from furniture to cabinets, was shabby beyond hope, something like the Goodwillesque furnishings of a college maintenance office. The desktop was littered with papers, books, yellowing newspapers. But I could tell instantly that the short, chubby man presiding over the mess was the first person I had met who had the perspicacity to solve the scooter case.

He waved me onto a lumpy sofa, folded his hands, and listened to my story—nodding, frowning, chuckling by turns until finally he held up his hand to stop me. "Enough already," he said, chuckling. "I know this story. I've heard it before. We are an exceptional people, we Guatemaltecos, true?" And he laughed anew. Then he took out some legal paper, scrolled it into an ancient Smith-Corona, thought for a moment, then banged out a full page of Spanish legalese. I signed the bottom of the page, he thanked me and said we were done.

"That's all you need?"

He grinned and tapped his brow. "I know the mentality. All the ministry needs is something legal to put on file."

"Well, what exactly have I signed?"

"Just a little statement, that's all, expressing your wish to forgo the title in favor of the other man."

"And that's acceptable?"

"Well, perhaps a little bribe will be necessary." He laughed again. "I hope you have enjoyed Guatemala. You will remember us, no?"

"Of course," I said. "You are an exceptional people."

Laughing, he accompanied me to the door.

The Post Office

TO RECEIVE A PACKAGE through the mail in Guatemala, you go downtown to the central customshouse. In the back of the building is a section called Fardos Postales, a large warehouse with green plastic sheeting for a roof, where your package awaits you.

You await your turn to present the form that was delivered to your mailbox, the form announcing the arrival of a package in your name. You show your identification, and the clerk wanders off into one of several gated enclosures, wherein hundreds of unclaimed or undelivered packages are stacked (thus lending credence to the story in the newspaper that there are two million pieces of undelivered mail in the post office).

If all goes well, the clerk returns with your slightly smashed package, but you don't get it just yet. It has been placed out of reach on a table, and now the clerk abandons it in favor of getting involved in a dispute concerning some Indian campesinos from the village of Patzicia. The Indians are in Fardos Postales in order to collect three boxes, but their mission is doomed from the start. The markings on the boxes indicate that the contents are gifts from a hospital in Italy—medical and pharmaceutical supplies. The campesinos have been sent by the doctor of Patzicia's clinic to retrieve the boxes. They have a letter charging them with this duty and explaining to all interested parties the nature of their errand. Four Fardos Postales clerks huddle around the clerk who holds the letter. Their faces show doubt and suspicion.

One clerk takes it upon himself to open the boxes. The other clerks, including the one who is handling the processing of your package, gather around to see. They discuss the contents, handle as many items as they can, poke open hermetically sealed containers of sterilized supplies. The campesinos stare straight ahead as the clerks discuss the fate of the box. The chief clerk arrives. He scrutinizes the letter. Well, he demands, where is your *franquisa*, the permission to import something without duties? The campesinos regard him, then one another, then the box. They mumble. "No franquisa." Too bad, says the chief clerk. Thirty-six kilos of medicine, that will cost a lot of money in import duties. A lot of money. The chief clerk totals up the duties on the medicine. He grins.

But now your package is being opened and your attention is drawn away from the plight of the campesinos. A clerk rummages through the wads of tissue and packing foam, and you see the package contains nothing of value—some Easter candy for the kids and a few other little reminders of home, all plastic and worthless. Woolworth's stuff. The clerk shoves it all back in the box and fills out a form describing the contents of the box. He takes pains with the description, like a catalog writer trying to get the words just right. This form is passed to a woman seated at a desk who uses a calculator to assess the taxable value of the items and to determine the appropriate import duty. When at last you are handed the form, you see that you are being charged six dollars—40 per cent of the value of the box (a completely fictitious not to mention ludicrous value, of course, left to the official's discretion) along with various charges for storage, handling, and even a fine, though the form does not specify the reason for the fine.

You have to take the form to another line, the line for "payment of fees." Once you reach the front, the typist takes your form and sets to work, first spending a few moments fussing over the placement of things on her desk. She types. It is a long form. You wonder why it is that in a country where so much depends on typed forms, the people cannot type with more than one finger. This particular form must be filed in triplicate. You pay and then take one of the copies back to the clerk, who examines it, nods, and makes as if to get your package. But at the last second he is diverted. First you must confirm receipt of the package by signing in a large ledger. Stick around Guatemala for awhile and you will record your name, address, passport number, age, and marital status in ledger after ledger. Where these ledgers go when they are filled up is one of the great bureaucratic secrets. You imagine a warehouse somewhere with thousands of filled-up ledgers, left for some future historian to ponder.

Now you have your package and a receipt. The rest is simple. On your way out of the building you show your receipt to a guard, proving you have not stolen the package. One more thing: before you can leave, the guard must record all pertinent, not to mention impertinent, information in *his* ledger. It is, after all, his job, his *raison d'être*.

"Fíjase"

ONE COULD NOT STAY LONG in Guatemala without some frustrating and baffling experience with bureaucracy. Dealing with *tramitadores* was frequently just as troublesome as dealing with the governmental agencies themselves. Very often you would go to the *tramitador*'s office only to learn from the underlings that he or she was not in, that it was not known when *el señor tramitador* would return, and that no one had any idea what progress, if any, had been made in your case. I dealt with four different *tramitadores*. One, an acquaintance I had made at a tennis club, managed to lose my wife's passport, a deed for which he was terribly sorry, but not terribly chagrined.

It was a given that I would not be allowed out of the country without one last bit of wrangling. What I wanted to do was simple enough: ship some crates of furniture, fabrics, and art back to the states. It *seemed* a simple enough thing. But the government of Guatemala, in a novel twist on the idea of customs, required that anything shipped *out* of Guatemala had to be inspected. As a consequence, I needed the services of yet another *tramitador*, one specializing in matters pertaining to customs.

First, I had to have some plywood crates constructed. When the crates were filled and ready to be sealed, a customs agent would come to inspect the contents, examine the bill of lading, then affix special stamps across the seal of the boxes so that they could not be opened again without breaking the stamps. Once this inspection occurred, the shipping company could move the crates to the port, where another customs agent would verify that they had been inspected and were indeed sealed properly. Only then could the crates be swung by the big cranes onto the Miami-bound boat.

My *tramitador* prepared the proper forms. As usual, one entire form was devoted to a lengthy request for the services of an inspector, written in the typical Spanish style for such documents, a style in which the humble requester fairly prostrated himself before the government official, begging the mercy of his attention, etc., etc.— all only so much slavish bunk in English, but quite convincing, sincere, and hence necessary by the conventions of polite Spanish. In short, a month ahead of time, I made my request. The boxes were soon readied, and the appointed day came. The hours passed, then late in the day, my *tramitador* called: there would be no inspection that day, but I should expect one the following day.

A week passed and each day it was the same story: not today, but tomorrow at 3:30, definitely. (I found the specificity of time an amusing and endearing touch; not only were they willing to lie about the day, but they felt the lie carried conviction if an exact time was attached to it.) Of course by then, after two years in Guatemala, I didn't believe a word of it, nor was I much put out by the delay. Finally, on the eighth day, I did not receive a phone call. 3:30 passed, and then 4, 5, 6 o'clock. A car drove up, and my *tramitador* hopped out—alone. He looked at the crates, praised the workmanship, and then took out an envelope. Inside were the stamps I would need to seal the boxes. He showed me how to do it, gave me the stamped bill of lading that proved the inspection had been conducted, and we were done.

"That's it? No inspection?"

The *tramitador* shrugged. "It's a small matter," he said, "one hundred quetzals took care of it."

This, I understood, meant that he had bribed an official into signing the bill of lading and handing over the stamps. I would have to give him some money to cover the bribe, of course. But I was a bit baffled: why was a bribe necessary when in fact my crates were clean—no drugs, no Maya artifacts, nothing objectionable?

"Ah," the *tramitador* said, lighting a cigarette and relishing the role of informed expert. "The reality of Guatemala is that a bribe, *la mordida*, is necessary just to get something done, never mind to get away with some crime. In Customs, for example, they will put you off, and put you off until, exasperated, you beg them to take a bribe just to get the business terminated. It's my job to await the suitable time, to recognize when the time is right, and to determine the appropriate bribe."

I wondered if he was disturbed about it, if Guatemalans ever got angry enough to demand a change, maybe get an inefficient, corrupt bureaucrat fired. He shrugged. It would never happen. Who could fire the guy? He's always the cousin of someone important. Look, the *tramitador* said, he'd been to the United States and had bought things there—cars, for example—and saw how a system could work with decent efficiency. He remembered getting a title for a car in Houston in fifteen minutes. And he a foreigner! But believe it or not, Guatemala would not function that way, it couldn't. They had built their economy, their lives even, around this intricate system of patronage and payment under the table. It could never be cleaned up.

But computers were more and more common in Guatemala, I pointed out. Wouldn't they help make things run more smoothly?

He scoffed. "If anything we will find a way to use the computer to improve the possibilities for corruption. And then the electricity is always going out. How do you use a computer without electricity?

Nothing will be done, I guarantee it. And when nothing is done, bribes are necessary."

He was more resigned than cynical, a pragmatist not a pessimist. He knew that in the end, the result was the same: you got your stamps, the box was shipped. Anyway, his job and the jobs of many others depended on this unwieldy, corrupt bureaucracy. It was like the defense industry in the United States: you could never dismantle it. Too many people depended on it and no one could imagine an alternative.

Everyone knew that corruption existed, but I think the one really surprising thing about Guatemalan corruption was how necessary it was just to accomplish ordinary errands, to conduct daily affairs. Sure, *la mordida* helped you to get away with something illegal, or to get out of a scrape. But you also had to rely on it just to take care of the everyday requirements of life—buying, selling, moving, working. It was everywhere, a vast network that implicated everyone. I can't pretend to know why it was so extensive and pervasive. Certainly one reason had to do with the incredibly low value placed on human services in Guatemala. To put it bluntly, human beings were bought and sold cheaply. Their work was so devalued by society they had to seek additional recompense and some measure of self-worth through corruption. Police, bureaucrats, teachers, clerks—most anyone on the public payroll—were badly underpaid. Accepting bribes made the job worth the effort. My impression, after living two years in the place, was that corruption, on small and large scales, permeated almost everything in Guatemala. It was unavoidable.

Religion

ON REFORMA, the wide, median-divided boulevard that traversed the fashionable districts of Guatemala City, there was a building with a white tent for a roof. This building served as the main facility for Verbo, a huge evangelical operation that included dental and medical clinics and other "outreach" programs. For whatever reason, Guatemala had become the most Protestant country in Latin America—perhaps as much as one-third of the population had converted. Verbo's growth was indicative of the stunning success Protestant missions had experienced in the country.

Protestant churches were springing up everywhere, little storefront congregations with names like Ebenezer, Galilee, and Misión Bautista, and big multifaceted outfits such as Verbo, Shaddai, and

Elím. There were approximately one thousand churches altogether, one for every nine hundred Guatemalans. Nor was it a strictly urban phenomenon. Protestantism seemed to travel by mule-back in Guatemala, for it had reached distant mountain hamlets that had only rarely been visited by Catholic priests.

In general, the new churches were not like mainstream American Protestant churches. Almost every missionary church in Guatemala was sponsored by what to me were the fringe Protestant churches, the Pentecostal kind with names like Living Water and Gospel Lighthouse. I saw almost no Presbyterian, Methodist, or Episcopalian churches in Guatemala, and those there were tended to be more like the Pentecostals than like their staid namesakes in suburban America. My colleagues at the university were surprised when I told them this. They had the idea that most Americans went to churches like Verbo and that the church service in the United States was essentially an affair of several hours with much handclapping, singing, and generally fervent enthusiasm. When I described for them a typical Presbyterian church service in the states, the kind I grew up attending, they said I made it sound more like a funeral. Exactly, I said.

So prevalent was Protestantism, so thoroughly had missionaries infiltrated the country, that Guatemalans presumed that any gringo in the country was either a tourist or a Bible banger, and probably both. My own colleagues even had doubts about me. One day I met one of the English teachers for lunch. He had arrived before me, and when I came in I found him morosely sipping a Coca-Cola. I ordered a beer and his face registered his surprise. "You drink alcohol?" he asked.

"Sure, why not?"

He admitted that he had assumed I was a teetotaler simply because I was an American working in the country for an extended time and therefore must be connected to a mission. With relief he ordered a beer, took out a pack of cigarettes, and we proceeded to have a fine, immoral lunch. On many occasions, I had to reassure new acquaintances in some overt or subtle way that I was not a missionary.

From what I could tell, the significance of the *evangélico* reformation—and the movement really was reforming Guatemala—had been overlooked or misunderstood by scholars. One very good book on Guatemalan politics, for example, saw the *evangélico* movement as merely a counterinsurgency ploy designed to challenge the effectiveness of Catholic liberation theology. While there was no doubt that the evangelical churches by and large supported the army and conservative political parties, the movement had a far greater and more extensive impact on the country than any strictly political interpretation allowed for.

The Protestants had been active in Guatemala since the 1870s, when President Barrios invited the Presbyterians to establish a mission there. Their numbers increased slowly but steadily throughout the first part of the twentieth century, but the *evangélicos* really grew in strength after the 1976 earthquake. For some reason, rubble-strewn Guatemala became a cause célèbre for North American fundamentalists after the quake. Dozens of sects sent down hundreds of missionaries and thousands of dollars for reconstruction and salvation. The *evangélicos* were highly visible in the rebuilding of the country, especially in the highlands, which as usual were ignored by the urban-minded politicians. As part of the reconstruction, fundamentalists succeeded in convincing people that the earthquake was sent by God for a reason: He was calling them to Him, and they, the *evangélicos*, were there to lead the way.

It worked. But this explanation alone is too simplistic and glosses over some of the important factors in the *evangélicos'* success. The reasons for that success were very complicated, though I spoke with many people who were quite willing to try to reduce those reasons to their simplest form, to explain away the phenomenon, as it were.

There was, first of all, the liberal-Left explanation. According to this interpretation, the explosion of evangelism was due primarily to its connection with US economic interests, both historically (as part of the expansionism that launched neocolonial exploitation in the late nineteenth century) and currently (as part of the global fight against communism). The evangelical success, in the leftist view, was something insidious, the result of attacks on progressive elements in the Catholic Church, the disintegration of traditional rural society, increased repression, and the aggressiveness of the religious Right in the states.

This aggressiveness amounted to nothing less than an "invasion," led by a media barrage of televangelists and mercy ministries. The televangelists and radio preachers hammered at the guilty conscience of the audience, while the mercy ministries addressed their physical needs by handing out medicine, food, clothing, and toys.

According to the leftists, these handouts were mere ploys designed to lure people into the churches and to make them dependent on the church. Once dependent, individuals and even communities could be more easily manipulated. Manipulation was the central goal of evangelism, according to this view, because evangelism was not only religion, but also an ideology, specifically a reactionary ideology that supported the army and the status quo and opposed itself to communism. Thus, the leftists saw evangelism as essentially a political/ideological phenomenon that had been made possible by a radically destabilized socioeconomic situation and by aggressive, dollar-wielding organizations that were able to work their will on the people because of their ability to manipulate charity and technology.

On the whole, there was a good deal of evidence to support this interpretation of the evangelical movement. The use of handouts to attract people to the church was quite evident, and indeed admitted to. Pentecostal crusades, for example, would hand out rice and beans to those attending revivals. Missionaries often gave out food, clothing, and medicine to people, then conditioned the future doling out of these items on church attendance, thus creating the Central American equivalent of Asia's "rice Christians." Many poor people had been "converted" in this way. These acts of charity were no doubt laudable, but sometimes a certain crassness and insensitivity went along with the charity. Rather than dedicating themselves to ministering to the physical deprivation of people, missionaries were decidedly focused on what they saw as the spiritual impoverishment of these "priest-ridden" Guatemalans. Charity was for them a means, not an end. Handouts were bait. Because the missionaries did not consider the nurturing of the body as their primary mission, in their zeal they sometimes ignored the implications of their actions and made some rather egregious gestures, such as the 700 Club's outreach campaign, during which missionaries handed out thousands of boxes of a diet chocolate shake mix. You would think that the crassness of this action would be more than obvious, but such was not the case. Those involved apparently were sincere in their belief that this was the Lord's work. One American I spoke with at the English-language church in Zona 9 failed to see my point when I questioned the purpose of giving away diet products. "Actually," he said, without a hint of irony, "there are a lot of vitamins and nutrition in that stuff. I drink two myself every day."

Certainly one effect of the handouts, whether intended or not, was the association, in the minds of Guatemalans, of Protestantism and prosperity. This "affluence factor" had a strong appeal not only to the poor, but also to the Guatemalan middle class. I don't know of any statistics on this matter, but my impression was that the middle class in Guatemala City was predominantly Protestant. Some of the largest congregations, such as El Shaddai and Verbo, were largely middle-class churches (though not exclusively) and it was clear that these people were attracted, in part, to the traditional Protestant notion that sober industry was rightly rewarded by God, that indeed one's material wealth clearly signaled God's approbation. On a national level, the wealth of the United States could be taken as evidence of righteousness; that is, the United States was wealthy and blessed in God's eyes because it was a Protestant nation. The handouts helped reinforce this notion among the poor: any country that could give away such quantities of stuff must be blessed in God's sight.

I could not tell whether these associations were intentionally exploited by US missionaries. In my experience, the missionaries—and I came to know quite a few of them in the capital—did not really seem aware that this affluence factor came into play. They were not people given to analysis, nor were they particularly perceptive folk.

The missionaries also exhibited a certain cultural blindness when they used advanced technology to communicate their message. The Christian television and radio barrages were only part of a large-scale technological campaign. The Wycliffe organization, for example, uses sophisticated technology to deliver its message. Wycliffe considers language the key to ministry, reasoning that the gospel and the word of the Lord are best heard in one's native language. In countries like Guatemala, where there are dozens of languages, some lacking written alphabets, the task is enormous. In many such countries, Wycliffe has set itself up as the Summer Institute of Linguistics (the name change is intended to draw attention to the supposed academic nature of the enterprise) with a central support staff in the capital and individuals working in small villages. Some work for years in these villages, mastering the language and translating one of the Gospels or the Book of Acts into the native tongue. But Wycliffe also relies on the latest gadgets in order to interest people in the message while they wait for the translations. I happened to meet a few of the Wycliffe missionaries, and while they were good people, I sometimes wondered if they fully appreciated the impact they were making on a given village, since the appearance and extended stay of a missionary and his family meant not only the introduction of the Bible but also the infiltration of American culture.

One of the Wycliffe people I met in the capital called himself the audiovisual specialist for the organization. His job involved driving around the highlands in a four-wheel drive van, bought with donations from his home church. In the van he carried video cameras, televisions, VCRs—the entire stock of an electronics store, it seemed. What he did, among other things, was to visit villages in the remotest parts of the country where the roads were barely passable, hauling along this electronics showroom for the sole purpose of playing video-taped reenactments of the Gospel stories to the villagers, most of whom had never seen television before.

I couldn't really understand what this approach accomplished, and when I expressed doubt, my friend assured me that the impact was tremendous. People really wanted to know more about the Gospels after seeing a bit of the story, he said (I tried to imagine how the cru-cifixion scene or the clearing of the temple might appear to the Indi-ans). I suspected that maybe it was television that they wanted to know more about, that technology, the medium, was more interest-ing than the message. But when I tried to explain this, my friend was puzzled. Just like the diet-shake missionary, he didn't recognize the potential for culture clash in his actions. He didn't perceive any pos-sible side effects that might go along with the importation of ad-vanced technology into a decidedly low-tech culture. After talking with him, I understood why anthropologists had been so concerned about the proliferation of evangelical missions.

The *evangélicos* could also be fairly criticized for their apocalyptic conservatism. Although they condemned Catholic liberation theol-ogy and the religious Left for un-Christian political involvement, I knew of no other group, religious or nonreligious, that was more per-sistently political in its interpretation of the Guatemalan scene than the *evangélicos*. They provided ideological and spiritual support for the counterinsurgency work of the army and the government. Many pastors cited the Gospel verses in which Christ tells his disciples to render unto Caesar that which is Caesar's, but ignored the apoliti-cism implicit in these verses, choosing instead to interpret Christ's words as a call to support directly the existing government. (Mean-while, related Pentecostal groups in Sandinista Nicaragua conve-niently ignored this verse altogether and rejected Caesar.)

The *evangélicos* were fanatical in their conservatism. On several occasions, I attended services at different churches, Assembly of God, Gospel Outreach, and Baptist, among others. And at every church, I was surprised at how quickly the associated missionary, whether American, Canadian, or Australian, turned our conversa-tion toward political issues (always assuming, of course, that because I was North American and at church we shared views). Missionaries emphasized the importance of an army victory over the guerrillas. Those who had been in the country a long time, decades in some cases, blamed the guerrillas and Jimmy Carter for ruining Guate-mala. Their fear of communism was boundless and they regarded the attempt to confront it as a heroic campaign supported by God. Even I had their blessing in this campaign. Twice a week I played basketball with a group of North American missionaries. After each game, there was a prayer, and in each prayer one of the missionaries asked the Lord to guide me as I worked on the dangerous San Carlos campus. (This same missionary was noteworthy for habitually wearing a T-shirt that read "Thank God you can still pray in the USA.") "Dangerous," of course, meant that the university—as everyone knew—was Godless and communist. Curiously, although they knew that I was working at the university under the auspices of the US government, they assumed that I also was in some way evangelizing at the school. I always had the impression that to them US government support was the same as church support, unless of course a Democrat like Carter had formulated policy. At any rate, they acted as though I had been given San Carlos as my special mission, and they were impressed by

Many missionaries, but not all, took an interest in Guatemalan politics because they believed that Guatemala played a key role in the approaching apocalypse. The East-West showdown was considered part of a larger struggle between God and Satan—a clean, simple, black-and-white issue, in which US support was necessary to defeat the devil. One day I attended the adult Sunday school class at the English-language church and listened to a very strange lesson. The teacher, an Oklahoman in his forties, suggested that because the strife prophesied in Revelations was part of God's plan, Satan was active in the world promoting *unity and harmony* so as to delay the apocalypse of the End Times, in which he, Satan, would be bound for a thousand years. According to the teacher, Satan was behind the antiapartheid movements in South Africa and the work of human rights groups the world over. He didn't quite come out and say that God's plan required apartheid, racial strife, and torture, but the implication was clear: he felt that Christians should support strife and *dis*unity because it brought the apocalypse closer.

This apocalypse, so the Bible said, consisted of certain stages or events. To the missionaries, the Great Tribulation was clearly already under way in Guatemala. But Christ would not come until thousands had converted and accepted him. For this reason, Gospel Outreach, the California-based church whose mission was to bring people into the fold in order to prepare for the Second Coming, turned its attention to Guatemala. In 1976, the leader of Gospel Outreach, Jim Durkin, decided that the devastating earthquake in Guatemala City was a Sign. He sent his followers to the obscure country, where they established Verbo, the church on Avenida Reforma, with the idea of bringing thousands, even millions, into the fold and preparing humankind for the Second Coming.

Yes, it was easy to criticize the American missionaries. But after being around them for some time, I felt that very often this criticism was based on exaggeration or misunderstanding. Furthermore, the critics were just as likely to interpret things in black-and-white terms as the missionaries themselves were. In other words, the critics were guilty of the very fault that they censured in others. For example, all sorts of wily and sinister machinations were imputed to the missionaries, and evangelism was made out to be an insidious campaign deliberately designed to contribute to the country's disintegration. Seen in this light, the *evangélicos* were considered one of the causes of Guatemala's social ills.

Yet, it seemed to me, the sudden surge in the popularity of evangelism could just as well be an *effect* of Guatemala's social ills, rather than a cause. First of all, the missionaries themselves were more naïve than insidious. Yes, they did weird things like giving out diet shakes and showing home movies of Jesus, but at the same time they *believed* that people benefited from these things, and they were earnest in their efforts. Of course, this belief was not enough to justify the results of their actions, which, critics were correct in pointing out, were far more harmful than the *evangélicos* realized. ("Innocence is a deadly thing," Graham Greene wrote of his Quiet American; and the more I witnessed of American involvement or, rather, the involvement of Americans, around the world, the more I realized that Greene got it right in creating Pyle, the prototypical American innocent.)

Nevertheless, the condemnation of evangelism did not adequately account for the fact that Guatemalans were willingly converting, that they were embracing this new interpretation of Christianity as a better way. Evangelism had many strong selling points besides free consumer goods. For one, evangelical church services appealed to Guatemalans. Instead of the repetitiveness and mystery of the Catholic Mass, an *evangélico* service offered rousing songs, handclapping, and other displays of simple enthusiasm. In the big urban churches, the buildings were fairly rocking with fervor, the noise of which could be heard out on the busy boulevards, even above the roar of traffic. The gregarious nature of Guatemalans found this approach to worship all but irresistible. Sometimes, too, the service allowed for abject displays of a sort of spiritual self-flagellation, in which the believer sprawled and wailed at the altar and screamed out despair over her (for it was most often a woman) sinful state. For some reason, these displays seemed more common in the storefront churches of poorer neighborhoods. On many occasions, I stood just outside the door to one of these tiny Pentecostal churches and watched as the worshipers worked themselves into states of frenzy, weeping and tearing at their hair.

The message emphasized in the *evangélico* churches also had strong appeal. Its essence—don't smoke, don't drink, don't womanize—was a direct assault on the fundamentals of Latin machismo, and one could understand why women were especially wont to embrace it. Evangelical Protestantism seemed able to change Guatemalan society, to reform some of its ills, more profoundly than any other agent at the time. It was doing something the military, the guerrillas, and USAID couldn't do, and the changes were clearly welcomed by many, many Guatemalans.

But Protestantism had also begun working some changes for the worse. The one change most apparent to me was a rapidly deepening hostility between the two main branches of Christianity in the country. Most Catholics had long regarded the *evangélicos* a little suspiciously, but tended to dismiss them as freakish. In 1989, however, a pastoral letter by Archbishop Penados del Barrio introduced a tone of hysteria into Catholic concerns over the growth of *evangélico* churches. Penados del Barrio attacked evangelism and accused it of being a tool of US imperialism. By advancing this conspiracy theory, the archbishop radicalized the issue for Catholics and in essence split society in two camps.

Actually, the *evangélicos* had radicalized matters long before the pastoral letter appeared. I was always surprised to hear *evangélicos*, especially the US missionaries I met, vilifying Catholicism as often as possible, and in quite harsh terms. Many asserted that Catholicism was a false Christianity used by the Devil to bind Central America in his chains, and I have heard the radio evangelists call Guatemala an important battleground against the pope and his priests, who apparently are agents of the Devil. The head of the Confederation of Evangelical Churches of Guatemala, Vitalino Similox, publicly declared that "most evangelical churches see the Catholic Church as the beast of the apocalypse."

The *evangélicos* apparently believed that a militant, aggressive stance toward Catholicism was part of their Christian duty. Indeed, Guatemalans of all faiths perceived that a new civil war had broken out in the country, one with religious rather than political consequences. Any occurrence with religious implications was interpreted in light of these tensions. When several Catholic churches were vandalized and valuable art and icons were stolen, the tensions between Catholics and *evangélicos* surfaced. The archbishop felt that the vandalism contributed to "a confrontation between the dominant religions of the country." Although there was no reason to assume Protestants were behind the thefts, Catholics were upset and suspicious because in their view President Jorge Serrano, an *evangélico*, had not done enough to protect the churches or halt the vandalism. In such an atmosphere, it was easy to believe that things would soon come to a boil. As one *evangélico* minister predicted, "Guatemala could become another Northern Ireland."

There were so many ambiguities in the *evangélico* movement that it was difficult to judge its impact on Guatemala. Clearly, the impact was great, working many profound changes upon the society, but were these changes for the better? Guatemalans themselves appeared undecided on this question. *Evangélicos*, of course, thought that the changes were for the better, while devout Catholics were adamant in their refutation. But in between was a large number of people—the nonpracticing Catholics and the irreligious—who were ambivalent. They regarded the *evangélicos* as somewhat freakish, and yet granted them a moral authority that no one else in the country could claim.

This ambivalence was most apparent in the attitudes of Guatemalans toward General Efraín Ríos Montt. Ríos Montt was a storied character in Guatemalan politics. In 1974, running as the Christian Democrat candidate, the general appeared to have won an easy victory, but the election results were annulled by more powerful military figures. In the late 1970s, after a period of exile, Ríos Montt began attending Verbo and soon became an *evangélico*. His political career was resurrected when in 1982 a group of junior army officers staged a coup against the sanguinary Lucas García and invited the retired general to head the junta (the general's status as a thwarted election winner gave the junta a measure of legitimacy). Thus, Guatemala had its first *evangélico* leader, and the general immediately received attention and money from hopeful fundamentalists in the United States. The Christian Broadcasting Network in Virginia sent significant contributions; in return, Ríos Montt assisted the spread of Protestant missions in Guatemala and began naming *evangélicos* to top government positions. Membership in Verbo quadrupled in the three months following the coup.

During his time as president, a scant eighteen months, Ríos Montt bemused the nation by delivering maniacal harangues every Sunday night on television—long-winded, fist-waving sermons in which he hectored the country for its immorality and godlessness. Ríos Montt's sermonizing appalled, angered, and embarrassed most Guatemalans. At the same time, there was noticeable improvement in the operation of the government. Corruption seemed less rampant, and the intensity of state-sponsored violence—catastrophically high under Lucas García—seemed to diminish somewhat. The death squads were less active in the capital, and news reports indicated that out in the country the general's "bullets and beans" campaign, designed to win over the "hearts and minds" of the Indians, was working tolerably well. These reports were false, of course, as later investigations by Amnesty International and Americas Watch and even the US State Department demonstrated. But the important thing was that in the capital, people *thought* that the general was cleaning up the army's act. (The worst place in the world for learning about the Guatemalan highlands was probably Guatemala City; no one knew what was going on "up there," and news reports, if they existed at all, were often wildly inaccurate or little better than government propaganda. The highlands, more remote to the capital than Miami, really seemed like another world.)

By the late 1980s, when Ríos Montt had been out of power for half a dozen years, people were willing to dismiss the silly sermons as a Ríos Montt idiosyncrasy, one they could tolerate in return for the order and honesty that they associated with his presidency. Thus, unexpectedly, as the 1990 election neared, the most popular candidate was Efraín Ríos Montt. Even staffers at the US embassy were caught off guard by this development. Some of my acquaintances there told me that they had not even considered the possibility of a Ríos Montt candidacy, let alone a victory for the old general.

As a candidate, Ríos Montt embodied the ambivalent attitude that Guatemalans felt toward Protestantism: fanatic and even a little crazy on the one hand, but honest, strict, and moral on the other. Even his campaign advertisements—five-minute spots on television—featured the same oscillating hand movements, the same mad eyes, and the same enthusiastic, shouting tenor that characterized his presidential sermons. But Guatemalans liked his message: order, an end to corruption, discipline. Despite the fact that the Supreme Court declared him constitutionally ineligible for the presidency (because he was a former president), he led all polls as the elections drew near.

Eventually Ríos Montt was barred from running and his name left off the ballot. But the general had succeeded in convincing Guatemalans that *evangélicos* had a greater moral authority than the corrupt politicians of the status quo, and this alone was a significant development in Guatemalan politics. Thus, when Ríos Montt was no longer eligible, voters switched their allegiance to an all-but-unknown candidate, Jorge Serrano, one of the *evangélicos* Ríos Montt had brought into government during his presidency. Out of nowhere, Serrano surged to victory in the final weeks of the election, and Guatemala had its second *evangélico* president.

After two years of observing and studying it, I could not say whether the *evangélico* movement was helping or hurting Guatemala. Like so many of the issues in Central America, this one was easier to understand and to judge from a safe distance, but once you moved closer, once you met some of the players, your perspective clouded and judgment proved more difficult. Before going to Guatemala, I would have said, with reasonable certainty, that the actions of an organization like Wycliffe were detrimental to the cultures of Guatemala because they brought more than just the Gospel to the Indians. They brought American culture, too, and its consumerism. Further, they tended to dominate the tribes to the point that the tribes became dependent upon the missionaries; in the long run, the presence of the missionaries threatened the cultural survival of the tribes. This line of thinking made perfect sense to me, and I accepted it uncritically.

Sure enough, once I went to Guatemala I was able to gather evidence that readily supported these convictions. I met Wycliffe people introducing televisions, VCRs, and video cameras to the highlands. I saw that they had assumed moral authority over the cultures they ministered to, effecting changes in education, in politics, and even agriculture. Most important, this moral authority was undermining the syncretic religious practices that had been part of the culture for five hundred years or more and were now discouraged because of their "immorality."

But damning as all this was, I was also forced to admit that the evangelical missionaries did a lot of good. They were, for the most part, good-hearted, well-intentioned people who seemed to care very much about the Indians. Theirs was a sincerity I did not often encounter in the USAID people, or the Guatemalan government's social agencies, or even among the many liberal watchdog groups that came down to decry abuses but did little themselves to alleviate the pain in individual people's lives. Too, the Wycliffe missionaries worked to preserve the native languages, and this at a time when few people gave a damn about the linguistic heritage of the Guatemalans. True, the anthropologists at the national university regarded Wycliffe interference as catastrophic, but I saw no one else working as diligently to save these languages as Wycliffe, and their preservation was of paramount importance. Furthermore, missionaries had not supported the army without some reservations, and on many occasions evangelical missionaries had interceded for the Indians and had saved lives by convincing the military to back off a bit. Clearly, it was difficult to defend Wycliffe participation in the literacy program sponsored by the national police and in other military programs that had pacification and not amelioration as their goal; but after meeting some of the people involved—kinder, gentler sorts—I had to conclude that the Indians were probably better off with the missionaries on the scene as a mitigating factor. An unchecked military was infinitely worse.

Restaurants

IN GUATEMALA CITY, American fast-food franchises had become a big presence: McDonald's, Burger King, Wendy's, Pizza Hut, and Showbiz Pizza could all be found on the major boulevards of the capital. These American franchises were rather expensive restaurants by Guatemalan standards. Even though the price of a hamburger was far lower than it was in the states, one quarter-pound burger alone cost more than the standard *"almuerzo económico,"* a complete midday meal served up at local restaurants for a bargain price. Consequently, the American franchises were strictly up-scale restaurants, affordable only to the middle and upper classes.

The most noticeable thing about American fast food in Guatemala was its emphasis on efficiency. Of course, in the states the entire business is built on getting the customers in and out as fast and as impersonally as possible, but in Central America life was just not lived that way. Nobody wanted to hurry through anything, least of all a meal. The fast-food code of conduct also directly challenged the Guatemalan tradition of leisurely transactions. Guatemalans liked to draw out all encounters between human beings; a sale must be negotiated, pondered, questioned; weather and family must be discussed before a deal could be settled. It surprised me that the McDonald's approach, with its emphasis on efficiency and speed, had won out over such an essential part of the Guatemalan mind-set. I don't know what sort of training program Guatemalan employees of McDonald's were put through, but whatever it involved, it succeeded remarkably. They were diligent and quick in the performance of their duties, so efficient I could only guess that their training must have involved some sort of indoctrination in the legendary Protestant work ethic. The results in Guatemala demonstrated that capitalists could be as successful as communists in reprogramming the mind. To see the McDonald's workers bustling about, responding to buzzers and beepers—well, it was as though you had, in entering the door, passed from the warm and easygoing Tropics into the frigid and mechanistic north.

McDonald's was not the only North American chain to succeed in coaching out of its employees the usual Guatemalan disregard for promptness. Domino's Pizza made one of the more startling and amusing attempts to import American efficiency. Domino's had made it big in the states by emphasizing "fast" over "food," their distinguishing characteristic being a promise to deliver a pizza to your door within thirty minutes of placing the order. When Domino's first came into Guatemala, I assumed that they would not even consider making the thirty-minute pledge there. Expecting Guatemalans to do something within such a strict time limit was tantamount to imposing a death sentence. At least that was the standing joke among the North American community in the city. This basic truth about the culture, however, had apparently not made its way back to corporate headquarters in the states. Domino's stood for speedy delivery no matter where in the world its name traveled. Corporate headquarters simply assumed that "fast" was valued worldwide and by God they were going to give Guatemalans the thirty-minute pizza. And by God they did. Using motorcyclists who roared around Guatemala's congested streets at breakneck speed (for driving is the one thing Guatemalans like to do fast), the Domino's people pulled off an amazing stunt: they kept their promise. For a while, anyway. When the motorcyclists started crashing and dying, the company imposed a speed limit and changed the promise to forty-five minutes.

This monomania for efficient pizza also produced one of the strangest spectacles you could hope to witness in Guatemala—the operation of a Domino's kitchen. I picked up a pizza there one night and could not believe what I saw. The employees had been trained to keep track of the time it took them to do their various tasks; in fact, the whole outfit was obsessed with time and teamwork. When one employee finished a task, the assembly of a medium cheese pizza, for example, he would shout out, "medium pizza—four minutes," to which the other employees would respond in unison, "Gracias." When a driver returned from a delivery, he shouted to the others, "Delivery—twelve minutes," and he in turn was answered with a collective "Gracias." When I placed my order, I was interrupted three times by the clerk's Pavlovian shout over her shoulder as her teammates proclaimed their times. And so it went all night in the Domino's store, a constant antiphony of time and thanks. Where this training gimmick originated I have no idea, for the pizza stores in the United States did not, to my knowledge, follow the same pattern. I wondered if it were, in the company's exaggerated concern for efficiency, an attempt to drill into people who naturally recoiled at such an approach to life the same obsession with time that we Anglos have. In other words, had it been deliberately devised specifically for

Latin Americans and other peoples less time-conscious than Anglos? If so, it was the most perverse demonstration I had yet seen of the neocolonial attempt to remold the Other in our likeness, an attempt to turn the Latin American employees into parodic automatons.

One of the pleasures still left to the traveler—and there are fewer and fewer as technology and universal consumer capitalism hurtle us toward a uniformly bland future—is the opportunity to sample restaurants. Guatemala does not have a sophisticated cuisine in the Mexican sense, that is, a cuisine that has developed beyond its peasant origins. Guatemalan food is simple, and simplicity is its great virtue. Still, good food was readily available in the country despite the general poverty. Many travelers, especially the British, have derided Central American food. I can only say that our experience shopping in markets taught us that the quality of the food available was vastly superior to what we bought in the States. Beef, for instance, was juicier and leaner. And the fruit and vegetables—well, there's no point in making a comparison. Guatemalan fruit and vegetables are simply the best I've ever eaten. Finding a great meal in a restaurant, however, was something of a hit-and-miss proposition. There were hundreds of little places downtown where in the early afternoon you could get a *comida corriente*—the daily special—for a dollar or two. This large lunch consisted of the staples—beans and tortillas—along with meat in some guise, and a vegetable, usually potato, squash, or yucca. These small family-owned restaurants put a chalkboard out on the sidewalk announcing their daily special. You walked around until you found one you liked. Sometimes the meals were mediocre. Sometimes they were excellent.

There were also some restaurants offering this *comida típica* on a grander scale. With names like Parador and Los Antojitos, these restaurants served "typical" Guatemalan food in a pleasing ambience: high, palm-thatched roofs, tropical birds squawking in cages, a marimba band, and more waiters than customers. Tourists rarely ate in these restaurants, but they were quite popular with the local business set, who went through their leisurely lunches with their calculators close at hand.

In Guatemala, given its history, any site no matter how pleasant can conceal the lurid. One day, I was lunching in the Parador with a friend from the university. It had been one of those days, perfect in every aspect, that get you smiling to yourself, pleased that you're where you are and certain that nowhere else could be finer than that place, that time. We were seated at a table on a patio, just far enough from the tree-lined boulevard for traffic to be inconspicuous and the air a bit fresher than ordinary. A marimba band played; a woman slapped tortillas into shape; an unctuous waiter kept us supplied with cold bottles of Gallo beer. Then my friend interrupted the reverie. "You see that wall over there?" He pointed to the inside of the restaurant, near the marimba band. "That is where they killed a leader of the Christian Democrats in 1974." Such was the geography and language of assassination in Guatemala. Any place could have such associations. In giving directions to a store, a Guatemalan might say something like, "It's on Sixth Avenue by the bank where they shot so and so." Or, "It's across the street from that gas station the *guerrilleros* bombed."

One rain-lashed day, I drove the kids to a birthday party at Showbiz Pizza, a horrific place where mechanical bears played Fourth of July music, and little token-operated amusement rides berated the partygoers with a cacophony of bells, shrieks, blasts, sirens, and miscellaneous wails. On top of that, the pizza was tasteless. The only possibility of surviving two hours in the place was to drink as much beer as possible. I sat with an acquaintance, a consultant for USAID who was often at these parties, our children being in the same class at the international school. We occupied a booth near the front—as far from the chaos as possible. The management, however, had made damn sure no one could escape the noise: they had placed televisions all over the restaurant that broadcasted—for God knows what reason—the musical pageant of robotic bears.

Showbiz Pizza fronted Avenida Reforma. From our booth we could look across the verge-divided boulevard at the US embassy. Flanking the pizza place was the three-story USAID building, and I couldn't help but think that the three buildings—embassy, USAID, Showbiz—stood in some kind of trinitarian relationship. The rain streamed down and saddened everything, a sort of holy rain dirging the day. It was September, the season of the *temporal* rains, and the mists were ever-present. This rain was cold, dreary, and long, not at all like the violent outpouring accompanying the thunderstorms of May and June. That very morning, I'd read about the landslides over in Zona 3, in the *barrancas* where the hovels of the destitute slid away with the cleansing showers. It was a yearly event, dozens dying because poverty left them nowhere to go, nothing to do but wait for the mudslide to bury them.

Looking around at the childish mayhem reserved for the well-to-do, I thought about the depressing permanence of places like Showbiz Pizza. Why couldn't Showbiz Pizza slide down a *barranca* in a rage of mud? But rain was not the ruin of places like this—we would never be rid of such places. Instead, the rain only made life more miserable for the poor. The *barrancas* filled and the slopes slid away taking scores of shacks down the ravine. Children everywhere played in puddles but only the poor became infected from doing so. . . . I began to wonder just what sort of world we'd been making, a world of artificial amusement and fabricated food, a world of canned music and T-shirts with cartoon cats gorging on junk food, a world where mud coursed through the hovels and people starved, mired in their own muck. Sitting in Showbiz, I could appreciate, for that moment, the guerrillas' anger—the urge and the need, too—but most of all the anger, that made them willing to machine gun the whole bloody business.

USAID

ACROSS THE STREET from Showbiz Pizza stood a nondescript glass box building that housed the US government's foreign aid operations, the Agency for International Development. USAID was highly active in Guatemala. With the newly elected civilian government in power and the United States eager to support what it considered a showcase democracy, Central America's great success story, USAID projects— projects that were intended to reinforce conservative economic policies—were proliferating all over the country, especially in the capital. One of the most impressive things about Guatemala was the way in which virtually every program, no matter how well-intentioned, ended up helping the wealthy much more than the needy. This was certainly true with USAID. In the highlands, USAID undertook an economic development program that coincided with and supported the Guatemalan army's pacification strategy and its counterinsurgency campaigns. USAID's rural development programs, in other words, were concentrated in those areas where the army was most active. For years, until the US Congress put a stop to it, USAID assisted directly in two of the army's most invidious operations—the model village and "development pole" programs in the Quiché region. USAID was not permitted to use economic aid to support military programs. But to no one's surprise, USAID money indirectly found its way into military-controlled relief organizations, such as the Comité Nacional de Emergencia and the Comité Nacional de Reconstrucción. My acquaintances at USAID took this fact for granted. What were you going to do, they shrugged, when the military controlled everything in Guatemala anyway? In private, US officials acknowledged that their "showcase democracy" was at best an illusion, at worst a sham. The military continued to run the show in Guatemala. So what could you do, they asked, when the money you gave to *any* government agency—whether the Ministry of Education or the Ministry of Health or BANDESA (Bank of Agricultural Development) or even the Electricity Institute—ended up supporting in one way or another the military's "pacification" of the highlands? Even road-building programs, long a USAID favorite, helped the military, since the army needed these roads to move people and equipment more efficiently. In essence, USAID assisted, though not directly or willingly, in the militarization of the highlands. But USAID people preferred to remain optimistic; after all, the US interstate system was conceived for purposes of national defense yet had also facilitated commerce. In the same way, they hoped, new infrastructure in the highlands and jungles would eventually help stimulate the economic development of those isolated regions.

USAID could point to other successes as well, particularly in its program of "democracy strengthening." Through USAID's Inter-American Center for Electoral Assistance and Promotion (CAPEL), the United States had helped fund the electoral process in Guatemala, focusing primarily on the popularization of Guatemala's latest flirtation with democracy. Ever since the CIA had overthrown a democratically elected government in 1954, Guatemala had been an embarrassment for the United States. The idea in the 1950s was to purge the country of its communistic tendencies and to establish a "showcase of democracy." Unfortunately, the purge eliminated not only alleged communists but also the more democratically oriented elements of Guatemalan society. The only remaining power in the country was the military, and the military knew how to consolidate that power, build on it, and effectively exclude those who would challenge it. The "showcase of democracy," Phase I, turned into a textbook military dictatorship. In some respects, the appearance of armed guerrilla groups in the early 1960s was a godsend for the United States because the renewed existence of a communist threat provided a convenient excuse for the failure of democracy. The military had to run the show(case), the thinking went, because it alone could effectively deal with insurrection.

But by the mid-1980s, after years of brutality and terror, the US government, admitting the failure of its look-the-other-way policy, urged the military to hold elections and turn power over to a civilian government. In 1986, Guatemala once again became a showcase of democracy; the United States even resurrected the same terminology that had been so embarrassingly inappropriate the first time around. Showcase, Phase II, was all the more important to the US government because the Reagan administration wanted to argue that Sandinista Nicaragua was undemocratic; such an argument was not convincing as long as "free" countries like Guatemala remained under military rule. Much of USAID's money thus went toward the creation and financing of certain institutions, such as think tanks and study centers, that promoted the democratization of the country. This was no easy task in a country where freedom of expression had long been severely curtailed and where tolerance of opposing views was all but unknown.

Certainly in many respects this "democracy strengthening" was an admirable project, one that did succeed in providing a basis for democracy. Elections came off, the constitution was upheld in numerous court cases, parties were formed and candidates campaigned (quite a few were assassinated, too, but the embassy didn't expect miracles). This burst of democratic activity was indeed a change, but not the unqualified success that the Reagan administration had hoped for. Many people in Guatemala, including some embassy people I knew, doubted that democracy had really caught on. Skeptical Guatemalans believed that the military lingered in the background, and that the current elected government as well as any future elected government would have to operate with the knowledge that wrong moves—that is, anything unacceptable to the military—would bring the generals out of the shadows. In essence, the military held veto power over any governmental decision. An acquaintance at USAID noted that Guatemala's government really had four branches—the constitutional branches (executive, legislative, and judicial) and the extraconstitutional branch of the military. "Checks and balances," he said, was a "paper concept" in Guatemala; since the military held the ultimate check, the balance was weighted in its favor.

But the military was not the only obstacle to democratization. As the new elections neared, and as the political parties proliferated, often with some USAID support or encouragement, it became more and more apparent that these parties were formed to serve personal ambitions; political ideas, particularly the furthering of democratic principles, did not inspire any of the candidacies. Guatemala's democracy was not a popular democracy; the people were left out of it. It was a democracy of principals not principles, of aspiration not inspiration. Democracy was simply a new game for the traditional power elites to play.

Curiously, some of the biggest obstacles to USAID's goal of democracy strengthening were other USAID programs. Over the years, some of USAID's economic policies had proven counterproductive to the development of a meaningful democracy. USAID sought to build an economy driven by free enterprise and capitalism, but rather than encourage systemic change, USAID tried to work within the framework of oligarchic capitalism. Especially in the 1980s, USAID accepted the principles of "trickle-down" economics, and accordingly awarded the better part of its economic assistance to the conservative elite, who controlled most of the nation's resources and industries. This elite oligarchy continually blocked any kind of fiscal or political reform in Guatemala, and as long as it, aligned with the military, possessed this kind of control, Guatemala remained an enormously inequitable society and its democracy was more show than showcase.

USAID was content to trust the unproven policy that wealth trickles down—something that did not work in the United States and really had no validity in a society where the elite so easily manipulated everything to its advantage. Even when Guatemala's economy grew substantially (in the 1970s, for example), the gap between rich and poor only increased. Thus, without some effective systemic change to redress this imbalance, USAID money only exacerbated Guatemala's problems, even when (perhaps especially when) the funded programs were, in USAID's judgment, "successful."

For example, USAID promoted the diversification of Guatemala's economy by encouraging the production of nontraditional crops, such as spices, vegetables, and flowers. This strategy certainly had its merits in an economy that depended too heavily on coffee and bananas. But the strategy proved far more successful for commercial farmers than for subsistence farmers. New crops, especially if they were grown for export, did not by themselves change the system of land tenure in Guatemala; indeed, they were likely to worsen the imbalance. This had long been the history of agriculture in Guatemala, even before USAID began its tinkering. If there was money to be made in an export commodity, then those who had access to land were going to make money, and if the market proved particularly profitable, the commercial farmers would increase their holdings—as they had ever since large coffee *fincas* replaced cochineal plots in the nineteenth century. Fewer and fewer owners held more and more land: this was the most basic fact of Guatemalan agriculture.

Consider the rise and fall of cardamom production in Guatemala. Cardamom, a spice not previously grown or consumed in the country, was introduced in the mid-1970s as an alternative to the traditional exports. The exportation of cardamom (primarily to the Middle East) turned out to be a lucrative enterprise. By the mid-1980s Guatemala produced 60 percent of the world's cardamom. USAID sponsored several programs designed to move peasant farmers into underpopulated parts of the country (called development poles), such as the isolated Transverse Strip of the north, and helped them to get started in cardamom. But, as often happened with agricultural products, other Third World countries (including Honduras and Costa Rica, likewise encouraged by USAID) had started growing cardamom, too. But the demand had not grown along with the supply; consequently, the market price fell to the point that the crop cost more to produce than it could be sold for. USAID's peasants, stuck out in the northern jungle, were left with a worthless, not to mention inedible, crop.

The idea behind nontraditional exports—diversification—was a good one. But the results were less than satisfactory for those who needed the most help. Cardamom and flowers cannot be eaten, and in Guatemala the rate of population growth was already well ahead of the annual rate of food production. As a result, USAID had to increase food aid to the point that Guatemala imported basic grains from the United States. Since the structure of Guatemalan agriculture remained essentially the same, with a few very large haciendas and a great many tiny subsistence plots—it was hard to see how nontraditional exports, by themselves, could help anyone other than those who were already rich. The statistical results of the program were acceptable—an improved balance of payments for the country—but these results were meaningless given that they were achieved at the expense of a more equitable society.

There were other problems with the nontraditional exports, including the significant problem of production costs. Snow peas, for example, were extremely costly to grow—at least ten times the cost of corn. This cost meant two things: (1) only those with money to invest could afford the risk, and anything dependent on world market prices is a big risk to begin with; and (2) generally, foreign companies—producers of the fertilizer necessary for growing the nontraditionals—made the neatest profits out of the arrangement; indeed, USAID money often went straight to US companies for the purchase of chemicals and specialized equipment. The balance of payments situation could thus actually worsen—without of course some careful fudging of the official statistics. The successes of USAID, in fact, were largely statistical—paper successes that would never truly redress the needs of Guatemala unless the structural and systemic problems of the society were taken into consideration. In case after case, USAID programs tended to further the antidemocratic and grossly inequitable agenda of the military and the elite, even as those programs were promoted and lauded for the wonders they were working.

USAID's programs surely merited some criticism, but it was also possible to argue that they did accomplish some good things. The USAID people I met at parties seemed like sincere, hard-working people, well qualified to do what they were doing, and concerned that

the United States do its best to assist Guatemala. For the most part
the people I talked to understood the problems Guatemala faced,
spoke intelligently about those problems, and had some decent ideas
on how to go about changing things. For example, every US government representative I spoke with recognized that the country's biggest problems were rooted in the alliance of the military and the oligarchy. In fact, USAID was responsible for one of the most damning
studies ever conducted in Guatemala, a 1982 study that found that
Guatemala had the most inequitable land distribution in all of Latin
America. The Guatemalan government, at that time directly under
military control, branded the report "communistic"—a good indication of the report's severity (yet another McCarthy-era remnant in
Guatemala was the belief that even the US government was infil-
trated by Communists who used every opportunity, such as reports
on land tenure in Latin America, to subvert freedom-minded oligar-
chies the world over). The American "experts" understood that Guatemala's problems were structural and that nothing would change
until the basic structure was altered. They understood, too, that a
few bandages and some cosmetics would do little, if anything, to
change the bruised and ugly appearance of that society.

This, anyway, was the understanding of those I met; at parties, over
drinks, they readily acknowledged that real change was impossible
in Guatemala unless the military was dismantled and the power of
the oligarchy curtailed. They also acknowledged that the projects
they worked on did very little to effect these changes. In short, they
seemed resigned to applying bandages and cosmetics.

Of course, they were never so cynical, even after several rum and
Cokes, as to suggest that their work accomplished nothing. They
were, generally, rather defensive about that work whenever its value
was called into question. I remember one party, a birthday party for
one of the embassy kids, when I fell into conversation with a man
working on economic development. We were sitting in lawn chairs
in the backyard of a very fine home, a large and modern place located
in one of Guatemala City's exclusive zones. (American embassy personnel were allowed to live only in well-to-do areas—for security—
and their monthly allowance for housing was more than enough to
put them into some very fancy houses.) A maid delivered a tray of
hors d'oeuvres. A bartender stood ready to refill our glasses with
whiskey or rum. And out on the lawn a magician performed for a
crowd of hyperactive blonde kids bemused by his Spanish humor. My
acquaintance was a thin man, youngish and a little pale looking. He
wore a guayabera shirt and sipped steadily at a glass of whisky. He
spent his time in Guatemala as a sort of liaison (he called himself a

"point guard") between USAID and several private-sector organizations that represented the oligarchy and the business community.
His job: provide financial, technical, and above all else philosophical
assistance to groups such as the Chamber of Entrepreneurs and the
Amigos del País, associations that promoted free enterprise and private sector initiatives. "I assist in any way I can," he said. "Basically,
I dish off the ball and let the local businessmen finish the play."

USAID was spending a lot of money—around ten million dollars—
to strengthen the private sector and to create a favorable climate for
investment. This, my acquaintance claimed, was an even more important project than the "democracy strengthening" that his colleagues in USAID were working on. It was more important because
"without economic freedom, political freedom was just not going to
happen."

My acquaintance had only been in Guatemala for a little over a
year. Before that he had "done pretty much the same thing" on one
of the English-speaking islands in the West Indies. That had been his
first USAID posting after his graduation from an MBA program in the
Midwest. He had joined USAID, he said, "out of a sense of adventure." So far, after a year, he liked Guatemala better than the islands.
"A bit more authentic," he said, "and not so touristy. Tourism is good
for the islands, of course, but it kind of spoils the atmosphere. Here
it seems more genuine."

Maybe so. But I wondered what he thought about Panajachel and
Chichicastenango, where tourism had, to my mind, run rampant
over the native culture. Tourism there was spoiling the authenticity
of the highlands, was it not?

It turned out that he had not yet been farther from the capital than
Antigua. Unfortunately, his work kept him pretty much tied to the
capital, and the embassy was still chary of the situation in the highlands. While ordinary tourists might have no problem there, it was
still considered a bit risky for government personnel—the potential
for kidnapping and all that. They weren't *prevented* from going, of
course, but they were discouraged from it and, anyway, like he said,
they were too busy in the capital. But he really wanted to visit Lake
Atitlán sometime before he left Guatemala.

I asked him how long he intended to stay in the country.

"Well, in this kind of work you don't really get much choice. You
get moved around a lot, especially when you're young and learning
the game plan. I'll probably be here two, maybe three years. Sometimes they keep you in a place longer, maybe five years if the project's
big league, but right now I'm working on this private sector strengthening thing. Probably when the foundation's laid and things are on a

firm footing here, I'll move on. Now that I'm learning more Spanish, I hope to stay in Latin America. The way Nicaragua's looking, if the Sandinistas lose the election, they're going to need the same thing there—support for the private sector and all."

Out on the lawn, the party noise reached a crescendo. The kids broke into cheering and clapping: the magician had just produced a bunny from a hat and given it to the birthday boy. We had seen this same magician at four or five parties before, and each time the routine was the same. But kids like repetition, and each time they eagerly anticipated the appearance of the gift rabbit. Already the thing was hopping around the yard, pursued by a host of snatching, grasping hands. For the next half hour, the bunny's ears and legs were tugged and twisted, and its nose was repeatedly pinched. I wondered how long the magician's rabbits managed to live after he gave them away. At the moment, it seemed an apt analogy for USAID's programs: a magician giving away rabbits to a bunch of spoiled kids who would only tease the thing to death.

Later, in mulling over what my USAID acquaintance had told me about his work, I began to understand the factors that limited the success of American foreign aid. The first factor concerned the philosophy behind the aid: "Private enterprise produces liberty." All right, but what did that mean in Guatemala, a country where capitalism already functioned in its most brutal form: the penny capitalism by which most of the Indian and ladino peasants tried to survive? It seemed to me that economic freedom thrived in Guatemala; after all, the government did nothing to regulate industry and it only sporadically enforced labor laws. What bothered USAID most, apparently, was any kind of government intervention in the economy, especially when that intervention favored national companies over foreign companies. The United States preferred to encourage private initiative (although USAID also spoke of "initiatives to encourage private investment," which to me sounded like government intervention on behalf of the rich), arguing—as did the Reagan administration back home—that the poor would have more chances to improve their lot if private businesses were making money. Investment meant jobs; wealth trickled down: this was the mantra of USAID's economic specialists.

USAID's strategy for implementing this philosophy was to create, foster, and finance private sector think tanks, associations, and economic assistance programs. This strategy led to the second factor limiting USAID's success: generally, USAID supported the well-to-do business elite. The United States especially favored a group of business leaders who were considered "modernizers." The modernizers included those who were farsighted enough to take advantage of the provisions of the Caribbean Basin Initiative and other measures designed to encourage exports. The organizations and think tanks to which these modernizers belonged spent much of their effort, and USAID dollars, on self-promotion. They tried especially to create an image of private business as a new force, the primary force behind the movement for democratization in the country. Organizations like the Amigos del País, an organization my acquaintance worked with, published books and brochures that supported the electoral process and called for stability in the country's institutions. Yet the Amigos del País already had a long history; before USAID ever existed the Amigos represented the conservative oligarchy and the essentially feudalistic economic system that remained the principal obstacle to a more equitable distribution of wealth. However they phrased their rhetoric, this oligarchy did not care for democracy, modernization, or even economic liberalism (after all, the private sector that USAID lauded had always received tremendous help from government investment and intervention); what it cared for was the perpetuation of an extremely lucrative arrangement. And USAID, in its eagerness to promote free enterprise, used its funds to support these organizations. The entrepreneurial rhetoric of their publications complained that "Big Government" infringed on economic freedom through taxes, minimum wage laws, and the like—even though taxation was all but nonexistent and the minimum wage, absurdly low to begin with, was routinely ignored. It was, in short, a segment of society that had long gotten its way and was principally interested in maintaining its privileges—reform was the furthest thing from its interests, unless by economic reform one meant lower export taxes, privatization of services, and the liberalization of price controls.

And yet the United States, in the name of reform, gave this segment large sums of money, money that in turn simply supported the same wildly unjust, cash crop–driven economy that necessitated US aid for the impoverished masses in the first place. Aid changed nothing; instead it perpetuated a system that ensured that charity for the poor would always be needed. In other words, aid money to the one group (the oligarchy) negated the aid given to the poor. USAID worked against itself. Curiously, the descriptive brochure titled "USAID en Guatemala" that I picked up at the embassy mentioned only rural development, nutrition, health, education, and balance of payments assistance as the type of programs that USAID supported in Guatemala. The color photos showed a campesino watering cabbages and a schoolroom of traditionally clad Indian children seated at their desks.

Both text and photos implied that USAID was hard at work combating poverty in Guatemala. Maybe, but at the same time USAID was helping to perpetuate the system that had created the poverty. The pamphlet made no mention of the type of "economic development" my point guard acquaintance was working on, and did not mention the financial assistance given to private businesses.

A third factor limited USAID's success in Guatemala: the limitations placed on the agency's own personnel. Not that they were unqualified; the expertise of USAID workers in their various fields was unquestionable. USAID, however, overemphasized expertise in these fields—whether economics, agriculture, or health—and underemphasized familiarity with a given country. My acquaintance was a good example. After two years on an English-speaking island in the Caribbean, he was transferred to Guatemala. The nature of his work remained the same: in both places he worked with the local private sector and sought to improve the climate for investment. But the context for that work was very different, and he had much to learn before he could begin to do an adequate job in Guatemala. His experience in the West Indies did not necessarily prepare him for Guatemala; yet USAID did not seem to take this basic fact into consideration. The agency's policy, apparently, was that if one had worked as liaison to the private sector in one Third World country, then one was qualified to do the job in another Third World country. While there was certainly some validity to this view, USAID's practice of moving its people from country to country every few years hamstrung their effectiveness. Even an expert in management or business administration could not be expected to learn about a complicated country like Guatemala in two short years, especially without prior knowledge of the language. Add to this brevity the restrictions placed on personnel—restrictions that kept them cloistered in certain zones of the capital—and you ended up with skilled technocrats almost perfunctorily applying their expertise regardless of the circumstances. USAID had a philosophy, a paradigm that each country—whether Trinidad, Guatemala, or Malawi—was made to fit; the philosophy could not readily be adjusted to fit the country. Economic development, USAID seemed to think, was accomplished in basically the same way no matter where in the world it went. An expert in economic development thus needed only basic background information in order to work in any given country.

These policies also clearly affected the psychology of the USAID people. It seemed to me remarkable that my acquaintance could do anything at all when he had to struggle just to carry on a normal conversation in Spanish. One obvious result of his language limitations was that those business leaders who spoke English well had more influence with him than those who spoke little or none; on this score alone, then, he had a skewed understanding of the country, and the whole thrust of US aid to the private sector shifted because of a "small" factor like this: from the start, certain Guatemalans had more say than others, had more of a claim on US monies, and had more opportunities to shape the USAID worker's understanding of the country. The same problem surely occurred in the highlands, where a US agronomist would probably deal better with Spanish-speaking ladinos than with Indians. In all dealings with Indians, the agronomist would have to rely on interpreters, whether ladinos or Wycliffe missionaries. Even if his interpreter was a Spanish-speaking Indian, that Indian would then have enormous power, and US aid would depend entirely on what he had to say.

Another thing: USAID personnel knew that they would probably be transferred to another country before too long. On a personal level, an impending move would necessarily preoccupy a person's thoughts and thus curtail commitment to the current job. On a professional level, an impending move could possibly cause one to feel less committed to a particular project or country, especially when there were problems. There would, in short, be a strong temptation to think, "What the hell, I'm out of here in six months," whenever a job got too "heavy." Furthermore, such a move would mean starting all over in a new context completely different from the USAID worker's previous experience. Indeed, even if he or she were transferred from another Central American country, such as Nicaragua, the great differences between the two—and they really were two quite different societies—would make the adjustment to the new country challenging. North Americans, especially at the government level, have never really caught on to the fact that the Latin American countries are quite different from one another, and that they cannot always be regarded as a conglomerate.

The USAID people I met seemed like good people. They were well educated and for the most part sensitive. Above all, they were thoughtful about Guatemalan issues. Furthermore, over the years USAID had gathered extremely useful information about the country and about Guatemalan society, as exemplified by the 1982 study on land reform. The information was there, the people were good—and yet USAID didn't seem to accomplish much. Because USAID, like the Peace Corps, had to work through an oppressive, corrupt government, and because USAID did not keep its people around long enough to truly learn about this complex society, much of the agency's potential for effecting change was constrained and wasted.

The Gringo Presence

ONE NIGHT I WENT to a party given by the embassy's cultural affairs officer. He had a fine house, decorated with furniture and art from the many countries where he had been posted—so much of it that the place looked like a museum of folk arts and crafts from around the world. I was looking over some of the collection when the cultural affairs officer came up to me.

"It's taken me twenty years to collect all this. Finland, Haiti, you name it, it's here. Glad to see someone appreciate it."

I did appreciate it. He had some of the best carved *santos* I had ever seen, and we discussed the differences between his—collected in the Dominican Republic—and the kind made by the *santeros* of New Mexico. Although as a Fulbrighter I was in Guatemala under the auspices of the USIS, the cultural affairs officer and I had not previously met. His assistant officer had handled all the arrangements with the university. In fact, he had never even heard of me, nor did he seem aware that USIS had arranged anything at all with the University of San Carlos. "We really sent someone into that lion's den? Christ, what were we thinking? But to hell with all that. Details. We get so many people coming down, I can't keep track."

Nevertheless, he was curious about my work, especially when I mentioned some articles I had written about American authors in Central America.

"I didn't know there were any," he said.

I mentioned O. Henry and Richard Harding Davis and a few of the travel writers like John Lloyd Stephens and Ephraim Squier. He had heard of Stephens. O. Henry surprised him: "*The* O. Henry? 'The Gift of the Magi' guy?" I told him of my interest in the differences between British and American writing on the colonial situation. I found it curious, I said, that British writers had produced so much on the colonies—culminating in great works like Forster's *A Passage to India* or Burgess' Malayan trilogy—while American writers had written almost nothing on US territories and protectorates, and certainly nothing of literary importance. Where was the great—or even the mediocre—American novel on the Philippines, for example? Why hadn't the guerrilla war we fought in the Philippines or our nearly fifty years of colonial experience there inspired our novelists?

The cultural affairs officer was frowning. "No, no, now wait a minute there, Professor. The United States has never had colonies. No, sir."

"Well, maybe not in the same way that the British did, but still the Philippines—"

"That was different. Apples and oranges."

In any case, the main thing, I insisted, was that no American literature of any importance came out of our experience abroad, whether you called that experience colonial, neocolonial, or imperialist.

The cultural affairs officer called his wife over. "Listen," he said, "listen, dear. This, this here professor . . . " For the first time I heard the drunkenness in his voice, though his eyes were still keen and glaring right at me.

"Yes, I know the professor. His children go to Colegio Maya with ours."

His face softened. "Do they, now? Well. Glad to have you here, glad to have you."

His wife smiled and steered him away to another group, and I was left alone with the *santos*. That was not the end of it, however. A few weeks later I found in my mail at the embassy a two-page typed letter explaining the distinction between British colonies and American protectorates.

Embassy parties always provided me with fine conversations of this sort. There were a good many parties at that, parties for every occasion from the Super Bowl to Easter egg hunts. I fell into conversation with everyone from an archaeologist who was excavating caves in the Petén to an orphanage director who was later arrested for child molesting. One of the strangest parties was a Halloween get-together held at the marines' house, a beautiful place set on a wooded lot in one of Guatemala City's finest neighborhoods. That evening, the place was overrun with goblins and skeletons and witches— scores of gringo kids hooting and hollering and sucking candy. The marines presided; wearing T-shirts and smiling, no longer the dour, uniformed toughs who stood guard in the embassy lobby, they were transformed into rambunctious, fun-loving teenagers. They called the kids, chased after them, and led them into an elaborate haunted house that had taken the marines a whole month to set up. I sent my children into the fray, grabbed a beer, and found an acquaintance who was deep into conversation with a Spanish-speaking gentleman. My friend introduced the Guatemalan as a colonel in the armed forces. The colonel blinked with modesty, inclined his head in a gentlemanly way, and shook my hand at length. I had interrupted at an inopportune moment. My USIS acquaintance, an attractive young woman and a decided feminist, was commenting on the lack of opportunity available to women in Guatemalan society—a point hard to refute. The colonel, who clearly had intentions of flirting with and perhaps seducing the pretty gringa, found himself in the uncomfortable position of defending Guatemalan machismo while attempting to hustle a woman. A bit drunk, he stumbled through the usual trite arguments about a woman's place, the centrality of the woman in Guatemalan domestic affairs, and so on, but the American woman would have none of it. "Ah, bullshit," she said in English. She had obviously lost interest in the conversation, but the colonel was unable to check himself. Resorting to the English he had learned in training exercises with the US military, he pursued the point.

"No, no es *bullshit*," he said. "Definitivamente no es *bullshit*."

He was like the foolish chess player who realizes that his strategy is doomed to fail but persists in it anyway in the wild hope that some quirk of luck will save him. But each comment he made put him more and more out of favor. Before long, he was addressing me and not my friend, perhaps hoping I would come to his defense. It was unfortunate, but true, he said, that no woman in Guatemala had ever shown any kind of political acumen. He did not mean to say that women were not intelligent, no, but female intelligence was of a sort altogether different from that needed in the Machiavellian world of Guatemalan politics.

It so happened that a few weeks before this party Rigoberta Menchú, the Indian activist who would a few years later win the Nobel Peace Prize, had been in Guatemala for a brief visit during which she had been confined to a hotel room because of death threats. I immediately thought of her and her growing international reputation—surely she was an example of a Guatemalan woman with leadership qualities, I said. My American friend smiled at me and winced, as if to say, "Now you've done it."

I remember the colonel's red, watery eyes as he leaned his face into mine, a redness brought on by the fine whisky the marines were serving. As he spoke he leaned closer and closer, until our faces were in a proximity normally reserved for lovers. But I didn't back away. I met his besotted stare. I especially remember his fine hands, smooth and delicate. Again and again, he lightly set his long, slender fingers on my forearm, and whenever he made what he considered a particularly incisive point, he punctuated it by pressing my skin more firmly and giving my arm a little shake.

"Why? Why, my friend, all this interest in that Indian woman?" His voice was soft and pained, imploring, like that of a mother begging an improvident child to stop indulging his destructive habit. "This woman, she's a guerrilla—we know that she is, we have the photos to prove it, and I know because I have seen these photos. Oh, yes, yes. It is she, in the guerrilla uniform and carrying the guns of the guerrilla. A soldier, that is what she is—a subversive soldier. She's no lady—a lady does not have a gun under her dress, eh? It's ridiculous the attention she receives. She's uneducated. She has not been in the country for the past ten years. She does not know the actual reality. Human rights? What does the whore know about human rights? How can she work for human rights from a five-star hotel in Europe? Do you know, she's been seen in the Chanel store in Paris wearing a sexy yellow dress and Rolex worth five—no, seven—thousand dollars! Yes! *La puta.*"

The colonel's anger seemed to intensify his drunkenness. He put a soft, trembling hand on my shoulder for support. Spittle sat on his lips, his eyes blurred, and he leered at me to repeat with indignation—the indignation of someone decrying heavenly injustice—his final judgment of Rigoberta Menchú: *la puta,* the whore.

His speech done, the colonel leaned against me and waited for my reaction to his words. I heard some howls from across the grounds of the marines' estate: several costumed children danced and leaped, screamed and laughed as one of the marines, dressed as a skeleton, charged them, bellowing the nonsense of the dead.

"Sí, la puta," I said.

The colonel smiled and backed away, certain he had made his point.

Sometime later, I told a friend at the embassy about the incident. The colonel had given me pretty much the straight army line on Menchú, my friend said. The army had been bruiting a good deal about those alleged photos, but they had never actually been shown to anyone at the embassy, to his knowledge. "They gripe a lot about this woman and expect us to sympathize. We tell them basically to stop whining. Let her talk. What's going to happen? The army's all but won the war. The guerrillas are reduced to little more than a bothersome pest, and now the generals want to go and create another Ho Chi Minh. You know what worries me? They talk about killing her. Next time she sets foot in Guatemala, they say, that's it. Bang, bang. Death squad. Idiots. Frigging morons. What the hell do they want to go and make a martyr of her for? One stupid move like that and it's going to be hell to pay. International scrutiny, money withheld by Congress, and all that. Leave it to the Guatemalan army to do something stupid—they'll do any damn dumb thing and then come crying to us because the world points a finger at them. And when we chew them out, they get all bent out of shape and say they didn't need the frigging aid anyway. Well, what do you expect, I say, what the hell do you expect?"

The height of the party season for Americans resident in Guatemala came on the Fourth of July. The main event of the day took place at the ambassador's residence when, in the late afternoon, the ambassador hosted a ceremony outside on the grounds of the residence, an extremely formal affair, which was obviously staged to impress the Guatemalans. Important dignitaries of Guatemalan society and the foreign community were invited to attend this solemn event, which included speeches, flag raisings, more speeches, national anthems, and still more speeches. The complete text of the ambassador's address was carried the next day in the newspapers. The Guatemalans, great lovers of formality and solemn occasions, relished the whole affair. One American diplomat told me that he had previously worked in the Dominican Republic and Nicaragua, two much more informal countries where the embassy's Fourth of July celebrations were more festive and casual, "a weenie roast or country barbecue, something like that." But in Guatemala, suit and tie were necessary, along with long-winded speeches and inflated rhetoric. Fortunately, a cocktail preceded and followed the ceremony, so it was possible to get a little light-headed and let the warm afternoon sun put one in a more fluid state of mind. Our little contingent of Fulbrighters, woefully underdressed, stood off to one side scoffing at the speeches *sotto voce* and trying to catch the attention of one of the numerous waiters who passed through the crowd with trays of drinks.

Evening fell, the speeches went on and on, and a few of us slipped away for a stroll on the grounds. The place was impressive: swimming pool, tennis courts, fountains, even a few Mayan relics, which the archaeologist examined carefully and declared fake. When we returned to the crowd, the ceremony was concluding with an unintentionally avant-garde rendition of the "Star Spangled Banner" by the Guatemalan army band and the launching of some miniature hot air balloons, a traditional part of Guatemalan celebrations. To get the balloons to rise, one lit a fire in the basket part and the hot air produced by the flames lifted the paper balloon skyward. This evening, however, technical difficulties caused some delay, and it took the concerted effort of the marines to get the things lit properly. Meanwhile, the band continued its experiment in dissonance through several Souza marches. At last a fire was lit and a balloon lifted up above the crowd. The band stopped, and everybody watched the ascent, exclaiming with delight on the pretty colors. Suddenly, about thirty feet above our heads, the paper caught fire and in a matter of seconds the entire balloon was consumed in flame. The crowd fell silent. And then the archaeologist, who had downed a few too many whiskeys, said in a voice a little too loud, "God almighty, just like the Challenger!" It was not really the most fitting conclusion to a celebration of our nation's independence, nor was the comment much appreciated by those within earshot, but the jaded Fulbrighters found it funny as hell, and we laughed and laughed and decided the day would not be complete without a trip downtown to the gringo bars for a proper drunk.

The gringo bars gave you a different perspective on the American presence in Guatemala. These were the bars frequented by young, bohemian foreigners, a mixed crowd that included those who were just drifting through the Third World and those who were committed to some cause, such as graduate research or social justice. You met everyone from the deadbeat to the dedicated.

The Europa Bar in Zona 1 was the more international and, because of its downtown location, the seedier of the gringo haunts. Backpackers from all over the First World, but especially from Germany and the United States, stopped off at the Europa for a few beers and for the latest reports on everything from white-water rafting on the Usumacinta River to the availability of opium poppies. There, I met Californians in the Peace Corps and Australians making $100,000 a year trading *típica*. I met people checking out the surfing possibilities in Central America (not good in Guatemala; excellent in El Salvador and Costa Rica); and I met several mercenaries who were "in country" to freelance the fight against communism. Because it was in Zona 1, the Europa also attracted the more transient gringos, those who had stopped in the capital for a few nights before heading out to the highlands and Guatemala's greater attractions.

One night in the Europa, I met an Australian mercenary who declared that he would buy everyone in the bar a drink if someone could name a country he hadn't been to. He waved a passport thick as a Gideon Bible in challenge. After a few obvious guesses—Afghanistan, Mozambique—which the Aussie met with derision, we tried the most obscure places we could think of: Gabon, Cameroons, Montserrat. He had stamps for them all. "Suriname," someone tried. "What about Suriname?" The Aussie grinned, licked his thumb, and flipped some pages. There it was: a smudged entrance stamp from Cayenne-Rochambeau airport.

"What the hell were you doing in Suriname?" the bartender asked.

"Oh, Suriname," the mercenary said. "Jesus, Suriname is good—full of fighting that place, the bloody black apes."

Two other bars, El Establo and Shakespeare's, drew from a similar segment of the expatriate population, but because these two bars were located on Reforma, down by the US embassy, the expats who frequented them were generally those who had established residency in the capital—journalists based in Guatemala, teachers at the American school, volunteers in the marginalized relief agencies, people trying to make a meager living out of translation or English teaching—people who would do most anything to stay abroad rather than return to the States. I had expected that those people who had chosen to live and work in Guatemala would do so because they loved the place. This was not, however, a common motivation. I heard far more criticism of the country than praise. To be sure, most everyone liked *something* about Guatemala, especially its scenery and natural beauty. And many liked, or said they liked, Indian culture (I sometimes suspected that by "Indian culture" they merely meant the clothing and other handicrafts).

But if these expats were less than wildly enthusiastic about the country, why had they come down, and why did they stay? Because in Guatemala they were important, or at least they could have the illusion that they were important people. It is one of the oddities of the neocolonial arrangement that marginal or ordinary characters from the metropolis find themselves, in the periphery of empire, elevated to positions of importance and held in esteem by the natives. I met many Americans—from swim coaches to filmmakers to (yes) literature professors—who had been nothing in the States—anonymous people going nowhere. Suddenly, in Guatemala they were respected. Beautiful girls from well-to-do families wanted to marry them. Newspapers interviewed them. They were invited to fancy dinners. Doors closed to them back home were wide open down in the hot countries.

In my case, for example, I was invited to all the bluestocking events in the capital—cocktail after cocktail at which my picture was taken for the social pages of the newspaper. This would never happen in the States. I was invited to speak at the book club meetings of the society dames. I gave public lectures that received press coverage. I was judge of a prestigious novel award, and was even referred to at the awards assembly—broadcast on radio—as "the eminent North American critic," an implausible overstatement of my credentials if there ever was one. In short, I was exalted solely because I was an American with a title, a title that did me no good at all in the States but meant everything in Guatemala.

Even ne'er-do-well Americans gained prestige in Guatemala. It did not require much money because Guatemalans *perceived* Americans to be wealthy, hence even impoverished bums were treated as if they were wealthy, and their impoverishment was explained away as an eccentricity of *los norteamericanos*. All you really had to do was play along, pretend you were wealthy. Anyone who figured this out stayed in Guatemala. Why go back to the States where you were a toiling, impecunious nobody? Better to stay and enjoy the life of privilege.

So in the gringo bars of Guatemala (and the same was true on an even larger scale down in Costa Rica) you met people who felt obliged to recite the litany of Guatemala's faults, but who could not possibly leave the place because their sense of self-worth depended on their remaining big fish in this small tropical pond.

In *The Colonizer and the Colonized,* Albert Memmi describes a similar situation in the European colonies of Africa. Colonials decided to expatriate, Memmi maintains, because they wanted an easier life. His definition of a colony, from the colonialist's point of view, is "a place where one earns more and spends less." More bang for your buck. Guatemala was never a colony of the United States, but for decades individual Americans residing in the country took a rather colonial attitude toward the place. Americans continued to expatriate to Guatemala and the rest of Central America because the countries were cheap—especially where human services were concerned—and because a white-skinned person had a certain inherent wealth and social standing, however undeserved. This desire to expatriate could be considered a "Third World itch": the urge among certain people, especially Anglos and northern Europeans, to seek out the hot countries, where their money goes farther and where they are held in higher esteem than at home. In the gringo bars, this itch was highly contagious. Almost every discussion was grounded in a need, on the one hand, to excoriate the people and institutions of Guatemala and, on the other, to revel in the easily affordable pleasures of the place.

The upscale version of the itch manifested itself at Zona 15's American Club, a large, secluded complex with tennis courts, swimming pools, ballroom, and a restaurant. An armed guard manned the checkpoint at the club's entrance. Small boys waited outside, hoping to be chosen as ballboys for the tennis matches. Waiters patrolled the poolside, taking food and drink orders and bringing around the chits for members to sign. There was little doubt about the intentions of the club; its members, business people and diplomats, wanted to recreate the Raj or some other idyllic colonial setting. Neocolonialism is often described as an economic or political system. But we have to recognize that neocolonialism is a mind-set as well, a psychological orientation that deliberately demarcates the boundary between the inferior native and the superior colonialist. If you really want to understand why the United States has so successfully exploited Central America for more than a century, you must take into consideration not only the political and economic system but also the psychological basis for such a system. The American Club presented a vivid tableau of that psychology.

On the night of the US presidential elections in 1988, a small group of club members, both Guatemalans and Americans, gathered at the American Club to watch the election returns on satellite television. I was invited by a friend from the embassy.

The banquet room was decorated in red, white, and blue streamers. About fifty people stood in clusters, holding cocktails and chatting, the Guatemalans dressed like members of a wedding, the Americans like fans at a ballgame. Over on one wall, Peter Jennings, larger than life, discussed the election on a giant screen. No one seemed too interested. Bush was expected to win easily enough, and the club members were content with the continuation of Republican policies.

Uncle Sam hats were handed out, but no one put them on except for three silver-haired women in evening gowns. Each time Bush was declared the winner of a state, the women blew on plastic whistles. When Jennings pronounced Bush the next president of the United States, they threw confetti and banged chairs and whistled even louder. The television sound was turned off, the lights dimmed, and dance music came over the sound system: a ragtime version of "Yankee Doodle Dandy," then Michael Jackson's "Beat It," then the Beatles singing "Michelle" and "Revolution." Jennings' talking head mouthed the lyrics and several couples danced. Then everybody sang a slightly distorted version of "God Bless America" before the party began to break up.

My friend and I drank beer at the bar and watched. Next to us, two American businessmen—fifty-something, paunchy, balding—drank martini after martini, their voices getting louder and louder until I couldn't help but eavesdrop.

"And she was willing to go through with it?" one said.

"What choice did she have? Her father would have run her out of the house and into a brothel. That's the way they are here. But Christ, what a mess it was. I couldn't find anyone to do it. You wouldn't believe how religious doctors here can be. I must have spoken to a dozen or more and they all wanted to lecture me about mortal sin. And I was offering a pretty penny, too."

"So what did you do?"

"Found some quack. I mean let me tell you—the guy was a butcher. Damn near killed her. And we couldn't even take her to the hospital—legal implications and all that."

"She still working for you?"

"Nah. I told her it was best for all involved if she quit. But I got her a job with a friend. He calls me up the other day—I didn't tell him any of this—and he says, 'You know that girl you sent over here? What a nice piece she is. I can't believe you'd let an ass like that walk away.' I just laughed and said, 'Watch out, George, she'll bust your balls and you're too old for that.''

The two Americans had a good laugh and called for more drinks. On a wall near the bar was a large topographical map of Guatemala. I went over to look at it. It was a good map, highly detailed, with a key that indicated which roads were paved, which roads could be traveled in all weather, and which were passable only in the dry season.

I studied the map for a round-trip route through the crumpled-paper topography of the highlands. A trip sounded good. The highlands—cool, remote, and mysterious—sounded good. I yearned for a chance to get away, to get out on those passable and impassable roads that led to another Guatemala.

PART TWO
ROADS AND TEXTS

Antigua

GUATEMALA CITY USED TO STAND about thirty miles west of its present site, but its original location seemed cursed. At the very least it was not a stable place. After an apocalyptic series of earthquakes, plagues, floods, more earthquakes, volcanic eruptions, and still more earthquakes—culminating with a massive quake in 1773—the citizens of Guatemala City got fed up and left. The capital of Guatemala was relocated to the Valley of the Hermit (Valle de la Hermita) and the name Ciudad de Guatemala went with it. The citizens left the rubble behind, a memorial to nature's puissance. The rubble was never removed.

After two hundred years that lack of initiative paid off. "Old Guatemala," Antigua, became Guatemala's principal tourist attraction precisely because the rubble left behind in 1773 was still lying there. A score of buildings—convents, monasteries, churches, schools, homes—lay in various states of destruction and desuetude. Against a backdrop of coffee plantations and three towering conical volcanoes—one still sending up plumes of smoke—Antigua was the very definition of Spanish colonial baroque, exactly the sort of thing North Americans and Europeans loved to gawk at and photograph. Even better from the perspective of tourists and tour promoters, economic opportunity brought the Indians in from the surrounding countryside, and their appearance enhanced the picturesque qualities of the place. Of course, the Indians also brought shopping opportunities—bales and bales of their unique clothing, and all of it dirt cheap.

In the latter half of the twentieth century, the highlands of Guatemala have thrived (in places) on a First World vogue for things native. Antigua, the gateway to the highlands, has done particularly well because it is close to the capital and has the added attraction of ruined baroque buildings. Whenever I visited, the tourists seemed to outnumber the local residents. Walking the streets, I heard more

English, German, and French than Spanish. Enterprising Antiguans had devised an additional attraction: language schools, where tourists could spend a few weeks or months studying Spanish. These schools were especially popular with the young bohemian tourists who intended to travel up and down the Americas but needed to learn a smattering of basic Spanish first.

Because of these tourists, Antigua was changing. Yogurt shops, health food stores, vegetarian restaurants, and rock 'n' roll clubs had opened up during the last decade, and Antigua was beginning to look like an American college town. Walking the cobblestone streets, I saw backpacks bobbing through crowds alongside Indians carrying loads on their heads. I saw blonde women wearing *huipiles*, the native blouse, and long-haired, bearded men wearing *caites*, the cheap sandals of the indigent. I even saw male tourists wearing *huipiles*. In the afternoon, Antigua's cafes were jammed with college students on vacation, dropouts, Green Party fellow travelers, and New Age religionists who were trying to go native. And they were all dressed in the kaleidoscopic *típica* that was the *dernier cri* of the set.

One day I was drinking coffee on the patio of one of these cafés when a beggar boy entered the patio from the street. The iron gate was shut, but he was so thin he passed right through the bars like a ghost. His bare feet slid on the tiles of the patio as he approached a table of foreigners, newly arrived language students it appeared. He circled the table mumbling, hand extended to the diners. Still new in the country and not used to the presence of beggars, the foreigners tried to ignore him. At last, one dropped some worthless coins into his soiled palm. The boy lingered, as though he had been purchased, until a waiter tried to shoo him away. When the boy didn't leave, the waiter advanced on him with a broom. The boy finally backed away, but before he could get through the gate, a sudden coughing fit convulsed him: tuberculosis, which was endemic in the country. The boy spat blood onto the tile and vanished through the bars. The blood clot seethed in the sun until the waiter came out and dumped water on it. The foreigners left their cheesecake untouched.

The First World vogue for native things was a late-twentieth-century phenomenon. For a long time, Anglos had only contempt for the Maya and their culture. The more recent guidebooks that I had read invariably claimed that "the main attractions for visitors are the highland Maya." Guidebooks from the 1920s and the 1930s, on the other hand, said little about the Indians other than that they were lurking out there in the highlands, "primitive but Christianized." Their distant past was considered much more interesting than their degraded present; even intelligent and appreciative travelers of the time, such as the archaeologist Alfred Maudslay and the novelist Aldous Huxley, were dismayed by the "primitive" culture of the descendants of the great Maya. Travel books of the time frequently disparaged the Indians; a salient example comes from Huxley, who commented: "Try as I may, I cannot very much like primitive people. They make me feel uncomfortable." It was not until the 1950s that the *South American Handbook*, the bible for Latin American travelers, began calling a visit to Chichicastenango to see the Indians a "must." Before the second half of the twentieth century, almost nobody took an interest in the indigenous Guatemalans. Traveler after traveler either belittled the Indians or ignored them. Given the current vogue, I was surprised to find that the indigenous Guatemalans had excited only pejorative interest in the past.

The first gringo ever to write a book about travels in Guatemala was the Englishman Thomas Gage. His book, *The English-American, or A New Survey of the West Indies* (1648), is a marvel. Whenever I went to Antigua, I tried to look past the yogurt shops, the vegetarian restaurants, the *típica* vendors on the plaza, and the baroque viceregal ruins, and I tried to imagine Antigua as Thomas Gage saw it in the 1630s, when it was still Guatemala City, the finest city between Mexico and Lima.

Gage had an opportunity unavailable to other Englishmen at the time, the opportunity to visit Spanish America. Because Spain jealously protected its New World colonies, few non-Spaniards were allowed to journey through the empire. Gage, a Catholic priest trained in Spain, was on his way to the Philippines as a missionary when he went AWOL, so to speak, in Mexico. For some reason, he had doubts about the Philippine mission and decided to strike out on his own. He chose to go south, traveling down the very spine of Spain's forbidden empire. His journey took him through Chiapas and then on to Guatemala City, that is, present-day Antigua. There, Gage succeeded in attaching himself to the Dominican mission and wound up spending over ten years in Guatemala. For much of that time, he was priest to the Indians of Mixco, Amatitlán, and Petapa and came to know them well, at least as well as any European of his day.

But that is only half of Gage's strange story. After returning to his native England, where the political power of the Puritans was growing rapidly, Gage's career took a dramatic turn. Quite suddenly, he renounced Catholicism and the priesthood and even became an ardent propagandist for the Puritans (in an attempt, no doubt, to make his conversion appear all the more convincing). Gage had an unfortunate inclination toward the unethical. He even went as far as to give evidence in a trial that led to the execution of his own brother, also a priest. A book about his experiences in the New World, the *New Survey*, was his most substantial work of propaganda. What Gage had to say about Guatemalan Indians has to be read in this light: the central purpose of his book was to condemn Catholicism and Spain's role in its propagation. Nevertheless, a significant portion of the text is devoted to a description of the Indians.

Because of his peculiar subtext, Gage appears to be sympathetic toward the Indians. After all, his intention is to argue that the Spanish, particularly the priests, vilely abused the Indians. To this end, he frequently employs phrases such as, "the poor Indians" and "the much abused Indians." But Gage's sympathy is not very convincing. They are merely victims, and their value for him seems limited to their status as victims. In fact, when Gage does attempt an amateur ethnography (in a chapter on native customs and a chapter on his experiences in Indian villages), he finds little more to say than that the Indians are "much given to drink" and superstition. Even though Gage learned the Pokomam language, he seems to have taken little interest in the Indians themselves. They are abstractions to him, not individuals. For example, the only individual Indians he speaks of, after seven years among them, are those in his parishes who were accused of devil worship (what Gage calls devil worship is quite clearly the practice of Maya religions, a practice that has survived centuries of such accusations).

It is interesting that, for all his accusations against the Spaniards, some of the cruelest acts of persecution recited in the *New Survey* are those Gage himself committed. His sympathy for the Indians did not run deep; as their priest, he resolved to eradicate their "heathenish practices." Indeed, these practices seem to have troubled him much more than they did the Spanish priests, who come across as somewhat tolerant or, as Gage would have it, "lax." On one occasion, Gage led a party into the mountains above Mixco where, in a cave, he discovered an "idol." He describes in great detail and with some relish how he smashed and burned this idol in front of the gathered village while he sermonized on the Second Commandment. This and other incidents in the book suggest that Indian culture did not particularly inspire him.

Gage initiated what has proven a fairly persistent motif in Anglo writings on indigenous Guatemalans: Spanish or ladino abuse is always decried, but Anglo observers leave little doubt that they are more concerned with Spanish sins than with Indian survival. When they do turn their attention to the Indian culture, the writers express the same sort of contempt that allegedly underlies the Spanish oppression.

A good example is found in the writings of John Lloyd Stephens, the explorer who was the first American to write at length about Guatemala. Two hundred years after Gage, Stephens arrived in Guatemala on a diplomatic mission for the US government. In the execution of his duties, Stephens managed to travel the length of Central America. His most renowned accomplishment was authenticating the existence of pre-Columbian ruins in Central America. Reports of such ruins had surfaced in the United States and in Europe, but no one before Stephens had convincingly documented their existence.

Stephens' travels resulted in another important, though less recognized, discovery: not since Gage's time had someone reported on life in the Guatemalan highlands. Most travelers to Central America at that time visited Guatemala City and Antigua, but few ever journeyed west into the little-known Indian country. In fact, Stephens found few Guatemalans who knew anything at all about the highlands, and the residents of the capital emphatically discouraged his notion of traveling into such a dangerous, backward land. When he eventually made the journey, Stephens saw Indian communities that had been only sporadically visited by whites, mostly Spaniards, since the Conquest.

Stephens was an intelligent, enthusiastic, and (for the most part) sympathetic traveler. To his readers, he comes across as a genial latitudinarian who criticizes only after experience has taught him that the criticism is merited. During most of his journey through Central America, Stephens is fair-minded; he generally assumes the best in people until proven otherwise. But when Stephens writes about the highlands, his tone changes. The Indians do not excite his interest; neither their physical appearance nor their culture inspire him in his text: "Here the people had no character and nothing in which we took any interest, except their backs," he wrote. This is a remarkable shift in tone for someone who for hundreds and hundreds of pages (the two volumes of *Incidents of Travel in Central America, Chiapas, and Yucatan* total more than seven hundred pages) has noted the minutest details about the places he has visited. In the highlands, he suddenly loses interest, dismisses entire villages in a single sentence, and ignores even the most salient details of the culture he encounters. For example, in over one hundred pages about his ride through the highlands from Guatemala City to Chiapas, Stephens makes only sketchy comments on indigenous clothing and never mentions the brightly colored blouses that inspire so many clichés in contemporary narratives. It is difficult to account for Stephens' sudden apathy. He doesn't lose total interest in the place, of course. In the spirit of American romanticism, he still writes enthusiastically about the natural beauty of the highlands, but his enthusiasm does not extend to native culture. In the few extended passages about Indian rituals, for example, Stephens voices his distaste for and even disgust at the primitive aspects of the Indian religion. Throughout his text, Stephens expresses a sort of sanctimonious dismay at the immorality of all Central Americans. He decries, among other things, common-law marriages, the prevalence of smoking among women, and the "abhorrent" Spanish practice of naming people Jesús—a practice that so embarrasses him he can only bring himself to write "Hezoos," so as not to offend his readers. But the Indians were clearly the worst of the lot for Stephens. Like Gage, he considered them idle, superstitious drunks, "a wretched spectacle of the beings made in God's image." Whenever Stephens deigns to mention the Indians in his narrative, he catches them in unflattering attitudes—drunken, lecherous, idolatrous. A typical image for Stephens (and for many American writers since) is "a drunken Indian . . . lying on the ground, his face cut with a machete." To be fair, Stephens did remark upon the need for closer study of the Indians, and he felt that "to study the Indians would be of great interest." But judging from his harsh treatment of them in the text, I have to conclude, despite my admiration for him, that he found the Indians interesting primarily for their supposed depravity.

Stephens is by no means the only writer to depict the Indians in this way. Virtually every American traveler for the hundred years after Stephens' journey insisted on a nearly identical interpretation of Indian culture. The same motifs persist in text after text. Writing in 1885, Helen Sanborn, daughter of a coffee baron, reported: "If you want to be convinced of the doctrine of total depravity, get some of the foreign residents of Guatemala to talking about the natives. They will grant them no excellencies whatever. They will tell you the people are false, deceitful, treacherous, and desperately wicked; that they are polite and say kind things without meaning a word of it, simply to flatter you and make you pleased with yourself and them; and that they never do a kindness save from a selfish motive" (*A Winter in Central America and Mexico*).

Guatemala's visitors and foreign residents persisted in this view for decades after Sanborn's brief visit. It was still common during my sojourn. On any given night in the Europa Bar or the American Club you could hear similar opinions, though there was a good chance that the speaker would be wearing something *típica*. Perhaps such cal-

umny was no longer the majority opinion, but in the early twentieth century, to judge from written accounts, few Anglos found anything good to say about indigenous Guatemalans. Repeatedly, these
accounts express astonishment at and even rapture over the natural
beauty of the country in one sentence, and disgust for the natives
in the next. English writer Rose Macaulay's 1930 novel, *Staying
with Relations*, exemplifies this Anglo disposition. Every single English character in the novel tediously disparages the Indians. They
are called "dumb," "dull," "lethargic," "immoral," "uncultured,"
"shocking," and "lazy as a rule." They are demeaned for having
"unfortunate complexions" and criticized for always wanting "more
money in order to afford more alcohol." Significantly, Indian villages
are considered a necessary part of the visitor's itinerary, but not for
the reasons accepted by today's *Fodoristas*: "Catherine was taken by
her relations about the forest and mountain slopes. They showed her
Indian villages full of small, gentle intoxicated Maya, old Spanish
churches, Maya ruins . . . and tremendous views of distant blue sier-
ras, great brown palms and illimitable forests, at which her heart
was astonished and fainted within her."

This single paragraph captures the essence of the visiting Anglo's
response to Guatemalan scenery—nature is fascinating, the ruins
and churches are interesting, and the Indians are dead drunk. Most
English and American travelers simply did not consider the indigenous Guatemalans an intrinsic part of the country's beauties, except
on those occasions when Indian depravity added to the exotica of local color. In the Anglo view of things, the Indians were noteworthy
only because of their debilities and moral failings, such as drunkenness and superstitiousness.

Another theme present in Anglo narratives is the belief that the
Indian culture must vanish, especially as it comes into contact, more
and more, with a technologically and intellectually superior civilization. This note was sounded from the moment travelers began to
visit the highland Maya, but it was especially strong in the early part
of the twentieth century. An article that appeared in *National Geographic* in 1910 provides a good example. The article, by one Edine
Frances Tisdel, is titled "Guatemala, the Country of the Future." Tisdel intends to dispel the notion common among North Americans
that Central America is "continually torn apart by internal strife,
devastated by earthquakes, and ravaged by disease—in fact a tropical
wilderness scarcely worthy of a visit." She asserts Guatemala's modernity (rather oddly calling Guatemala City "one of the best-lighted
cities in the world"), and notes the explosion of progress in the country that makes it "worthy of a visit." But notice what Tisdel cites as

evidence of Guatemala's modernity: "the beauty of the cities, the rapid extension of the railroads, the cultivation and enormous proceeds of a wonderfully rich and fertile soil, all convince us of the progress of a people living amidst a wealth of scenic beauty and a perfection of climate rarely equaled." According to Tisdel, Guatemala's charms are found in nature and in the progress brought by foreigners. She notes in particular the country's new railroad, which, she assures her readers, is "owned by an American syndicate and . . . absolutely under American control." She also marvels at the "remarkable" work of German coffee planters in the highlands and the United Fruit Company in the lowlands, whose efforts have transformed tropical wilds into a land of beauty and profit.

Obviously missing from her list of the country's attractions are the Indians. Tisdel mentions the indigenous populations in her article, but seems to regard them as a quaint phenomenon, useful primarily for their inexpensive labor: "The servants are mostly Indians and are exceptionally good. They learn quickly, and with a little patience can soon be converted into model domestics." This Indians-as-domesticated-animals theme recurs in her article: "It was not far from here that I visited, at a place called Cantel, to my mind one of the greatest tributes to American energy and enterprise in the country. Nestled in a fertile valley is a large cotton factory, the only one of its kind in the republic. Think of a model factory employing some 400 or 500 hands, where every bit of machinery used has been brought on the backs of Indians or mules. The factory hands are all Indians, mostly women or children, the dexterity of the latter being fairly astonishing." Since all the work mentioned in this paragraph is done by Indians, it is difficult to see where Tisdel's vaunted "American energy and enterprise" figure in. Furthermore, it is apparent that basic social justice, such as child labor laws, is not considered applicable to Indians, who remain, in Tisdel's view, mere brutes in a marvelous land of progress.

The title of Tisdel's article, "Guatemala, the Country of the Future," is significant. Turn-of-the-century Guatemala was to North Americans a country that would "take its place on an equal footing with other nations of the world" because "the steady increase of American and German interests here is fast opening for our benefit one of the loveliest countries in the world." The future did not include Indians, who were clearly relics of the past. Tisdel goes so far as to say that "the country *was* for centuries the home of the Maya-Quiché Indians" (my emphasis). Her use of the past tense is typical of a sentiment prevalent among early-twentieth-century travelers, even those who were fascinated by the Indians: that the Indians were anachronistic, their time was past; they must modernize or pass into history.

Most North American travelers, perhaps because their own country had already taken care of its "Indian problem," had no trouble believing that Guatemala's progress required the anachronistic Indians to yield to modernization. In their narratives, these writers voiced support for the "long and peaceful" administrations of dictators such as Cabrera and Ubico, who supposedly brought progress to the country by "modernizing" the Indians. Joseph Henry Jackson, the well-known editor of *Sunset* magazine, summarized this viewpoint best in his 1937 travel book, *Notes on a Drum*: "You can't judge the situation in Guatemala by comparing it with our own. You have, in your Indian, a human being whose standard of living is so far below that of our meanest working man that the two cannot be mentioned in the same breath. . . . Yet if you leave him to his own devices your country will be bankrupt in no time. No, a firm hand is necessary if Guatemala is to get anywhere at all. And President Ubico has that firm hand."

Jackson was quite aware that modernization meant the end of Indian culture. While journeying in Guatemala, he took an interest in the Indian villages, their artistic productions, and the like; nevertheless, he was quite willing to see that culture vanish for the sake of progress: "the Indian is being taught discipline through service in the army, is learning about hygiene, becoming used to the Spanish language which will eventually give him a sense of belonging to his country instead of merely to his tribe. Schools are being built, shoes are replacing flimsy sandals. The color and atmosphere of the villages will disappear quickly, yes. But it is all part of the forward movement to which Guatemala is now firmly and happily committed."

Jackson was no crass tourist. A respected literary critic, he was a man whose sober opinion counted highly among his readers. But for him, and for many other Anglos in the first half of the twentieth century, Indian culture was merely quaint. He did not rue the potential extinction of that culture. Nor did Aldous Huxley. An eloquent spokesman for freedom in the Western world, Huxley did not consider the Guatemalan Indians eligible for that freedom. Commenting on Ubico's forced labor laws (Joseph Henry Jackson had also approved of them), Huxley wrote, "Voluntary labor at the point of a bayonet— the notion, to us, is extremely distasteful. But, obviously, when you are confronted with the urgent problem of domesticating a wilderness, you cannot afford to be very squeamish in your methods of getting the work done." Ironically, a substantial portion of Huxley's little travel book, *Beyond the Mexique Bay* (1934), which is ostensibly about the Caribbean, Central America, and Mexico, actually is concerned with the emergence of fascism in Europe. Huxley's horror at oppression in Europe does not extend to the Americas, however, where dictators like Ubico instituted fascist policies.

Once we recognize that such attitudes were prevalent for most of the history of the Anglo-Maya encounter, it is not so difficult to understand why the US government has for decades supported a military that at times has waged a nearly genocidal war against the Guatemalan Indians. Government policy is slower to change than intellectual fancies and the interests of bourgeois tourism. I would guess that many an American diplomat until quite recently would more or less subscribe to Huxley's statement: when progress is at stake, you can't afford to be squeamish in your methods of achieving that progress, especially in a wilderness like Guatemala. The Reagan administration argued that the military in countries like Guatemala and El Salvador needed more latitude than was normally accorded the military in more stable countries; the implication was that some abuse of human rights was inevitable as the military worked toward stabilizing the country. Certainly the elite of Guatemala still believed, as Jackson had, that such abuse was "all part of the forward movement to which Guatemala [is] firmly and happily committed."

Concerned more with progress than with the survival of indigenous culture, the elite in the late twentieth century were caught off guard by the First World's recent fancy for things primitive. The sudden concern for cultural survival baffled them because they still regarded the Indians in much the same way that Stephens, Jackson, and Huxley had. They were quite simply shocked that the world now seemed suddenly to embrace the Indians and wished to protect them. How was it possible, they wondered, that people were promoting this Rigoberta Menchú, an untutored Indian *woman*, for a prestigious award like the Nobel Peace Prize? Had the world gone mad? Put on the defensive, they became more reactionary and more insistent than ever on the need to "modernize" the Indians (even as they sought to capitalize on the vogue for *típica*: many of the shops in the capital and in Antigua were owned by ladinos).

It was pleasant to sit on a wrought iron bench in Antigua's plaza—the guidebooks called it "quaint"—with the beautiful cone of Agua towering above and romantic ruins standing or half-standing in bougainvillea shade no matter which direction you looked. All around the plaza, Indians from the surrounding villages had spread their goods on the ground—blouses, hats, pants, blankets, masks, backpacks, belts, tablecloths—thousands of things made from the polychromatic fabric unique to Guatemala. Hundreds of gringos strolled around, examining the merchandise, taking photos, tentatively haggling over prices. There were well-to-do middle-aged tourists on a two-week blitz tour. There were retirees traveling at a slower pace, their Winnebagos parked off the plaza, where several curious Antiguans looked them over, trying to fathom the apparition of such beasts. And everywhere there were young gringos with their backpacks, their "flimsy sandals," and their notecards of verb declensions, heading for the cafés after morning lessons at the language schools. All these gringos, unlike their predecessors, were enamored of the Indians. They knew they should like the Indians because their guidebooks gushed about the picturesque qualities of the indigenous populations, about their highland villages, and about their cultural artifacts. The foreigners had arrived in Guatemala expecting to respond with approbation to the Indian world, expecting to buy quantities of native handicrafts, and expecting to take lots of photos (or shoot lots of video footage). The last thing they wanted was the extermination of the Indians, or even their modernization. The success of their tour and of their photos depended on confirming the expected primitiveness of the Indians. After all, that was why they came to Guatemala. The tourists wanted things just the way they were supposed to be: picturesque, exotic, primitive.

In the plaza, I would often see another group of gringos—drifters whose drifting had come to a dead end in Guatemala. One man, a juggler by trade, spent his days juggling three sticks out by the fountain (sometimes he also appeared in Panajachel on Lake Atitlán). He held one stick in each hand and batted the third stick around and around, batting and balancing it with the two that he held. He would keep it going for hours, from midmorning until late at night, staring at the sticks, only occasionally glancing at his bemused audience. He had long, matted hair, a spectacular navel-length beard, and very weird Rasputin-like eyes that might have been frightening had he been twirling knives instead of sticks. He was, in fact, pretty good with the sticks. I never saw him miss. Middle-aged, wealthier tourists, just descended from a Mercedes-Benz coach for their hour in Antigua, liked to photograph the juggler. These stolid tourists seemed to find something quaint and charming about the counterculture. Sometimes they dropped a few coins at the juggler's feet, maybe to thank him for adding interest to their slide shows. The juggler ignored them.

Another plaza regular was a jewelry maker, apparently from France, although it was hard to tell because his speech was some slurred hybrid of French and Spanish. He set up a blanket on the plaza's cobblestone, next to the native vendors, where he attempted to sell some misshapen bits of paste jewelry and a few necklaces made from broken bits of shell. He too had long matted hair, and an odor that usually ensured that the benches near him remained vacant. Occasionally, he entered the cafés and dangled a few of his creations in front of the espresso drinkers who, far from being offended, seemed to take an interest in his baubles.

One day I was sitting on a bench in the plaza. The stick juggler batted and balanced his sticks. The jewelry vendor stared and stank. Near the fountain, a blind guitar player plucked a Spanish folk song, background music for some lightly clad tourists of immense bulk who wandered by, now stopping to take a picture, now haggling with a dirty gamin who could not seem to make himself understood.

A massy woman in short pants stopped her waddle. "Whazzee saying?" she asked one of her companions.

The other wore a red sun hat and blue sunglasses. "Whazzit matter, Emily, give him some of those centavo things and get rid of him. Lookit how dirty his feet are."

For a moment, the whole group stared at the indicated feet. The boy picked up the coins that Emily had dropped in front of him and then held very still under the tourists' gaze. The guitar player twanged three consecutive flat chords, and then the tourists abruptly turned their attention to the fountain in the plaza's center. One of them began reading from a guidebook about the plaza's history. Then the group crossed the street, the boy trailing respectfully behind, where they bent over the blankets of trinket vendors. Their voices carried across the plaza.

"Oh, Marge, did you get a picture of that hippie with the sticks?"

"That hair. Imagine how long since it's been washed. Oh, look at these cute napkin rings."

When I left Antigua, I came across an accident. The road out of town was very steep, narrow, and full of curves. Accidents happened all the time when cars tried to pass slower vehicles on the curves. Occasionally, an old bus overloaded with Indians and maybe a backpacking gringo or two would veer off the road and plunge a couple hundred feet into a ravine. Crosses along the road marked the sites of these disasters. The accident I came across was not quite so spectacular, but it looked gory enough. A car and a pickup were smashed together. A sleek tour bus was stopped on the narrow margin, looking as out of place as one of Hannibal's elephants in the Alps. It wasn't hard to tell what had happened: the tour bus had been descending the mountain slowly, the car had tried to pass on a curve and had collided with the pickup. Now a cluster of people stood around the corpses waiting for the ambulance and the police to arrive. A row of tourist faces stared from the gray windows of the bus. Several of the tourists had left the coach and were now circling the wreck, video cameras held up in place of their faces.

Lake Atitlán

THE PAN-AMERICAN HIGHWAY twisted, rose, dipped, and rose still more as I drove west, away from Guatemala City and toward Mexico. The usual tourist route followed the Pan-American from Antigua to Lake Atitlán, an exhilarating sixty-mile drive of sharp curves and steep grades that required two hours to negotiate.

I wish I could have approached the lake for the first time just as John Lloyd Stephens did—on mule back—or, better yet, on foot. All places of great natural beauty should be approached and encountered in this way. An automobile ruins the experience; a tour bus is ten times worse. Think of the millions of people who first see the Grand Canyon from a tour bus or car window as they cruise along at forty miles per hour: all intensity is lost. Only a walk of several miles (well, one mile at least) can adequately prepare you for the sudden, awesome sight. Stephens also had the great advantage of approaching Atitlán completely without expectations, or even warnings. By now, so much has been said about Atitlán, so many superlatives have been spent on the lake's description, that one visits the place expecting to be swept away. Most people already have the lens cap unscrewed long before they reach the first scenic overlook (where, in fact, a sign advertises Kodak film). I hate travel when it is reduced to the act of confirming what others have already said.

But, damn it, I have to say it anyway: Lake Atitlán is the most beautiful lake in the world. After the first scenic overlook, from which the lake and its three volcanoes appear in the enchanted distance like some fairy realm, the traveler is inevitably captivated. Even jaded travelers are shocked into thinking, Can such a place exist?

I turned off the Pan-American and took the road to Sololá, a village that gazed over the lake from a thousand-foot-high vantage. After Sololá, the road began a dramatic descent of over fifteen hundred feet to the lakeshore. The road was practically carved into the cliff side. The only way to negotiate it was by braking with the motor in first gear—even at twenty miles per hour the car could not handle the hairpins and coils of the narrow road. The views were stunning.

There were some four scenic overlooks in the five miles from Sololá down to Panajachel on the shore. One stop was not enough: each overlook gave a different vista that must be taken in, studied. The light changed. The color of the water changed. The height of the volcanoes changed. Clouds shifted to conceal, to reveal, to darken, to heighten, to highlight. Even the most reticent photographer ran out of film.

Panajachel, the town at the bottom of this descent, has been affected by foreigners more than any other town in Guatemala. In 1935, when Sol Tax began his renowned anthropological studies of the Atitlán communities, Panajachel had a population of eight hundred, mostly Indians who subsisted through small-plot agriculture. Huxley, visiting just before Tax arrived, called it a "squalid, uninteresting place, with a large low-class Mestizo population and an abundance of dram shops." But in the 1940s a paved road to the lake was completed and it happened to end in Panajachel. For a long time, Panajachel was the only lakeside community with easy access to the outside world. More important, it was the only community to which tourists had easy access. As soon as the guidebooks mandated a visit to the lake, tourists came in herds, drawn to the lake like large mammals to a Serengeti watering hole. By the late 1970s, Panajachel's economy was entirely driven by tourism. Millions of dollars a year were spent in "Pana" (as the tourists now called it), which was obviously no longer the "squalid, uninteresting" town that Huxley had visited.

Guatemalans sometimes refer to Panajachel as "Gringotenanago." Many foreigners, especially Germans and Americans, have decided to stay in Pana more or less permanently. They (along with a few Guatemalans from the capital) have opened up hotels and restaurants to cater to other foreigners. For some reason, maybe because at first a trip to Pana is still something of an adventure, the town attracts an eccentric caste—even more so than Antigua. Many of the foreigners resident in Pana are bohemian drifters, counterculture dropouts and disaffected refugees from the hippie movement. The decor and ambience of Pana combine Mayan and psychedelic; I expected at any moment to turn a corner and find the Grateful Dead playing "Truckin" on marimbas.

Just why these gringos chose to settle here was, to me, something of a mystery. It couldn't be the scenery alone—Lake Tahoe is beautiful, too, and much closer to San Francisco. No doubt they wanted "to get away from it all," but if that were their motivation, why choose a country that had experienced a bloody, decades-long civil war—especially when that war had been waged within miles of their chosen retreat? The presence of foreigners, it was true, prevented Pana from suffering the worst of the civil war; still, from time to time there had been intrusions on the tranquillity. In 1981, for example, guerrillas bombed one of the larger hotels. And heated fighting had occurred in areas around the lake, especially near Santiago Atitlán, where in 1990 the army had killed fifteen Indians.

The most likely reason for Pana's popularity was the strange, un-defined attraction that the Indian culture held for westerners. For people who wanted to buy Indian fabrics and *típica* clothing, Pana was a paradise. The long street that led from town to the beach was lined with vendors who displayed their handiwork on tall wooden frames. Some vendors called out to passersby, encouraging them to take a look or make an offer. Other vendors sat in the shade and watched the parade of gringos. Some, exhausted from the journey to Pana, slept. Sales were few and far between, for too many vendors with too many items for sale lined the streets of Pana. At any given moment, there were thousands and thousands of more or less iden-tical items on display. The supply far exceeded the demand. The In-dians of Pana had experienced exactly the same phenomenon of capi-talism that the coffee producers had experienced, and on an even more brutal scale: too much product meant little, if any, profit. Sure, the tourists were a great source of income for the villages around Atitlán; millions of dollars had been pumped into the local econ-omy and Pana had benefited tremendously, no doubt about it. But only so much *típica* could be sold, and this boom would eventually turn to bust.

In the two years I had been visiting Pana, the prices for *típica* had stayed about the same, and for some products had even gone down. Meanwhile, the quetzal, Guatemala's poetic currency, had lost half its value and steep inflation had increased the prices of basic food-stuffs by at least a third. The real income of Indians was decreasing, despite an increase in tourists. Already you detected a note of des-peration: wherever tourists walked in Pana, little groups of girls fol-lowed imploring them to buy trinkets. If a gringo sat down on the beach, dozens of peripatetic vendors descended on him. And across the lake in the Indian village of Santiago, tourists arriving by boat were immediately accosted by vendors and by children charging money to have their pictures taken. For new visitors, this hard sell was overwhelming. Even for old Pana hands it was an annoyance. Among the first things a tourist needed to learn in Pana was the cruel tactic of ignoring other human beings, of waving them off like gnats.

A kind of brutality underlay the street fair atmosphere. The local Indians were in fact relegated to a sideshow, reduced to begging, even though they were supposed to be the principal attraction of the place. One could argue that tourism was good for the area, that it had brought progress and jobs to Pana, and I had no doubts that this was so. But progress is not inherently good, certainly not in a society as inequitable as Guatemala's.

The tourism of the future in the Third World can take several different forms. One form is the developed, planned resort like Cancún. Another is the native village like Panajachel packaged as an exotic nonwestern experience for those disaffected with the western world. Both depend on illusions. Cancún peddles the illusion of a tropical paradise, with everything sanitized and controlled to the point that mosquitoes are sprayed and the beach is graded. Panajachel sells the illusion of spiritual bonding with the primitive. Of course, the gringos of Pana would never admit it, but the resorts like Cancún are probably more beneficial, if not necessarily more just, for the natives—not that I care to see any more Cancúns on this earth. Cancún is artificial, but at least nobody was displaced when it was built. Instead, hundreds of Mexicans were moved in to work at the resort. In Pana, on the other hand, the natives were pushed out to make room for the spiritually disaffected gringos who came to "bond" with them. The Indians are left to scramble on the sidelines, engaged in cutthroat competition with each other, while the gringos sipped cappuccinos in cafés and write letters assuring their friends back home that they have found "inner peace" in Pana.

One evening in Panajachel, I met two women from Pittsburgh in a restaurant called the Flyin' Mayan Yacht Club. In the States, they had led normal middle-class American lives—suburbanites who commuted downtown every day, reared kids, made house and car payments. They had each traveled a bit when younger—Europe once, Mexico a couple of times. One had been on a cruise—the honeymoon of a marriage long since terminated. They were fed up with careers, with bosses, with sexual harassment. They were tired of house and car payments and the like. Their children had grown up and moved out, and now, bored with their jobs (they were research assistants in a law firm), they didn't know how they were going to face the endless round of days for the next twenty years until retirement.

Then one day during their lunch hour they went to an arts and crafts fair and saw Guatemalan weavings for the first time in their lives. They were fascinated and bought several *huipiles.* It so happened that the blouses had been made by a women's co-op in San Juan la Laguna, and a card attached to the blouses told about the village, Lake Atitlán, and the Tzutuhil Indians who lived there. Jean and

Sarah knew right away that they had to visit Guatemala on their next vacation. As Sarah put it, "Something stirred inside us and we just knew this was the place to go."

So they came down, spent three weeks in the highlands, mostly on the lake, loved it, and dreaded the prospect of another tedious winter in Pittsburgh. "You can call it a midlife crisis, I guess," Jean said and laughed. "We just couldn't take it anymore, so we sold everything and came back here."

"Well, it wasn't quite as impetuous as that," Sarah said. "First we made some test runs." Their plan was to go into the *típica* business. They would live most of the time in Pana, buy a stock of *típica*, and take it to the United States to sell. They were surprised, on their test runs, at how easy it was. Soon they were taking orders from boutiques and shipping the stock. Now they only needed to go to the states with pictures of what they could obtain for the boutiques. Nearly everything sold well, but backpacks and belts were the best sellers, especially in college towns like Austin, Madison, and Eugene. They knew that the vogue might someday pass, but they weren't concerned. They had good savings and could live very comfortably on little money here. They were planning to buy a house, take Spanish lessons, "make a total change."

But what made life in Pana so much better? I asked.

Well, first of all, there were some obvious things. It was cheap. They could afford a cook and a maid. They worked only when they wanted to. They spent their days doing things they liked—reading, sailing, walking. "It's so peaceful here," Jean said. But there were less tangible things as well: "There's something spiritual about it. It's hard to say exactly, but it's like here the karma's right."

"I'd say there's something holy about it," Sarah said.

"Panajachel is a holy place?"

"Well, in a way, yes. Sometimes when the clouds come in over the lake, like in the evening, it's like the spirits are moving. I could meditate on that mist for hours."

Jean nodded at everything Sarah said. They were in complete agreement: Lake Atitlán was a site of great spiritual power, a place of special spiritual intensity. They even thought that the volcanoes and earthquakes were maybe a manifestation of that spiritual power. More important, they were sure that the Indians had special insight, a heightened awareness, something Americans could never have unless they forgot everything and relearned the Indian way.

"I guess you could say our ultimate goal is to retool like that," Jean said.

"Go native?"

"Think native, anyway. The Indians have a total concept, a sense of the whole, the one. It's beautiful."

This kind of talk, which I was hearing quite often in Guatemala, was exactly what troubled me about the gringo infatuation with the Guatemalan Indians. Where was this idea coming from, this idea that the Indians had some mystical key to the universe? I just couldn't understand it; it seemed to me that this was simply another gringo imposition, a fantasy like the many other fantasies we have had about so-called primitive peoples. I asked Jean and Sarah how they knew this about the Indians, that they had a "total concept," and all that.

It wasn't so much that they knew it, but they *sensed* it—and you had to be open-minded, receptive to this kind of thing, they said. Otherwise, you would miss it, like the majority of the tourists going by on the street outside.

One day I went down to the Panajachel beach to look for a launch crossing the lake to Santiago Atitlán, a village renowned in guidebooks for its Sunday market and its traditional charm. Of course, anytime guidebooks enthuse about "charm," you can count on finding the place commercialized. In Panajachel, I saw the warning signs: a sleek boat, hotel logo painted on its stern; a herd of camera-heavy tourists; a dozen touts running along the beach shouting "¡Santiago, Santiago Atitlán, Santiago!"

I walked down the beach looking for something less ostentatious. A little way down, I found a weathered tub, an old man and a boy peering down a hatch at a sputtering motor.

"¿Van a Santiago?" I called above the roar.

The two looked at each other, deliberating.

"Vaya," the old man said at last, as though consenting to a difficult request. "Santiago."

I liked his what-the-hell attitude, and figured a slow crossing would let me see the lake better. I jumped aboard, found a bucket near the bow that would serve as a seat, and settled down for the voyage, my feet in two inches of bilge water. Half an hour later I was still settled on the bucket, and the boat was still tied to a rotten log, rocking in the waves created as the tour boats shoved off, and the bilge water now lapped the top of my shoes. The boy had already been dispatched to town, and now the old man, grumbling, stepped into the lake, walked ashore, and disappeared into the Sunday throng.

Down the beach, another launch, less imposing than the hotel boats, was boarding a group of American college students. I decided it was time to abandon the leaky tub. Nobody paid any mind as I climbed aboard with the college students, at least half of whom were wearing little headphones, black wires dangling from their heads to their waists. Somehow, they kept up conversations despite the head-phones, their clipped speech louder than necessary. The main topic of conversation concerned social justice.

"Look at that."

"Exploitation."

"That's so gross."

"Our taxes support."

I looked ashore for the object of their commentary, but found noth-ing dramatically emblematic of Exploitation, though everything in the scene, ourselves included, bespoke exploitation in some way or another—the glassy front of the tall Hotel del Lago reflecting Atitlán sky; the soldier buying a Coca-Cola from an old woman; the tall blonde tourist surrounded by little indigenous girls showing her their weavings. Or perhaps they meant the tour bus parked in front of the market stalls; but no, it could not be the tour bus, for now a middle-aged man—khaki pants, a shirt made from *típica,* canvas photogra-pher's bag—came out of the bus and toward the boat. Once aboard, he spoke to the nodding kids.

"Now when we get across the lake, we'll go straight to the Habitat homesites, where Carole will meet us. She'll show us around then take us to the co-op. They promised to have someone there if you want to buy anything."

The students nodded and nodded, but whether to their leader's words or to their personalized music, I couldn't tell.

The boat chugged away from the dock into open lake. Panajachel shrank and the volcanoes rose up above us into a deep blue sky. I'd never seen anything so impressive as Atitlán's skyline: rugged cliffs all around culminating in the three volcanoes that just then wore skirts of wispy clouds. The leader of the students busied himself with lenses and filters as he went through a roll of film. His charges played with cassettes, backpacks, sunglasses, lip balm, tanning oils, and each other while the boat churned and sputtered past the little lakeshore villages. Isolated at the bottom of the cliffs for centuries, accessible only by water, the villages honored saints great and small: San Marcos, San Pablo, Santa Clara, San Juan. Onion fields and corn patches had been scratched into the scant land available between cliff and lake. Wearing their traditional full-length skirts, women stood or kneeled in the water, scrubbing clothes, while a few men paddled along in small dugout canoes. This was Atitlán as it had ap-peared for centuries past.

But out toward the middle of the lake, you could see the future: a dozen windsurfers and three or four jet-skiers, harbingers of the recreation area Atitlán was fast becoming.

The captain of the boat was a young Indian who had abandoned native clothing for western wear—a plaid shirt, jeans, straw cowboy hat. He kept his gaze fixed on the distant shimmer of the village of Santiago and seemed to ignore the American girls who lolled in various attitudes around the boat deck, shirt sleeves and shorts rolled up to expose white flesh to the sun. We were near the middle of the lake, about five miles out from Panajachel. Here the lake was very deep, at least a thousand feet, though purportedly the deepest point had never been discovered. The lake is unusual not only because of its great depth but also because it has no river outlets. At some point in time, centuries past, volcanic eruptions sealed Atitlán off, and now its waters can drain into the Pacific only by means of underground seepage.

Indeed, the lake was mysterious in a number of ways: its unearthly beauty, its unsounded depths, its cyclical rising and falling, its lack of outlets, and its instantly changing weather, placid days dissolving into sudden violent tempests. The lake definitely had personality, almost as if it were some mysterious complex organism.

I asked the boat captain about the lake's famous storms, which occurred when sudden afternoon winds called the *xocomil* roiled the waters and could turn a tranquil boat ride into a nightmare. Could he tell when the *xocomil* was coming?

When the clouds swallow the volcanoes, he said. Not slowly, as usually happens, but suddenly, in a matter of minutes and when the waters turn a very clear blue, just before the waves begin. The *xocomil* came from above and below. But these signs didn't matter once you were out in a boat. When the *xocomil* blew, you could not get to shore soon enough.

According to the people of the captain's village, the spirit of Atitlán was once an ant who fell to the bottom of the lake. A nymph rescued him when she saw that he cried tears of pearl. She changed the ant into a human baby and left him in a fisherman's net. The fisherman hauled up the baby and took him home to his childless wife. They named him Xocomil. As he grew, the boy was constantly getting into mischief and he spent long periods of time in the wild with jaguars and serpents. When he was a man he developed the power to change forms. He abandoned his parents and went to live atop the volcanoes. From time to time he rushed down from the peaks and entered the lake, where he would dance and cavort with the nymph who had saved him when he was but a mere ant. So wild was their lovemaking the waters shook and the waves turned white and all vessels were endangered. The good side was that the subsequent rains watered the earth and brought corn to the people.

Xocomil was apparently in control of his urges that day, and we made our passage safely across to Santiago Atitlán, a village precariously set on the volcano slope that rose right out of the lake. Seen from the boat, Santiago Atitlán seemed composed of primary elements: lava rock boulders, stone terraces, bamboo and thatch huts, rough cobbled streets, cactus fences, Tzutuhil Indians clad in rainbow colors. Tourists gazing up at the town from arriving boats could not help but see this as the quintessential Indian village.

Whenever a boat put in at Santiago—an event that occurred several times a day—scores of Atitecos made their way down to the dock to work the arriving tourist crowd. Four or five women pressed against each tourist, holding up weavings for the strangers' admiration. Children came scurrying down the rough stone streets of the village shouting, "¡Saque mi foto, saque mi foto!" The asking price had risen to a quetzal—about twenty-five cents—for a photo of a child dressed in the traditional outfit: red skirts with white and purple blouses for the females, purple-and-white-striped pants on the males. The women wore long red bands wrapped into halolike headdresses. Certainly both the village and its residents were beautiful, precisely the sort of thing tourists found photogenic; and most tourists were all too willing to hand over money for the chance at a photo, however staged.

Perhaps some tourists noted the irony that the money they spent in Santiago was clearly contributing to the degradation of the very culture they had come to see. Prosperity had brought changes to the village: video stores, satellite television, boom boxes blasting pop hits from the States. When they weren't "in costume" for the photographers, young Atitecos were more apt to be wearing Disney T-shirts and playing with the plastic turtle warriors of an American cartoon. It took a bit more work now for tourist photographers to get that perfect shot of a quaint, primitive village.

After walking around Santiago, spending rather more time looking at the other tourists than the place itself, I entered a small restaurant for lunch. The place was empty except for two men seated at a table, both ladino, who turned to watch my entrance. They acted surprised at my sudden appearance, and I had the immediate impression that they had been engaged in some furtive activity. One stood up and came over to me, rubbing his hands, smiling unctuously.

"¿Sí, señor?"

The other man stuffed some papers in a portfolio and grinned at our proceedings.

"I would like lunch," I said.

"¿El almuerzo económico?"

"Yes, fine, the daily special."

He waved me into a chair and disappeared behind a door. I heard him yell indistinct words. Several pots clattered, followed by angrier yelling, then a querulous female voice.

The other man continued to grin at me while I sat, somewhat self-consciously, and looked over the minimalist decor of the place: three imbalanced wooden tables, a half-dozen metal chairs stamped with the rooster logo of Gallo beer, and four completely bare walls recently painted a painfully bright blue.

The man, squat and doughy in his chair, cleared his throat melodramatically, then said, in English, "You are maybe American?"

"Maybe American, that's sounds about right."

"New York? Washington?"

"Albuquerque," I said. He frowned. By now I was accustomed to this reaction and knew I would have to explain. "New Mexico. It's near Texas."

"Ah, Texas. Dallas. My favorite television drama. Linda Gray." His grin widened. He took pleasure in demonstrating his vast knowledge of the United States.

I nodded my appreciation.

"What do you think of our little *pueblo*?" he asked.

"It's very . . . picturesque."

"Ah, yes. Very pretty. All the gringos they like it too much. My Indians are picturesques, yes?"

"Your Indians?"

Again he grinned in triumph. He reached into his pocket and passed me a business card.

"I am senator of Santiago Atitlán, at your orders."

This was my first encounter with a member of Guatemala's notoriously corrupt congress. I was surprised to meet one in Santiago, but not too surprised to find a ladino representing Indians.

"You were elected?"

"Of course."

"You live here then?"

"Live here?" The idea was laughable. "No, no. I have business here—pharmacies all over the country. But my cousin"—he waved toward the now-silent kitchen—"he lives here. He operates this restaurant and the video store."

"Do the Indians like movies?"

"Too much! The Rambo, the kung fu . . . "

While he spoke, I tried to frame a question I just had to ask the senator from Santiago, a question that must be phrased delicately. Recent demonstrations in Santiago had led to disturbances, then violence, then an army attack during which at least fifteen Indians had been killed. I wondered what spin the senator might put on the trouble.

"In the capital, I read about problems here in Santiago, violence . . ."

He let out a low whistle. His eyes rolled in their fatty sockets. "Violence, oh you bet. My Indians they bring me all the problems. The guerrillas, they say, come into the town, yes, and grab the men and take them to the mountains, yes. The guerrillas they kill us, the *inditos* say. And I call the president to say, we need more army now."

"The guerrillas are a big problem?"

"*Big* problem."

After my lunch, complete with beer compliments of my new friend, the senator from Santiago Atitlán, I returned to the dock. The launch I had arrived in was just now departing, loaded for the return with locals, no tourists except for one young German who spent the subsequent passage fending off a pig that tried to gnaw on the straps of his backpack.

Once again I fell into conversation with the young captain. I told him I had just met the senator from Santiago, and I repeated what the senator had said about the guerrillas.

The captain shook his head. Guerrillas? No, the problem was the army. I was a little surprised at his forthrightness. The Indians around the lake were now used to the inquisitiveness of foreigners, and some anyway—especially those like the captain who offered services to the tourists—seemed more willing to shed the obdurate guise with which Indians had long confronted strangers.

"The guerrillas don't cause trouble?"

"Poquito." Only a little. The guerrillas sometimes came to the villages and forced everybody into the plaza for a town meeting. They spoke to the people. Don't join the civil patrols, they said. Don't listen to the government. There was no democracy until there was justice. They must keep solidarity. Then the guerrillas collected money, a war tax they called it, and left before the army arrived to "liberate" the village. The army lieutenant would be angry and say, "Why do you listen to those subversives?" And the people would say, "Because they carry guns." Maybe the army wouldn't do anything that day, but the people would be scared because the army might come back and there would be deaths and beatings and people would disappear. Not just in Santiago, the captain said, but over there at San Juan, and there at San Marcos, too. He pointed out villages around the lake. "In all these villages, the army is responsible for the violence. The guerrillas they are like the puma hidden in the jungle. We hear of its dangers but almost never see it. But the army is like the *xocomil*, it comes at any moment, without warning, killing those it catches."

Before I left Pana, I went to visit Sarah and Jean in their rented house, a pleasant little place with a patio and small garden. Inside, there were scores of crystals and amulets and little smoking pots of incense. Like many middle-class suburbanites in the States, Sarah and Jean had entered middle age nearly spiritually dead, and they were desperate for some kind of awakening. They had turned to the gimmicks of the New Age fringe for assistance in that awakening. Guatemala was somehow a more propitious place for the functioning of these gimmicks; at least many of the Panagringos seemed to think so. They professed love and respect for the Indians, but the fact remained that the gringos had moved in on Indian land, altered the local economy and way of life, and now wanted to confiscate Indian religion or whatever they perceived to be Indian religion. Given the long history of disregard, contempt, and hostility that gringos had felt for these Indians, it seemed curious that it had suddenly become so fashionable to appropriate culture from the Maya. I wondered whether it was a fad, or whether in fact some shift had taken place in the mind-set, in the *Weltansicht* of the First World. And was the shift necessarily good? Now that we were so interested in "primitive" cultures, did our interest signify a new manner of encountering the Other? Or was it just a new way of fashioning the Other into the image most desirable to us?

I left Panajachel and the lake, driving up the steep highway to Sololá, past the waterfalls, past the *miradores*, where newly arrived tourists had stopped for photo sessions. But the lake was obscured just then by another sudden *xocomil*. Clouds filled Atitlán's basin, blotting out the lake and its villages. Rain pelted down on Panajachel and on the other disappeared villages and on the tourists getting down from their motor coaches.

Just past Sololá, I came upon a curious sight: at the entrance to the local army post stood an eight-foot-high replica of a pair of army boots, molded from plastic, painted in vivid camouflage colors. A couple of cars were stopped at the side of the road while their occupants hopped out to take pictures. The boots were no doubt part of many photo albums and slide shows of Our Vacation in Guatemala. I wondered how many of the passing tourists knew that from this same base with the Disneyesque boot out front came the death patrols that terrorized the villages around Lake Atitlán. How many knew that even as they snapped their photos there were, behind the razor wire–topped gates of the base compound, nightmare cells where villagers were tortured, raped, and killed?

Chichicastenango

THE THIRD POINT in Guatemala's tourist triangle was Chichicaste-nango, a small village of Quiché Maya Indians only about twenty-five miles from Atitlán, though the drive was so rigorous it took an hour to go between the two. In fact, the rigors of this road had kept Chichi isolated until the twentieth century. Stephens, the first Yankee to journey across the highlands (in 1840), passed through on his way to the Utatlán ruins but did not think much of "Santo Tomás," as he called it. Nor did archaeologist Alfred Maudslay and his wife, Anne, when they passed through later in the nineteenth century. Another British travel writer, J. W. Boddam Whetham, who found very little of interest in Guatemala on his journey in 1875, called Santo Tomás "an inhospitable village" (*Across Central America*). A trickle of tourist traffic began only in the 1930s when a man named Alfredo Clark opened a hotel in Chichicastenango and drove visitors up from the capital for a look at an honest Indian town. By the late 1950s, the *South American Handbook* had declared a visit to Chichi a tourist "must," and tour buses by the score began negotiating the hairpin turns up to the village.

On Thursdays and Sundays, Chichi was turned into one vast market with vendors coming from all over the region to sell their products and produce. The tourists came by the hundreds and were confronted once again—as in Antigua and Panajachel—by thousands and thousands of textiles and garments. Everywhere I went I saw the same glut of *típica*. For most tourists, the textiles had value primarily as souvenirs and conversation pieces. Only a few people took a true aesthetic interest in the weaving. In such circumstances, the bottom of the market would soon drop out, the prices would have to fall, and the quality of the weaving would seriously diminish.

The *South American Handbook* was right: market day in Chichi was a must for the tourist. But the village was fascinating for other reasons, too, and in order to see the "real Chichicastenango" one had to stay over for the nonmarket days. Most tourists, seeing only the market and maybe the inside of the church, missed what Chichi was all about. It was a tourist destination, but not a tourist site; other than the market, nothing the Indians did was for the benefit of tourists.

The remarkable thing about Chichi was that, despite this twice-weekly influx, the Quiché Indians remained largely unaffected by the disturbances of the tourist hordes. They continued to observe their customs and traditions as though they were oblivious to the invasion. The Quiché Maya possess an impressive fortitude and spiritual focus. Almost nothing disturbs them when they are attending to their religious duties. For the Quiché Maya, physical reality and spiritual reality are not distinct but intimately interpenetrated. This interpenetration is explained by Linda Schele and David Freidel in *A Forest of Kings*:

> The principal language of our reality in the West is economics. Important issues in our lives, such as progress and social justice, war and peace, and the hope for prosperity and security, are expressed in material metaphors. Struggles both moral and military, between the haves and the have-nots of our world pervade our public media and our thoughts of the future. The Maya codified their shared model of reality through religion and ritual rather than economics. The language of Maya religion explained the place of human beings in nature, the workings of the sacred world, and the mysteries of life and death, just as our religion still does for us in special circumstances like marriages and funerals. But their religious system also encompassed practical matters of political and economic power, such as how the ordered world of the community worked.

The steps to the Santo Tomás Church seemed to rise right out of the market. Every hour of every day, some religious observance—usually the burning of incense to the accompaniment of a chant or prayer—took place on these steps. Most visitors to Guatemala considered these ceremonies one of the more noteworthy spectacles in Guatemala, a spectacle that afforded excellent photo opportunities. Somehow, despite the intrusions and disruptions, despite the clicking of cameras and the clucking of tourists, the Quichés persisted in the observation of their rituals. On several occasions, I watched the ceremonies carefully, expecting the participants to betray some self-consciousness, however slight. They *had* to be aware of the crowds and the cameras, I thought, and would therefore exaggerate the more dramatic elements of the ritual. But if they did, I could not detect it. The shaman-priests of the Quichés came and burned incense, said the appropriate prayers, and entered the church to light candles and to offer gifts of flowers, money, and even alcohol to the saints. To the tourists, especially those with video cameras, it was great theater. Unperturbed, the shamans maneuvered around groups of tourists or ducked past the jutting lenses of video cams, their faces locked in the stereotypical obdurate stare of the Indians, a stare that Anglos over the years have described as stupid, obtuse, and rude. As I watched the Quiché rituals in Chichi, I came to appreciate something different in this stoic appearance. If anything, the Indians' faces revealed not stupidity but intense determination, concentration, and focus—qualities that for us are commonly associated with athletics, but that the Indians reserve for reverence and worship. Imagine North Americans feeling intense and focused during a church service: no, it rarely happens for us—on the golf course, maybe; in the sanctuary, almost never.

At Chichi, tourism became voyeurism. There was always so much going on—the crowded, noisy market, the rituals on the steps of Santo Tomás, a ceremonial dance outside El Calvario chapel, the explosion of firecrackers in the morning, a procession—that it was easy to think it all a show put on for the tourists' benefit. But in Chichi it was not a show. The "spectacle" was part of daily life for the Indians, ritual that must be performed in spite of, not because of, the tourists. Wherever tourists went in Chichi they were treading on and through someone else's devotional rites. Two different worlds whirled past each other, momentarily inhabiting the same space but unable to comprehend each other. Bizarre scenes resulted from this encounter: a Quiché man walked on his knees over rough cobblestones, crying out his agony, while a tourist trailed behind him, filming the man's act of penance on a camcorder; a tourist group climbed up the crowded steps of Santo Tomás, hoping to get a photo of the plaza from atop the church's platform, and in the confusion a heavy-set tourist kicked over an incense burner, apologized loudly in English to the woman kneeling there, then fumbled in her purse and waved a ten-quetzal note at the Indian woman; a *cofrade*, a member of a brotherhood devoted to the worship of a particular saint, was standing outside El Calvario, wearing the traditional outfit indicative of a special occasion and holding an ebony and silver staff, the symbol of his office, when a tourist approached and asked him how much he'd take for the staff: the tourist's money belt was already open when the *cofrade* without a word turned and disappeared into the sanctuary.

Inside the church of Santo Tomás, the smoke of *pom* incense swelled and billowed around the dark, chilly nave. Candles burned everywhere—in every nook, at the foot of every statue, on the floor at the back of the nave where there were no pews. The large, eye-catching objects in the church represented the contributions of "ladinoized" Christianity to the Quiché religion: a bloody, tortured Christ; a dolorous Virgin; saints in various states of agony and ecstasy. The smaller details pertained to Quiché symbolics: bundles of pine needles, for example, or splotches of spilled aguardiente. These smaller objects were down low, where they could be touched and experienced; the Christian objects were higher, larger, and out of reach. There was clearly a struggle for space in the church, a struggle between two competing systems of belief. The Quiché objects won on a grassroots level; for grandeur, all eyes gazed up at the altar, the paintings, the statues. The church decor reflected the syncretizing nature of the Guatemalan Indians. One could understand why some priests had been reluctant to completely accept the Quiché elements: Christianity might hold their minds, but the Maya religion held their souls.

The spatial arrangement was reversed on a nearby hillside where the idol of Pascual Abaj was located. Up there, the Christian elements were relegated to the side and Maya objects moved to the center. To reach the idol, you had to take a trail up a hillside about a mile or so outside of town. I was walking on the road that led to the trail, a back road that bordered one of Chichi's three surrounding ravines, when I was intercepted by a young boy.

"El ídolo?" he asked.

"Yes, I'm going to the idol."

He fell into step with me. In Guatemala, young boys commonly worked for the tourists as touts or guides. In my experience, they tried to be helpful, they were eager to show off what they had learned, and they needed the money to help their families, so I had no qualms about "hiring" them to guide me. This boy, Tomás, walked with a limp and spoke softly.

"Here," he said, and we turned onto a trail that led past several huts. At each hut, Tomás called out something as we passed the doorway, and each time a female voice from within the huts shouted a response. The trail climbed into stands of pine tree, and soon I could smell the idol—incense and alcohol on the breeze indicated that we were approaching the sacred site.

Tomás led me to a small clearing in the trees, and there it was: a blackened stone about three feet tall, squatting on a pile of tumbled stones. The scene looked a little like a battlefield, as if all those stones had contested with one another. One—the idol—had emerged the victor; the others were strewn about. The victor, sitting atop the pile, had begun to take on crude anthropomorphic features, a process that must have been abruptly abandoned, for the facial features of the idol were unfinished, an aborted metamorphosis. Candles and incense pots had been placed at the idol's base. Scattered around the clearing were feathers, the leaves used to wrap incense, and small, emptied bottles of aguardiente.

While we were climbing to the idol, Tomás had answered my questions about school, family, and town. He had volunteered information, pointing out objects of interest—an unusual butterfly, an old stone wall, a cave. But once we arrived at the idol, he fell silent. He met my questions with vague nods. When I asked about other idols, in caves perhaps (an archaeologist in Guatemala City had told me that caves were important sites in Maya religions), Tomás did not answer at all. I decided to forgo the questions.

Later, I thought about Tomás' reticence, and I wondered if the whole thing wasn't some sort of ploy. It was curious, I thought, the way he intercepted me. Of course, boys offered guide services all the time in tourist spots like Chichi, but why wasn't Tomás hustling business around the market where the tourists concentrated? Why was he standing out on a back road where only an occasional tourist wandered? In an odd way, I was reminded of the "watchers" at tourist sites in the Soviet Union, the people in the background who stepped forward whenever tourists got off course. More pertinent, I was reminded of the words in the *Popol Vuh* (trans. Dennis Tedlock), the Quiché sacred book: "Do not reveal us to the tribes when they search for us," the gods tell the Quichés. The Quichés remained very secretive about their religion. Perhaps Pascual Abaj was some sort of decoy idol, the one designated to placate the occasional curious tourist who just had to see an idol. The Quichés would take these curious tourists up to Pascual Abaj in order to satisfy their curiosity about "pagan rites." No doubt most people were satisfied, and no doubt most confirmed their stereotypes about paganism by glancing around the Pascual Abaj site and snapping some photos for the folks back home.

In the late twentieth century, travel has proven easier than ever. We can quickly and cheaply get most anywhere, even to places that a few decades ago were remote and inaccessible. It is as if the physical boundaries have disappeared. When I visited Chichi, however, which was once one of those remote places, the dream of any true traveler, I couldn't help but think that the mental boundaries remained as strong as ever. In fact, they were stronger, since tourists who visited Chichi simply confirmed their preconceived notions. They saw only what they had expected to see in the Indians—things like colorful markets and pagan rites. In other words, tourism can, and frequently does, inhibit cross-cultural understanding because technology has made superficial tourism all the easier. Quality touring is less likely than ever.

Over drinks in the bar of the Mayan Inn, the tourists would say how impressed they were, how they found Chichi so fascinating. What they were really saying, of course, was that, as tourist experiences went, the ceremonies were impressive and very well staged. The gringo tourists, regarding it all as a pagan show, generally missed the powerful religiosity of the Quichés. This was nothing new: outsiders had long denied legitimacy to the Indians' religion. Thomas Gage took pride in exterminating their "idols" in the 1630s. The Spaniards habitually destroyed the sacred texts of the Maya. As late as 1957, the foreign priest stationed at Chichicastenango tried to abolish the *cofradías,* and a Catholic Action mob, made up mostly of ladinos, hurled the Indians' idols into a *barranca.*

Visitors generally came to Chichi only for the market, a peek in the church, a drink at the Mayan Inn, and (for the more adventurous) a hike up to Pascual Abaj. And that was it. Overhearing tourists talk in the Mayan Inn about what they had bought and what they had seen and filmed during their day in Chichi, I realized that most people had not really seen anything at all. Worse, they often misunderstood what they had seen, so that they were taking back and spreading mistaken notions about the Guatemalan Indians. Global tourism did not seem to help the First World understand the Third World any better. In fact, it seemed to help harden the stereotypes that were already in place.

To begin to understand the Quichés better, one must turn to an amazing text found in Chichi at the beginning of the eighteenth century: the *Popol Vuh.* This document, a collection of Quiché histories and legends, was discovered by a Spanish priest, Father Ximénez, in the archives of the old church of Chichi. He copied the document, which was written in Quiché, using the Latin alphabet, and translated it into Spanish. His is the only surviving copy of the Quiché text (it is now in the Newberry Library in Chicago). The original was apparently written by an unknown scribe some time in the 1560s.

Actually, to call the *Popol Vuh* a "document" is misleading, for it is really one of the great works of world literature, certainly the greatest work of pre-Columbian New World literature to survive Bishop Diego de Landa's sixteenth-century destruction of Maya texts. In beautiful and striking poetry, the *Popol Vuh* tells the story of creation and of the emergence of the Quiché people prior to the arrival of "the Castilian people." For example, here is how the moment before creation is described: "Whatever there is that might be is simply not there: only the pooled water, only the calm sea, only it alone is pooled. Whatever might be is simply not there: only murmurs, ripples, in the dark, in the night."

The poet succeeds in capturing the tension, the anticipation, and the imminence of the moment of creation. Creation happens because the nothingness, the emptiness *requires* something to burst forth. Something *must* happen, and yet unseen and unknown forces—perhaps the mere inertia of nothingness—prevent the moment from realization: "Now it still ripples, now it still murmurs, ripples, it still sighs, and it is empty under the sky. . . . It is at rest; not a single thing stirs. It is held back, kept at rest under the sky."

After some deliberation, the gods begin the act of creation. The *Popol Vuh* poet emphasizes that together the gods are the *logos* and *nous* behind the universe, for it is the "word" and the "genius" of these "great knowers" that cause the universe to form: "And then the earth arose because of them, it was simply their word that brought it forth. For the forming of the earth they said "Earth." It arose suddenly, just like a cloud, like a mist, now forming, unfolding. Then the mountains were separated from the water, all at once the great mountains came forth. By their genius alone, by their cutting edge alone they carried out the conception of the mountain-plain, whose face grew instant groves of cypress and pine."

This is tremendous metaphysical poetry, part Genesis, part pre-Socratic philosophy. In fact, to my mind, the entire first section of the *Popol Vuh* rivals the pre-Socratics in metaphysical speculation; had it been written in sixth-century B.C. Greece, western philosophy would surely take a greater interest in it—perhaps some scholars would declare the *Popol Vuh* poet the foremost of the pre-Socratics. But of course, since it was written by unschooled Indians, we are content to call it a collection of myths and legends and leave it at that.

Speech—the equivalent of the biblical Word or the Greek *logos*— is of paramount importance in the *Popol Vuh.* The gods bring forth creation by speaking. And the gods' first disappointment with this creation concerns the inability of the new creatures to speak. Two principal gods, named Heart of Sky and Sovereign Plumed Serpent, "planned the animals of the mountains, all the guardians of the forests," but some of the other gods, observing these creatures, point out a basic flaw in the design: "Why this pointless humming? Why should there merely be rustling beneath the trees and bushes?" The gods are extremely disappointed that the creatures do not speak and are thus unable to name the names of the gods. They implore the animals: "Talk, speak out. Don't moan, don't cry out." Unfortunately, the animals "just squawked, they just chattered, they just howled. It wasn't apparent what language they spoke; each one gave a different cry."

The gods realize that their creation is pointless without a creature that can speak, give praise, and observe their holy calendar. So they try again, first fashioning some creatures with earth and mud. These, however, simply dissolve away, a clear failure. Next they attempt to carve beings out of wood. This species proves somewhat more successful in that they are "human in looks and human in speech." The species even multiplies successfully. Still, something is not quite right; the speech turns out to be mere mimicry, and the gods realize that "there was nothing in their hearts and nothing in their minds, no memory of their mason and builder." Furthermore, these robotic manikins are grotesques: "Their faces were dry. They were not yet developed in the legs and arms. They had no blood, no lymph. They had no sweat, no fat. Their complexions were dry, their faces were crusty. They flailed their legs and arms; their bodies were deformed."

Disgusted with these creatures and frustrated by their own creative failure, the gods devise a horrific apocalypse, "a humiliation, destruction, and demolition." Heart of Sky brings down a flood on the heads of the wooden creatures. But unlike the flood accounts in Genesis and Gilgamesh, the *Popol Vuh* poet is not content with mere rain. The wooden manikins are done in by a series of tortures and devastations:

> There came a rain of resin from the sky.
>   There came the one named Gouger of Faces: he gouged
> out their eyeballs.
>   There came Sudden Bloodletter: he snapped off their heads.
>   There came Crunching Jaguar: he ate their flesh.
>   There came Tearing Jaguar: he tore them open.
>   They were pounded down to bones and tendons, smashed and
> pulverized even to the bones. Their faces were smashed because
> they were incompetent before their mother and their father, the
> Heart of Sky, named Hurricane. The earth was blackened because
> of this; the black rainstorm began, rain all day and rain all night.

Severe punishment indeed for linguistic incompetence. But not severe enough for the gods: in a brilliant conclusion to the apocalypse, the manikins' possessions revolt and destroy their owners: "their water jars, their tortilla griddles, their plates, their cooking pots, their dogs, their grinding stones, each and everything crushed their faces."

Each thing in turn rises up, chastises the manikins for their tyranny and their incompetence, and then crushes the faces of the hapless creatures. "The people were ground down, overthrown. The mouths and faces of all of them were destroyed and crushed." All told, it's a pretty impressive apocalypse, but somehow the manikins are not entirely exterminated. The *Popol Vuh* concludes that "this is why monkeys look like people: they are a sign of a previous human work, human design—mere manikins, mere woodcarvings."

Along with an explanation of creation and an account of a flood, the *Popol Vuh* shares many features with Genesis and other such mythologies. First, it explains the origin of astronomical features, such as the Big Dipper, and other natural phenomena—like the monkeys in the apocalypse passage. Elsewhere, for example, the *Popol Vuh* recounts an Ovidian type tale that explains the origin of the whippoorwill's unusual gaping mouth. Second, like all mythologies and heroic epics, the *Popol Vuh* tells of a journey to the underworld—which for the Quichés was a place called Xibalba, ruled over by seven lords. The twin heroes who journey there must pass hellish nights in Xibalba's chambers—Razor House, Cold House, Jaguar House, and Bat House. Third, like Genesis, the *Popol Vuh* asserts that woman was created after man, that the gods became concerned that humans had too much knowledge and were too close to deistic powers, and that a confusion of languages led to the separation of humans into different linguistic tribes.

These similarities are intriguing. But the *Popol Vuh* also sets forth some differences, particularly some subtle points of conflict with Christianity, that provide clues to the Quiché worldview and their remarkable ability to resist the devastations that have been visited upon them. The *Popol Vuh* was composed sometime in the 1560s, approximately forty years after the Conquest. Two generations of Quichés had been instructed in Christianity, and yet there seems to be very little Christian influence, if any, on the *Popol Vuh*. Indeed, the only references to Christianity in the text, while not directly critical, seem to imply a rejection of Christianity or at least dissatisfaction with it.

Christianity is mentioned twice in the *Popol Vuh*, and the location of the references is important: at the very beginning and at the very end of the text. The poet of the *Popol Vuh* frames the holy book with obeisance to the Christian God, although it is an obeisance tinged with discontent. "We shall write about this now, amid the preaching of God, in Christendom now," the poet proclaims, using the Spanish word, "Dios," for God—one of the few Spanish words to appear in the narrative. For the Quichés, "Christendom" has meant the suppression of their religion and, most important, the destruction of their sacred writings. The poet is motivated to write, in fact, because "there is no longer a place to see "the Council Book, the *Popol Vuh* of the Quiché."

The last line of the *Popol Vuh*—"everything has been completed here concerning Quiché, which is now named Santa Cruz"—provides a poignant and ironic conclusion to the work. All the history and glory of the Quiché people have been obliterated—even their name is conquered by the Spaniards: the sacred name Quiché has been changed to the Spanish words for "Holy Cross." As a conclusion to the text, these foreign words jar the reader; they have a sad sound to them; no doubt they reminded the Quichés of the bitterness and gall they felt under "the Castilian people." The *Popol Vuh* makes no overt statements of resistance, but the tone of the beginning and ending of the text suggests an obdurate stance. The "Christian frame" of the *Popol Vuh* is not unlike the Quichés' current practice of praying in the Catholic church and lighting candles for the saints before going into the woods to pray before an idol.

And while there are no direct challenges to Castilian/Christian authority in the text, the reader does find some allusions to Christianity that imply a subtle conflict between Quiché and Christian theology. The most interesting of these allusions concerns the creation of human beings. The gods, as we learn at the beginning of the *Popol Vuh*, have difficulty creating a race that will properly praise and respect their creators. One of their attempts involves fashioning a creature out of earth and mud, but this attempt is an utter failure because the material doesn't hold together: "it was just separating, just crumbling, just loosening, just softening, just disintegrating, and just dissolving." One of the gods, examining the mud creature, states, "It won't last. It seems to be dwindling away so let it dwindle."

It would seem that in this account the poet of the *Popol Vuh* is subtly alluding to the Genesis creation story, in which God creates Adam from mud; and in so alluding the poet is rejecting the Genesis version as somewhat ludicrous. The true creation of human beings could not be effected with a material so unpromising as mud. Later in the *Popol Vuh* the truth is revealed concerning "the making, the modeling of our first mother-father with yellow corn, white corn alone for the flesh." The belief in corn as the primary substance, the material from which the gods could construct the human prototype, goes well back to the pre-Columbian Maya, who frequently depicted on pots and in murals human heads emerging from stalks of corn. The poet of the *Popol Vuh* thus rejects the new theology, taught to the Quichés dogmatically and sometimes with force, by asserting the ancient teaching and arguing for its obvious validity over the absurd instruction of the Castilians.

Near the end of the *Popol Vuh*, the poet comments on the purpose of a Council Book, such as the one he is writing. The poet states that the Quiché leaders could foretell the success or failure of ventures by consulting such a book: "They knew whether war would occur; everything they saw was clear to them. Whether there would be death, or whether there would be famine, or whether quarrels would occur, they knew it for certain, since there was a place to see it, there was a book. Council Book was the name for it."

The poet, transcribing this same Council Book, hints that what we have been reading, ostensibly a collection of stories and legends, also contains a key to secret knowledge. In a twist worthy of Cortázar or Borges, he tells us, in effect, that there is another way to read the book we have been reading, a secret code that transforms those stories into a kind of magic book that can be consulted when the diviners need to predict the outcome of important events. The poet does not, however, provide any clues for solving the code: like so much of the Quiché world, it's there, but we cannot see it. Its face is hidden, and will remain so as long as the Quichés are living "amid the preaching of God, in Christendom now."

Utatlán

THE ROAD NORTH OUT OF Chichicastenango took me away from tourist territory. Only a few gringos traveled into the remote highlands: the ubiquitous missionaries, some human rights workers, journalists. People with a purpose. The paved road ended in Santa Cruz del Quiché, a ladinoized town twelve miles from Chichi that was now the center of military operations in the highlands. The road was traveled mostly by trucks—decrepit transport trucks hauling livestock, people, and construction materials, and the dark, dull green trucks of the military hauling troops and ordnance. Occasionally, a jammed bus jounced along, music blaring within, huge sacks and baskets tied to the roof.

Santa Cruz was heavily militarized, like a Vietnamese village. Helicopters circled an airfield. On the outskirts, several checkpoints monitored access to the town. When I approached the checkpoint, a soldier dropped a crude pole across the road. A life-sized soldier painted on a board extended his palm, the word ALTO (Stop) emblazoned on his helmet. My papers were scrutinized, all data were written down in a ledger, and permission was grudgingly granted. The road into Santa Cruz was lined by a wall topped with razor wire, and there were storks' nests every quarter mile or so, machine guns jutting from the peepholes. Tourist country seemed far, far behind; and yet only twelve miles away suburbanites from the Midwest were buying textiles.

Utatlán, the site of the ruined post-Classic Quiché capital, is located just outside Santa Cruz. A dirt road drops down into a *barranca* and then climbs up to a plateau, where the city is situated. No doubt the site was chosen for defense, and it must have been formidable in its time. But now Utatlán is nothing but grass-covered mounds, with a few sections of stone sticking up here and there. The most interesting part of the ruin is a tunnel where native rituals still take place. The dense smoke of incense fills the cave, and in fact the majority of visitors to Utatlán are Indians who come to perform some sacred duty.

Not much was left to see in Utatlán, but the place had as rich a history as any site in Central America. The principal events of the conquest of Guatemala took place around Utatlán in 1524. When the Spaniards arrived, Utatlán was the political and religious center of a kingdom that controlled most of present-day Guatemala. The Quichés were a sophisticated and creative people with a complex calendric system and cosmology, as evidenced by the *Popol Vuh*. A city of temples, houses, and ball courts, Utatlán had been the principal Quiché city for approximately 150 years when, in 1523, Cortés sent Pedro de Alvarado south from Tenochtitlán to learn what he could about the powerful city the Aztecs called Utatlán (the Quichés called their capital Cumarcaj). Already Cortés had received one hundred ambassadors from the Quiché capital who promised him that they wished to be "subjects and vassals" of the imperial majesty, Charles V. Later, Cortés' allies in Soconusco complained that Utatlán had harassed them for being allies of Cortés. "So to learn the truth of this," Cortés wrote Charles V, "I dispatched Pedro de Alvarado." It is interesting to note that the professed purpose of the expedition was to gather information. In other words it was a fact-finding mission. If indeed that was Cortés' intention, he chose the wrong man to head the expedition, for Pedro de Alvarado, more rapacious than Pizarro and more megalomaniacal than Cortés himself, could not content himself with fact finding. He was by then too full of the romance of conquest.

Alvarado was born in 1485, an Extremaduran, like so many of the conquistadors. He had a predilection for adventure and conquest, and he was involved with most of the major New World expeditions of his time: Velásquez's conquest of Cuba in 1511; Juan de Grijalva's venture to Yucatan in 1518; and Cortés' campaign in Mexico. Bernal Díaz described him as handsome and brave and noted in particular the impression Alvarado made on the Indians of Mexico. When Moctezuma asked his spies what the Spaniards looked like, they singled out Alvarado as the finest specimen of the strange beings.

According to Díaz, they told Moctezuma that Alvarado was a man "of very perfect grace in face and person, that he looked like the sun, and that he was a Captain, and in addition to this they brought with them a picture of him with his face very naturally portrayed, and from that time forth they gave him the name of 'Tonatio,' which means the Sun, or the Child of the Sun, and so they called him ever after" (*True History of the Conquest of New Spain*). This description was just one of the many misinterpretations the Aztecs made concerning the Spaniards.

In his letters, Cortés considers Alvarado "valiant" and describes him as "elegant both in person and appearance, and distinguished for his capacity in training soldiers" (the letters are included in Alvarado's *An Account of the Conquest of Yucatan in 1524*). Even the perspicacious Bernal Díaz thought Alvarado "of good size, and well-proportioned, with a very cheerful countenance and a winning smile." Díaz went on to note that Alvarado "was very active and a good horseman, and above all was very frank-hearted and a good talker, and he was very neat in his attire but with rich and costly clothes. He wore a small gold chain around his neck with a jewel, and a ring with a good diamond."

From these contemporary accounts, a stunning picture of Alvarado emerges: he was devilishly handsome, athletic, frank, eloquent, neat, elegant, graceful . . . and a psychopathic killer. One can hardly imagine meeting such a man, coming face to face with that "winning smile." It is worth noting that all three observers (the Aztec spy, Cortés, and Díaz) confuse appearance with substance. It would seem that everyone encountering Alvarado mistook his beauty and grace as a sign of worthiness, that he was an exceptional man in both appearance and person. And yet history documents few men as vicious as Alvarado. His record of cruelty began in Mexico when, left in command while Cortés was away, he massacred Aztecs indiscriminately. Even Cortés, no angel of the Conquest himself, had to chastise Alvarado for his actions.

Cortés may have sent Alvarado on a fact-finding mission, but he must also have anticipated the havoc his sanguinary captain would wreak, for the rest of the story follows ineluctably. Alvarado met the Quichés at Pinal, south of Quetzaltenango, where he supposedly defeated Tecúm, the grandson of the Quiché ruler. Invited to Utatlán for the formal surrender, Alvarado arrived in the city but immediately became suspicious that the Indians were plotting something. Only one narrow causeway permitted access to the city, the streets were too narrow for his horses to maneuver, and women and children were conspicuously absent from the city. Alvarado played it safe and withdrew to the outskirts, telling his hosts that the horses needed to be exercised on the open plain. Inexplicably, the leading men of Utatlán accompanied the Spaniard outside the city. Alvarado was not one to pass up an opportunity: he seized the rulers, accused them of duplicity, found them guilty, and burned them at the stake.

Eight days of fighting followed. The Spaniards needed the assistance of the Cakchiquels, a traditional enemy of the Quichés, before they could capture the capital. Finally victorious, Alvarado destroyed Utatlán. He left nothing behind but piles of rubble.

Other than rubble, Alvarado's legacy includes two brief letters, written to Cortés between 1524 and 1525 from the battlefronts in Guatemala. The letters (there were four, but two are lost) were appended to Cortés' own letters to Charles V, and while Alvarado's writing is not so fascinating as Cortés', his words do reveal some interesting things about the initial encounter of Europeans and aborigines in Guatemala.

Alvarado writes a breathless prose. He doesn't trouble himself with explanations or the niceties of description. It is a blitzkrieg style that matches Alvarado's march through the land. Here is a typical sentence: "And next morning I left for this town, and at its entrance found the roads closed and many stakes thrust in, and when I was entering into the town I saw certain Indians cutting a dog in quarters in the manner of a sacrifice, and in the said town they made an uproar, and we saw a great multitude of the people of the country, and we attacked them, breaking them up until we drove them from the town, and we followed them in pursuit all we could."

This is quite a bit of action for one sentence. Alvarado does not linger over details, nor is he interested in explaining the bizarre parts of his narration. Although supposedly on a fact-finding mission, Alvarado displays no curiosity whatsoever about the Indians, their customs, manners, architecture, art—nothing of the like graces Alvarado's account. He isn't even interested in the land; the few descriptions of terrain in his letters appear only to explain tactics or other military information: "This land is very full of gullies; there are gullies two hundred *estados* in depth, and on account of them, one cannot carry on war and punish these people as they deserve."

Furthermore, Alvarado never seems to encounter an individual worth describing or even naming. His only attempts at communication are threats: "I threatened to make war on them as traitors rising in rebellion against the service of our Lord the Emperor and that as such they would be treated, and that in addition to this I would make slaves of all those who should be taken alive in the war." What matters to Alvarado is that these New World savages must be conquered, or, to use his phrase, "pacified." In one town, his forces actually invaded the *homes* of villagers in order to continue the killing: "And after entering in the houses we struck down the people, and continued the pursuit as far as the market place." On another occasion, he pursues the fleeing Indians "for two leagues and a half until all of them were routed." With pride, he tells Cortés that he "made the greatest destruction in the world" and "killed and imprisoned many people."

Alvarado kills the Indians with such conviction because he believes they are the very incarnation of "evil," a word he uses again and again to describe their actions. Everything they do he regards as evil—whether it is blocking the streets of their towns against him or fleeing from him or ignoring his messages. He thus feels justified in slaughtering them, and justification is a constant concern for Alvarado. He is clearly worried about Cortés' judgment; he feels compelled to give his commander some reason for his brutal actions. To defend himself against possible censure, he asserts the evilness of his foes. Thus, in writing about his destruction of Utatlán, he explains to Cortés that, "as I knew them to have a bad disposition towards the service of His Majesty, and to insure the good and peace of this land, I burnt them, and sent to burn the town and to destroy it, for it is a very strong and dangerous place, that more resembles a robbers' stronghold than a city."

Another document recounts these same events differently. In the *Annals of the Cakchiquels* (trans. Daniel Brinton), a record of Cakchiquel Indian history kept by their priests, the events of that year are recorded, but with a different emphasis. The Cakchiquels had long been the enemies of the Quichés and had initially supported Alvarado in his battles. Nevertheless, the text of the *Annals* emphasizes Alvarado's cruelty; according to its authors, the lords of Utatlán came before Alvarado and paid him tribute, only to suffer "many torments from Tunatiuh." The *Annals* do not mention any attempted deceit on the part of the lords of Utatlán; instead, Alvarado appears as the instigator, the aggressor, a man devoted to the excesses of slaughter: "nor was the heart of Tunatiuh satisfied with war," the *Annals* tell us. For the Cakchiquels, there is no doubt who is the evil savage: Alvarado.

From the ruins of Utatlán, I could see the outskirts of Santa Cruz and some of the neighboring hamlets. A helicopter hovered in the distance. Nearly five hundred years had passed since Alvarado burned and destroyed this town, and yet the conquest continued, pretty much following Alvarado's paradigm. Just like Alvarado, the army used the word "pacify" to mean "conquer and destroy." Alvarado destroyed numerous villages on his march through the highlands; the army, too, had destroyed scores, even hundreds of villages. Alvarado relied on Indian troops and used one tribe to fight against another; today, the Guatemalan army gang presses Indians from one region and uses them to assist in the slaughter of tribes in other regions. Alvarado relied on the king of Spain for his support, and the army has relied on the United States. There is even a parallel when it comes to human rights: the king of Spain from time to time expressed concern over the treatment of the Indians so that those on the front lines, like Alvarado, felt compelled to justify their slaughters. Thus Alvarado's use of doublespeak has its equivalent in the army's manipulation of language in order to justify massacres to the US government—though in neither case has the imperial power monitored the situation all that closely.

The Conquest was reenacted again and again in the highlands. Even the traveler passing through was aware of this ever-recurring, unending drama. I saw the staged version, or rather one of the many staged versions, near Utatlán in the village of Joyabaj. There, in the middle of August every year, the villagers performed *el baile de la conquista*—the dance of the Conquest. This dance was an important annual ceremony in villages throughout the highlands. Each village had its own variation, but the core event of the drama—Pedro de Alvarado's legendary battle with Tecún Umán, the Quiché prince—remained the same everywhere.

During the days of preparation, the plaza of the village was consecrated by the local shaman; then a stage was constructed and pine needles, palm fronds, and cypress branches were strewn on the stage and around the plaza. Fireworks were exploded and incense burned outside the church. Then on the designated day, the villagers gathered to see the performance of the dance-drama.

It begins with music: a small drum, called a *tun*, beats a dirgelike rhythm for a small flute, the *chirimia*. The Indians, elaborately costumed and painted, enter the plaza. They wear masks, their painted faces intense and philosophical. Fantastic headpieces, whose colors and patterns suggest stylized animals or mythical beasts, top the costumes. Now the Indians make way for a grotesque figure. This is the shaman, whose bright red face and bulging eyes make him look like a Dantean devil. The shaman introduces the dance by foretelling a war "the likes of which has never been seen in this land." This war will spell doom for the great Quiché prince, Tecún Umán. At first, Tecún denies the authority of this prophecy (in no culture are prophets believed until it is too late), but immediately word comes to the Quiché people that Moctezuma of the Mexican kingdom has been defeated by "a foreign king," and that the "notorious captain" of this king, "who is called Pedro Alvarado and who caused great ruin in his pilgrim war" is coming to the Quiché kingdom.

Then Tecún announces that he too has dreamt about the destruction and enslavement of his people. Despite these omens, the Quichés prepare for battle. The shaman reappears and promises that he will bring down curses and spells on the invaders and help to defeat them.

After all this preparation, the Spanish enter the plaza on horses. They are dressed in an exaggerated, almost oriental version of a European conqueror: golden beards, pink faces, tricornered hats topped with feathers, and elaborately embroidered breastplates. There is a distinct contrast between the masks of the opposing forces. The Indian faces seem more human, more thoughtful. The faces of the Spaniards are frozen in a wide-eyed, vacant stare, more zombie than human. Their ghostly blue eyes make the Indian fear of *mal ojo*, the evil eye, believable (the Indians fear blue eyes, believing that meeting the stare of a blue-eyed person would bring on the *susto*, a deathlike condition in which the victim is rendered physically and spiritually paralyzed).

Alvarado speaks first for the Spaniards as he performs a dance that takes him to each corner of the plaza. At one point, working himself to a frenzied pitch, Alvarado bellows:

> War! War! Unceasing, against those who intend
> To stain the Fatherland's escutcheons.
> War! War! Soak the native banners
> In waves of blood.
> War! War! On hill and in valley.

There is little doubt about Alvarado's essential character. War, destruction, and conquest are on his mind from the beginning, before he even meets the Indians. His troops, caught up in his bellicose enthusiasm, swear their fidelity to their captain and to the king of Spain, then confirm their desire to destroy and pillage. One foot soldier pledges that he will give "these Indian swine twenty thousand kicks in the ass." Alvarado, satisfied with his soldiers' commitment to war, decides to send two envoys to the Quiché king with a message: the Quichés are to surrender and accept the faith of the one true God. These two "ambassadors" are the first Spaniards to encounter the Quichés. They first meet an Indian woman, so beautiful that one ambassador confesses an interest in her. But then the same Spaniard sees an Indian man, and cries out:

> Look, Carillo, how horrible is this Indian
> How infernal his appearance
> How red he is all over, body and face.

For the Spaniards, Indian women are desirable, but the men are ugly, almost inhuman creatures deserving of slaughter.

Shouting at the Indian, the Spaniard who was so attracted to the Indian woman, says, "Barbarian, stop jumping around and listen if you are capable." His haughtiness is soon repaid: word comes from Tecún that if the ambassadors wish to speak with him they must be bound and blindfolded. In a key moment of the dance, the Indian shaman blindfolds and binds the Spaniards. The amount of time dedicated to this binding suggests that it is an important psychological moment of the drama for both dancers and audience. The Spaniards, forced to submit to bondage, are humbled before the Indians.

It seemed to me that the crowd anticipated this scene and derived some satisfaction from seeing the Spaniards ill-treated. The Indian dancers representing these two Spaniards exaggerated their roles by swaggering and shouting brusquely—they were like the villains in staged wrestling shows inviting and inciting the wrath of the audience. Watching the encounter of Spaniards and Quichés, the audience hissed and whistled at the Spaniards and cheered the bondage. The "Spaniards" provoked the audience by raising fists, pointing fingers, and strutting about the stage.

When the Spaniards are led to him, Tecún harangues them for their rudeness and lack of education. The audience loves this—Tecún threatens to whip them into tiny pieces, he so dislikes their appearance and their barbaric behavior. But instead of doing so, he sends them back to Alvarado with his message of defiance. Now both sides prepare for war—the Spaniards eager for booty and the Indians full of foreboding.

The climax of the dance, the actual battle between Tecún and Alvarado, occurs rather abruptly. The two sides advance on one another, Tecún calls Alvarado out for man-to-man combat, Alvarado advances to meet Tecún, makes a speech, laughs mysteriously, then strikes Tecún. The Indian prince, mortally wounded, dies after a short speech.

The dance drama ends with a somber funeral procession, the flute and drum contributing a dirge. Tecún is carried to the feet of his king, who, devastated by the loss of his best prince, decides to accept the religion of the Spaniards. Word is sent to Alvarado that the Indians desire baptism. The epilogue of the play thus consists of their baptism into the Christian faith. It is a strange ending. First, the Quiché king announces that he has had a dream "so weird and mysterious that in it I saw the error of my ways." In the dream, an apparition spoke to him in his own language: "I am the Holy Spirit," it said, "the True God. Leave your false illusions and superstitions." Alvarado, convinced of their sincerity, has the Indians kneel, and then he baptizes them in the name of God. The Spaniards say to the Indians: "Proclaim Mary, and not your false gods." Curiously, and somewhat incongruously, the Indians answer: "Viva the Spaniards who made us Christians. The Quiché empire is exterminated." On that note, the dance ends.

It seems plausible that the dance of the Conquest originated with, or at least was sanctioned by, the Catholic Church. Its denouement is concerned not so much with Tecún's death as it is with the Indians' conversion. Suggestions of Spanish cruelty are muted (indeed the only torture that takes place is perpetrated by the Indians), and even Alvarado appears more as a crusader than a conqueror at the drama's end. Furthermore, much of the dialogue employs the second person plural (*vosotros*), which is nonexistent in American Spanish and known only through its use in biblical Spanish. It thus seems likely that a priest had a hand in the drama's origin.

The contemporary version of the dance, however, is staged by a village's *cofradía*, the brotherhood of elders who tend to the worship of the village saint. The preparations for the dance include the performance of the appropriate *costumbres* by a shaman. These *costumbres*, or rituals, predate Christianity and have been incorporated into the modern Maya's syncretism of Christian and pagan practices. The dance of the Conquest cannot be performed until a shaman pours alcohol on the ground, blesses the performers and musicians, and makes the appropriate prayers. According to anthropologist James Sexton, these include prayers to the spirit of King Tecún. This insistence on preparatory ritual is interesting because one subtext of the dance-drama concerns the ineffectuality of Maya *costumbres*. The Indian witch doctor promises to thwart the Spanish with his spells, but of course the spells fail. Throughout the drama the Indians refer to and call upon their gods, but these appeals go unheeded. By the end of the play, the Indians admit that they have been deluded. In fact, the last lines are spoken by the witch doctor, who announces that from this day forth, the Indians will accept the faith of Don Pedro de Alvarado.

When the play in Joyabaj finished, the dancers, still in costume, came before the crowd in a mixed line—Spaniard, Indian, Spaniard, Indian. They shook hands and then embraced.

The Ixil Triangle

TO THE NORTH OF SANTA CRUZ, the road turned very rugged. About eighty-five kilometers of climbing, descending, curving, and still more climbing brought me to an area of Guatemala called the Ixil Triangle. The Triangle is a small section of the far northern part of the department of El Quiché where the only speakers of the Ixil language are gathered in three tiny towns—Nebaj, Cotzal, and Chajul. The Triangle was pretty much the end of the road: to the west and east towering mountains blocked passage, and to the north the terrain was gouged by ravines as it descended into the impenetrable jungles of the Petén. The only way in was by the long grueling road from Santa Cruz.

The road crossed the Chixoy River, which northeast of the Triangle flowed into the Usumacinta and formed the boundary with Mexico. After crossing the Chixoy, the road climbed up a steep ridge, a breathtaking ascent in which the car, churning against the grade, veered back and forth across the ridge, valleys on both sides dropping farther and farther below. At the summit I left the dry landscape behind and entered into a dense subtropical pine forest. Far below, in a bowl-shaped basin bordered by mountains, Nebaj's neat image rippled through the heat waves, a mirage in a desert, a jewel in a stream.

On the road to Nebaj, I encountered a civil patrol (*patrulla de autodefensa*) for the first time. In only a few years, the civil patrol had become an institution in Guatemala that now involved nearly one million men, or one-eighth of the total population. The government's idea was to enroll the male civilian population of a town, or *aldea*, in a voluntary defense force—something like the minutemen of the American Revolution—that would assist the army in combating guerrilla terrorism. In effect, the army conscripted all the adult males ("adult" meaning age thirteen and older in some places) in the rural areas of the highlands and forced them to volunteer for periodic, unpaid duty. Each hamlet had to organize itself and report its efforts to the commander of the local army base. The commander then reviewed the villagers' efforts, rewarded them with a few old carbines, and gave them instructions on how to defend themselves against communist "subversives." Duty was supposed to be voluntary, but the military's supervision of the patrols meant that it was, in effect, mandatory. The army asked the patrol leaders to compile a list of anyone in the village who refused to serve. Refusers could then be accused of being in sympathy with the subversives. Even President Cerezo acknowledged that "less than one-third of the civil patrollers serve voluntarily."

Actually, the villagers had good reasons for disliking service, reasons that had nothing to do with supporting subversion. First and foremost, time spent on the patrols was time lost in the fields or at work. Patrol duty cost an already impoverished people money that they simply did not have. Second, the army quickly discovered that the civil patrol system could be manipulated as part of a psychological campaign for the hearts and minds, as General Ríos Montt had put it, of the Indians. For example, the army liked to stage rallies in which the civil patrols from all the *aldeas* were obligated to participate. At these rallies, the army led the patrols in group-bonding exercises, such as burning guerrilla flags, marching, charging mock targets in unison, cheering, parading, and singing the Civil Patrol Anthem. And of course there were indoctrination speeches, which identified the group's common enemy (international communism) and gave the patrols a common cause with the army (defense of the glorious *patria*, the fatherland). For the purposes of the exercises, patrols were even given weapons, though the army generally didn't trust them enough to let them keep the arms.

The civil patrol system proved a great vehicle for terror. For example, the army liked to use the civil patrols as scouts or bush-beaters in their search-and-destroy missions. When an army patrol went into an area where guerrillas were thought to be operating—a gorge, say, or a mountainside—they compelled the local civil patrol to lead the way. Armed only with muskets and perhaps an old carbine or Winchester, the civil patrols were clearly no match for well-armed guerrilla squads, and many civil patrollers lost their lives in such encounters. Once again, the army was simply following Alvarado's example. The conquistador had used Indians from one tribe as scouts in the homelands of different tribes, and these scouts were frequently killed as they searched the forests for hiding warriors. In fact, Alvarado saw this "voluntary" service as a test, much as the contemporary military does. When Alvarado took up a Cakchiquel offer of assistance in the attack on Utatlán, he did so, he wrote, in order to "find out what their [the Cakchiquel] disposition was, as well as to strike terror in the land"—exactly what the army did with the civil patrols. With civil patrols and guerrillas clashing in unequal combat, a natural antipathy soon developed, especially on the part of the patrols, which had no choice but to see the guerrillas as the enemy. Thus, the army benefited by saving soldiers' lives and by eliminating any sympathy villagers might have had for the guerrillas.

But the army used the civil patrols for more than just guerrilla tracking. Its most insidious move was to force the civil patrols into the role of village watchdogs or spies. The leader of each civil patrol had to report suspicious activity to the authorities—and "suspicious activity" in this case could mean anything, including the apparently innocuous activities of storing corn (obviously food for the subversives) or carrying a Bible (a sure indication of an interest in liberation theology). In the logic of the army, a lack of anything suspicious to report was itself suspicious; thus the civil patrols were forced to invent observations and reports of suspect activity. Divisions soon developed in communities whose members were encouraged to spy on one another (the Guatemalan army, it seemed, was not opposed to *every* aspect of communist societies). What's more, the army deliberately exacerbated these rifts. Human rights groups reported that some villages were forced into making the most horrifying decisions a community could ever face.

Consider for a moment what some of these villages went through:

The army shows up in the village one day with a group of prisoners—suspected subversives, according to the commander—who live in the *aldea*. Look, the lieutenant says, these guerrilla sympathizers were living among you; now we're going to let you handle it. We'll be back to find out what you've done. The alleged subversives have lived in the village all their lives, and the villagers know perfectly well that there's nothing "subversive" about these men. But what is to be done? The villagers, all too familiar with the army's mentality, perceive immediately that the army expects them to execute the "prisoners," their own neighbors and relatives. Any other decision, in the army's view, would suggest that the entire village is in league with the subversives, and there are scores of examples all over the highlands of what the military does to villages suspected of collusion with the guerrillas: a slaughter will surely follow any decision other than what the military expects. Even the accused men recognize this and acquiesce in the decision. In fact, one of the accused insists that their execution is the villagers' only choice: some must die so that the village may be saved. It is a cruel and pitiless world, but it is so.

The villagers pass a long and anguished night, a night of keening and wailing by the women, a night of prayer and oblations by the men. In the small church they light candles and place bundles of pine needles at the feet of the saints. Near dawn, the villagers feel more hopeful. Perhaps they are wrong, perhaps they have misinterpreted the army's intentions. Perhaps they could explain to the lieutenant that they know these men, they have questioned them closely and are satisfied that they have no connections to the guerrillas, that they are possibly confused with some other men who have gone over to the guerrillas, because God knows some have been deluded by the false message of the subversives. Or perhaps they could all leave for the mountains, spend a week, two weeks, in hiding. Maybe the army will forget about them, they are such a small and unimportant village. Then one of the younger men speaks up. He has been in the army, serving several years after he was gang-pressed one day in Santa Cruz (it was a fiesta day, and all the young men had come in from the *aldeas* for the occasion, and the army, knowing this would be the case, was waiting with large transport trucks, and at the height of the fiesta the trucks arrived in the plaza and soldiers started grabbing all the young men—there was nothing one could do to escape, for to resist was to invite a beating and torture). He tells the villagers that the army will surely return and will surely destroy the village if they do not execute the men. He has seen it before. He knows their mind. There is no escape: they will hunt with helicopters, they will pursue them into the mountains, they will burn everything. He has known the likes of this lieutenant: they become obsessed over these things and turn into animals. He has heard their words, witnessed their actions.

At dawn, the last prayers are recited. Everyone in the village hugs the condemned men. An elder speaks and asks the men to forgive them. He also asks all the villagers, even the youngest among them, to remember this day, to remember what the white men have done to them. The condemned men beg the villagers to care for the widows, the children, and the corn in the fields. Outside the church, before the morning mist has lifted, two civil patrollers who have served in the army and who know about death and killing, carry out the executions. It is a messy job, because the only gun in the *aldea* is the old, inaccurate Winchester the army has given to the patrol. The five prisoners are felled by the first shots, but three do not die, and the executioners must administer a *tiro de gracia*, a death blow. In the church, the praying villagers hear loud reports, cries, muffled shots, roosters crowing. Then silence. The executioners enter the church and fall sobbing before a statue of the Virgin. The widows renew their keening, and theirs is the only awful sound until, faintly at first and then louder and louder as it draws closer, their wails are drowned out by the beating, beating, beating of a helicopter that approaches and hovers over the hamlet.

A civil patroller waved me to a halt. The road was barricaded. Someone had ingeniously fashioned a swiveled gate out of a pole and a powdered-milk can filled with concrete. The can served as a weight at one end of the pole, thus allowing the whole mechanism to be raised and lowered for what little traffic the isolated road supported. Next to the road stood a very crude watchtower made from four felled trees and some old planks. One man—a teenager, really— played lookout. About a half dozen others gathered by the car and looked at the papers I handed them. I had seen these civil patrols here and there on the main highways, but their posts were always on ridges up above the road. The government didn't want to disturb the tourists driving to Atitlán or Chichicastenango. It was best, in fact, if the tourists knew nothing about the patrols. But way out here, on the remote back roads of the highlands, even gringos were obliged to stop and declare their intentions. Clearly, the appearance of a foreigner made these patrollers nervous. They knew what gringos looked like, of course—a good number of journalists and missionaries still came up this way. But what did these Cubans and Russians look like, the ones whom the army captain had been so vehement about in his speeches? Maybe this was an agent of international subversion? How could one tell?

"Norteamericano," I reassured them. "Periodista [journalist]."

"Sí, sí," they said. They frowned over the papers, and looked unsure. Obviously they didn't even want to be there, nor did they want to be dealing with something as uncertain as a foreigner. No one said anything, but the papers were handed back to me, the gate was raised, and I passed on. "Gracias," I said and waved as I went past. They politely said "Para servirle [at your service]," and waved back. But when I glanced in the mirror and saw them all standing in the road staring after me, I knew they regretted having let me pass. Maybe they were wondering whether they had just made a big mistake, one the army lieutenant would punish them for. For my part, I fervently hoped there weren't any more patrols before Nebaj.

There weren't. Instead, when I arrived in Nebaj groups of soldiers were patrolling the grassy streets. A machine gun nest guarded the main entrance of the town. A slogan painted on a wall read "¡Pueblo y ejército por la Paz: No al comunismo, sí a la democracia!"—People and army for Peace: No to communism, yes to democracy! Every cor-

ner of the central plaza was guarded and I noted another soldier man-
ning a large gun in the bell tower of the church. In Nebaj, these things
had become commonplace, but I could not imagine a more incongru-
ous setting for this kind of intense militarization. Nebaj was beautiful, every bit the jewel it had appeared from the highway summit. I
walked along streets that were little more than wide, grassy paths.
Mountains provided a green and blue and purple backdrop to every
horizon. Smoke rose from the houses and huts, and mists rolled in
and out constantly, sometimes shrouding the village entirely so that
I couldn't see fifty feet.

Most beautiful of all were the people, especially the women in
their outfits, their *traje*. By the time I got to Nebaj, I had seen enough
of Guatemalan weaving to begin taking it for granted, to see it without really noticing it any longer, as if it were another part of the scenery. But the *huipiles* of Nebaj demanded attention. There was a
genius to them that defied description; it was more than the intricacy
of the pattern, more than the pretty coloration: the *huipiles* of Nebaj
spoke. They told something, a story both ancient and contemporary, in which zoomorphic and anthropomorphic figures appeared,
danced, disappeared. The dance had meaning; the figures signified
something; the patterns revealed the psychic state of a whole people.
These weavings were as compelling and suggestive as a Jackson Pol-
lock painting. The Nebaj *huipiles* were more than clothing, more
than costume: they were textiles become texts, each *huipil* contributing to a larger, centuries-old text(ile), the collective work of thousands of weaver/scribes. Walking around Nebaj, I saw each *huipil* as
a fragment of a huge, unending hieroglyphic text—one that for me
must remain elusive and mysterious, though I felt certain the Ixil
could read these texts and could see in each individual weaving what
my untrained eye could not.

But everywhere I went in Nebaj, these multivocal, profound, complex, suggestive, and significant weavings yielded before a costume
of another type: the soldiers' camouflage uniforms, the significance
of which was limited to a single, brutal, relentless, and repetitive
message, the same message monotonously intoned by the stamp of
jackboots, by the thud of mortar fire, by the beating of helicopter
blades. Compared to the multilayered significance of the Indian
blouse, a product of a culture often considered unsophisticated and
primitive, the military *uni*form appeared inarticulate, its meaning
univocal and unambiguous—signifying nothing more than a savage
bellow. Maybe I make too much of mere clothing, but out on the
streets of Nebaj, the obvious contrast in the juxtaposition of the two

outfits demanded some explanation: I wondered how anyone could think that the soldiers came from a sophisticated, complex culture, or that the Indian culture was impoverished and "primitive."

In Guatemala, this constant juxtaposition of beauty and cruelty was startling, and nowhere more so than in Nebaj. In many respects, however, it was difficult to understand why it should happen here. What could be so important about a tiny town at the end of a dirt track? The government focused so much attention on the Ixil triangle because one of Guatemala's main guerrilla groups, the Ejército Guerrillero de los Pobres—the Guerrilla Army of the Poor—had chosen to base its operations in the Ixil region. Guerrilla groups had operated in Guatemala since 1960. The three main groups—FAR (Rebel Armed Forces), EGP, and ORPA—were united for diplomatic purposes (but not militarily) as the URNG. The EGP began operations in the early 1970s. They decided to focus on the Ixil region because it was remote enough to frustrate the army's attempts at retaliation and because they felt that the impoverished indigenous population would make good revolutionary material. The guerrillas, it should be emphasized, were outsiders in the Ixil region, and were mostly ladinos or whites who promoted a European ideology, Marxism. Therefore, the civil war being waged in the Ixil region was a battle over ideologies that were foreign and pretty much irrelevant to the Ixils' social reality. Both the Guatemalan army (as well as its supporters) and the guerrillas (along with their outside supporters) assumed that the Ixils did not know what was best for themselves, and both sides wanted to impose their vision on the Ixils without deigning to discover the relevance of these visions. The Ixils remained on the sidelines, or more accurately, smack in the middle, in no man's land. In the late 1970s, the Guatemalan government, under military control, went after any kind of community organization, especially co-ops (many of which were started by USAID, not the EGP). Co-op activists were branded as communists, hunted down, and murdered. As a result, many Ixils joined the guerrillas, hoping to find some protection, and some joined to fight for a more equitable society. The army responded with redoubled brutality and turned the Ixil Triangle into the focal point of its counterinsurgency projects. These projects involved a calculated attempt to restructure Ixil society under the control of the army. The civil patrols, an amnesty program, and the construction of "model villages" were all part of the army's effort.

Against the advice of friends in the capital and against the recommendations of all the guidebooks, I decided to drive the twenty-kilometer road from Nebaj to Chajul, an Ixil village where the religious statuary in the church was supposedly dressed in military uniforms. The first thing I noticed upon leaving Nebaj was the condition of the road: far better and wider than the roads that had brought me to Nebaj. The army had widened and improved the road for its own purposes, of course, and it was possible that USAID or the US Army Corps of Engineers had assisted; both frequently cited road building as one of their principal contributions to the development of Guatemala's infrastructure.

I also noticed immediately that a large swath of land on either side of the road had been burned. Miles and miles of margin were charred and barren of vegetation—vegetation that, according to the army, could conceal subversives intending to ambush army convoys. Nor had the army scrupled about the huts and homes that once lined the road. They, too, had been burned, and the remaining walls had been smashed lest they provide cover for snipers. All cornfields were left blackened and useless: the army made damned sure the guerrillas would find no food on these peasant plots. It was rumored in the capital that the army had used napalm in the highlands. I couldn't say. Certainly other tactics from the war in Vietnam had been imported. It was hard to believe an army would use napalm on its own country, but I saw the scorched earth and I wondered.

On an uphill curve just outside of Nebaj, I met with a stream of liquid spilling down the edge of the road. The smell of gasoline invaded the car. Up ahead, a green bough—the highway signal for "danger ahead" in Guatemala—lay in the road. I slowed down, maneuvered around the bough, and cautiously continued into the curve. Two soldiers waved me to a stop. Fifty yards away, another dozen soldiers stood in a group gawking at a transport truck fitted with a huge gasoline tank—much like the trucks that delivered water to the slums that had no running water in the capital. The truck had apparently caught its two right side tires in a rain-eroded gully at the far right edge of the road. As a consequence, it had somehow veered off the road and overturned. Gasoline spilled from a gash in the tank.

"What an accident," I said to the two soldiers who had stopped me.

One of the soldiers giggled, the other put his arm on the roof of my car and leaned his head into the driver's-side window. "The road is closed," he said.

"I was hoping to go to Chajul."

"Chajul, no. The road is closed."

"I have an important meeting with the priest at Chajul," I lied, hoping to play on religious sympathies.

"We have orders. The road is closed."

It was obvious that I was not going to see the church with the religious statues dressed in military uniforms. The giggling soldier, perhaps in response to my disappointment, suggested that I visit Acul instead. He pointed out a path that led up a hillside. Acul was just over the next hill. I could leave the car here and walk *dos cuadras*—two blocks—to Acul.

I had heard about Acul. It was one of the so-called model camps where refugees had been forced to relocate after their villages had been destroyed. I had assumed that these camps would be difficult to visit, but this soldier, trying to be helpful, seemed to think that Acul was the local point of interest, a must for the tourist. His suggestion was revealing; so many journalists and other curious foreigners had visited Acul that it had become, in essence, a model model camp, the one the army used as its showpiece to deflect international criticism of the model-camp concept. The soldier had simply assumed, not unreasonably I must admit, that I, like all the other foreign visitors to the area, would want to see a model camp. His assumption suggested to me that the army was making a concerted effort to impress journalists and human rights observers with the quality of its model camps.

These model camps had in fact been strongly criticized in the foreign press and by human rights organizations. The military had set up the camps as a way to address the refugee problem in the highlands, a refugee problem that the military itself had created. So many villages had been attacked and destroyed—as many as four hundred, according to estimates—that people, especially widows and children, had nowhere left to live. Many had fled to Mexico, and many tried to survive by hiding in the forests. Those who had been captured or who had given up were brought to the camps. In appearance, these camps suggested both the strategic hamlets the United States had constructed in Vietnam and the concentration camps of World War II. No one doubted that their principal purpose was to provide a measure of control over the indigenous population. The alleged humanitarian aspects of the project—health and education—were secondary at best.

When I set out on the footpath for Acul, the serious soldier called after me: "Be careful."

"Why? Are the guerrillas active lately?"

"Guerrillas, no. Snakes, yes."

The soldier's "two blocks" proved to be more like two miles. At last I came to the top of a hill and down below, in a valley, was Acul, or, rather, the new Acul, which had been constructed in the early 1980s after a series of massacres and army attacks had obliterated the original village. Only a small adobe church was left from the old

Acul. The army had constructed its camp on the site of the destroyed village. The refugees who were to live there, mostly women and children, were required to assist in the construction. The idea was to move the residents of old Acul—along with some refugees from other villages—into a central supervised location, ostensibly for their own protection, although the soldiers watched over the residents more than they watched the hills for subversives. Originally, the new village was surrounded by barbed wire, but quite a few journalists and human rights workers had visited Acul, and the army finally realized it had to display the place in its best light.

Acul, in fact, had become a kind of showcase village, the very paragon of what they were calling an "ideologically new, antisubversive community." By the late 1980s, there were some twenty-four model villages housing seventy thousand people. Wood plank houses had replaced the original lean-tos; the barbed wire came down; street signs went up. Some army intellectual had labored long and hard to give the streets significant names—Calzada de Libertad, Avenida Soldado Guatemalteco, even an avenue named for Taiwan, whose embassy had supported the model village program by selling bicycles to inhabitants of model villages on a low-interest repayment plan (according to the Guatemalan government's daily newspaper, the Taiwanese hoped the bicycles would help the Indians "continue, on their own, on the path toward civilization"). The army and the government were, in fact, quite proud of Acul and the other model villages and were eager to show them off to visitors. Their enthusiasm convinced the US State Department, anyway, which reported that the "model village rural resettlement program" had reconstructed and settled forty-nine villages "on or near their original sites." The report, which does not explain why the original villages had to be resettled at all, notes approvingly that "each town has a potable water supply and electricity, at least one school, a church, postal and telegraph services, private bus service, and a health clinic." The model villages were even lucky enough to have "a military detachment nearby to provide security."

Hypocrisy and doublespeak, to be sure, but standing on the hillside, looking down on Acul, I realized that more than just hypocrisy was working here; something even more invidious figured in as well. Acul's identical houses lined up in so many rows reminded me of the public housing developments in Guatemala City and, by extension, the American projects that they imitated. Acul was built according to the same worldview that had constructed those projects. The model camp represented the imposition of this worldview on those who were now more or less forced to live there. Acul was no longer an Indian village—the Indian village had been destroyed, eradicated. Acul was now a westerner's concept of a village. The Indians who had been moved into Acul were confined and constrained by this concept.

Acul was in fact quite similar to those collections of mobile homes and cinder block houses that are found wherever the interstate freeways cut through Indian reservations back in the States. The US government built those model villages, complete with all the conveniences (or rather, those things that white Americans considered conveniences, such as stove, refrigerator, air conditioner) and moved Indians out of their traditional hogans and away from their pastures, just so that they could be closer to an interstate and hence closer to "civilization," because, well, after all, doesn't everyone want to be closer to McDonald's and Wal-Mart? When the Indians said they didn't find the conveniences convenient, white Americans just couldn't believe it—why would anyone want an adobe beehive oven when you could have an electric range?—and attributed the rejection to the Indians' ignorance about modernity and their stubborn, archaic adherence to traditional ways that were, when it came right down to it, nothing more than superstitions. And that adherence to tradition, the white Americans might as well have added, was pretty much what had doomed the Indians to begin with.

In building Acul, the Guatemalan government followed the principles that underlay US Indian policy: eliminate the traditional and replace it with the basics of western progress. In this way you could break down the aboriginal culture, assimilate the Indians, and contribute to the progress of the nation. Acul and the other model villages were just the latest in a series of attempts to modernize the Indians. And here's why more than just hypocrisy was at work in Acul: the army and the ladino elite pretty much believed that the "model village rural resettlement program" was a *humanitarian* effort, a laudable attempt to help the Indians move forward, to modernize, to become more like the rest of us. Down in Acul they didn't show you the health clinic, the literacy program (where the Indians were taught to recognize the evils of communism), and electrical generators just to dupe you. No, they showed you all this because they were *proud* of it, and they were sure that you, a white person, would agree with the necessity of bringing the Indian into the twentieth century—even if she kicked and screamed a little bit when you dragged her in. Guatemala could never progress, they told you, as long as the Indians were dumb and dirty. By westernizing the Indians, the army was helping them and helping Guatemala, and what was so bad about that? Didn't a superior culture have a right, even a duty, to lead an inferior culture toward progress? The Guatemalan government and the army couldn't understand criticism of the model villages because they saw the programs as an attempt, a positive attempt, to improve the quality of life for the Indians. To the army, the western way had proven superior, so naturally everyone should want to westernize—and if they didn't want to, well then they just didn't know what was best for themselves; by forcing them to accept it—when necessary—you were really doing them a favor.

One of the central conflicts in the human rights crusade thus concerned worldview. Many human rights campaigners assumed that the "evil" Guatemalan army knew it was evil and acted evilly by choice. But there was more to it than that. Certainly some in the Guatemalan army were evil, but the majority I honestly believe were rational, sober-minded people. And this fact, I realized as I gazed down upon Acul that day, made what was going on in the highlands even more frightening. I had learned from being in Guatemala that many in the army thought they were doing the right thing—right by God, by country, even by reason; they believed that, far from being wrong-minded, their efforts had the Indians' best interests at heart, and that the future of Guatemala would be the better for what they were doing now. Is this so strange? Most white Americans assume the Navajos are better off living in air-conditioned mobile homes than in "filthy" hogans, and we find it incredible that our generosity in "giving away" these mobile homes to the Navajos is challenged. Most of us accept western values and western ways as universals. We are simply unwilling to believe that other worldviews may have validity, hence we consider the imposition of our values and our ways to be an acceptable, even a necessary, thing. Just as the British in India felt that they had an obligation to "do the right thing" and put an end to the "abominable" practice of suttee, the Guatemalan army felt that it, newly appointed bearer of the white man's burden, was obligated to impose western values and western ways.

Understanding the worldview of the Guatemalan Indians is not easy for westerners. We assume that the Indians themselves cannot really explain this worldview, not rationally, in our terms, anyway. We assume that they are bound by tradition and enslaved to superstition. Their "sullen" faces appear "inscrutable" to us (again, I am using terms common in our travel literature), and even those of us who are predisposed to think kindly of the Indians often have difficulty regarding them as fully conscious human beings. For example, Severo Martínez Peláez, a respected Guatemalan historian educated in the best western tradition, has written that "the Indians do not possess a definition of themselves" and that they "do not know their history." This patronizing attitude is common, not just among the Guatemalan army and Guatemalan elites, but also among the many foreigners in Guatemala who claim to be aiding the indigenous peoples, whether those foreigners are communist guerrillas, Protestant missionaries, or social workers. Time and again I've heard Peace Corps volunteers—generally good-hearted liberals—complain that the Indians are reluctant to accept whatever technological innovation the volunteer is attempting to implement in a particular village.

Several texts challenge this facile, patronizing attitude toward Indians. One of the most important for westerners seeking to understand the Indian worldview is the testimony of Rigoberta Menchú, the Quiché woman who won the Nobel Peace Prize in 1992. Apart from telling us about Quiché customs and values, Menchú leads us to three important revelations concerning her culture. First, the Quichés understand their historical and current plight. Too often, we assume that primitive people exist in some kind of mental fog, instinctive as animals and lacking the same fully developed historical consciousness that we have. We think they are not capable of analyzing their circumstances or of recognizing what has happened to them over a long period of time. In other words, we believe that, since they do not know where they have come from, they will not see where they are being taken, and will thus go gently into the night of extinction. But in Menchú's testimony we learn that the Quichés keep certain ceremonies intended to educate children about the history of their people and, in particular, to "remind them that our ancestors were dishonored by the white man, by colonization." The history that the elders impart to the younger Quichés is different from "the way that it's written down in books," where the Quiché story is either told from the white man's perspective or ignored altogether. Thus, Rigoberta Menchú points out that not only do the Quichés know their history, but that they also know the biased version of it in the history texts sanctioned by the dominant western culture. The Quichés have chosen to reject that version and, through ceremony, pass on a proper understanding of their history to their children.

Second, the Quichés reject the western world. In particular, they reject what they see as a crass commercialism in the West, a commercialism that encroaches on their world and threatens their cultural survival. From early in life, the Quichés learn (from their elders) that the things of the whites and the ladinos—whether objects or ideas—are not to be trusted. This rejection of things western is not, however, merely a conservative primitivism that fears what it does not understand. The Quichés understand what they are rejecting, and they have good reasons for rejecting our materialism. These reasons are clearly set forth in certain rituals, where the children are taught to keep their culture pure and unadulterated. The Quichés are unschooled in our sense of the term, but Rigoberta Menchú makes it clear that education is of central importance in the upbringing of their children. For the Quichés, however, this education is imparted through ritual rather than worksheets.

For example, Menchú describes a prenuptial ritual whose specific purpose is to teach children about western materialism. All the people come together for the ceremony. The elders place objects from western culture before the gathered community and "explain the meaning of each of those things." One of the products singled out for disparagement is Coca-Cola: "Our grandparents say of Coca-Cola: 'Never let your children drink this dreadful stuff because it is something that threatens our culture.'" The upshot of the lesson is that the Indians "must not mix [their] customs with those of the whites."

The Quichés also reject the use of machinery. Machines, they say, come between people and nature, and they also provide ladinos and whites the means to subjugate and control Indians. Menchú summarizes the teaching of the elders in this ceremony:

> There's a discussion about all the things that happen in the country. They talk about cars, about the *ladinos'* bathrooms, and about the rich. They do it to shake themselves free of it. They say that the bathrooms of the rich shine like new dresses whereas we, the poor, have nothing but a hole to go to. And our cooking pots are different from theirs too. But they also insist that we don't desire what the rich have. We have hands to make our pottery with and we don't want to lose the skill. They say: "These things may be modern but we mustn't buy the rubbish they have, even if we have the money. We must keep our ways of making our own." Our village does not have a grinder for our maize. This is not because we could not get one. Many landowners would gladly install one to grind the maize for the whole village. But our people say no. The ladinos bring their machines in little by little and very soon they own everything.

> *I, RIGOBERTA MENCHÚ*

The third revelation in Menchú's testimony is that the Quichés are not passive victims. They have survived five hundred years of oppression that has at times reached near genocidal intensity. Yet the Quichés have thrived under circumstances that have led to extermination elsewhere in the Americas. Even today, the indigenous peoples make up over 60 percent of Guatemala's population. Menchú provides some insight into this remarkable survival, a survival made possible by their ingrained resistance to the forces that threaten their culture. The Quichés do not reject machines and carbonated drinks because they are a backward and retrograde people. They reject them because they recognize that the infiltration of such things leads to the corruption and inevitable destruction of Quiché customs—customs that have served for thousands of years. In her testimony, Menchú emphasizes that Indian resistance involves vowing "to keep our secrets safe generation after generation, to prevent the ladinos learning anything of our ancestors' ways." The Quichés, as well as the other Maya peoples, have resisted all intrusions and have kept the secrets of their culture hidden. "Not even anthropologists or intellectuals," Rigoberta Menchú says in concluding her testimony, "no matter how many books they have, can find out all our secrets." This is an interesting conclusion, because it subverts the very purpose of the text we have just read (her testimony), which is an anthropologist's interview about Quiché customs (*I, Rigoberta Menchú* is a transcript of interviews that anthropologist Elisabeth Burgos-Debray conducted). It also completes her rejection of western culture; in her final statement, she resists western rationalism and the intellectual analysis that our approach to the Other is based on. Thus, virtually all of western culture, from its products to its epistemologies, is rejected as dangerous and destructive for the Quichés.

The Biotopo del Quetzal

FROM THE IXIL TRIANGLE, I took a nearly deserted gravel road across the very center of the country toward Verapaz, the mountainous region where Bartolomé de las Casas, the famous critic of the Conquest, did his missionary work. The road followed the Chixoy River through barren canyons and dry valleys.

After reading Rigoberta Menchú's testimony, I noticed signs of exploitation everywhere in the highlands. The effects of this exploitation were evident not only in the indigenous cultures, but also in the environment. Driving through the highlands, it was hard not to conclude that western attitudes had destroyed one of the world's most beautiful landscapes. Guatemala, a country of stunning beauty and variety, had been despoiled to the point that its environmental conditions had become a matter of international concern.

The most obvious problem outside of the contaminated capital was deforestation. Everywhere in the country, and most particularly in the highlands, I saw huge tracts of cleared land where forest once stood. Entire hillsides, once covered with cloud forest, were now divided into small plantations of corn. Erosion had completely devastated some hillsides, leaving them brown and scarred. As much as 35 percent of the land was already seriously eroded, and another 30 percent was at risk. In places where repeated slashing and burning had rendered the land all but useless, the forests were reduced to grazing pasture. Guatemala, a name that means "land of the big trees," had lost two thirds of its tropical rain forests, and there was no immediate hope of reversing the trend.

At least environmental issues were receiving more attention. In the capital, for example, billboards and television ads promoted a tree planting campaign, and the cement industry claimed to be deeply involved in the reforestation of the interior. Educated people were becoming more aware of the extent of the problem, and a few members of Congress had voiced concern over the environmental impact of some government projects. Still, hope for halting the devastation of Guatemala's forests was limited because no one was willing to address the major structural changes—economic and societal—that were needed before long-term solutions could be implemented.

Guatemala's environmental crisis was extremely complex. Inequitable land distribution had forced subsistence farmers into attempting to cultivate marginal lands high on mountainsides or deep in jungles. Despite their fecundity, tropical rain forests grow in rather poor soil, a laterite soil, which is inadequate for farming. Because its nutrients are in the trees and not in the ground, a deforested jungle is a wasteland unable to sustain crops for very long. This is a basic and well-known fact: clearing rain forests for farmland is a doomed and wasted effort. Yet the Guatemalan government (supported by USAID) sent landless campesinos into the Ixcan and Petén regions and encouraged them to clear the forest. In forty years, the population of the Petén, Guatemala's jungle region, grew from fifteen thousand to more than three hundred thousand. The inevitable happened: after two or three years the soil gave out, yields diminished, and the campesino had no choice but to move on, clear more jungle, and still more after that. The cleared land was good for nothing but pasture, and the campesinos ended up selling their land to cattle barons, who in turn made good money exporting beef to the United States (much of it going into pet food). Thus, the land colonization program failed in every way imaginable: it ruined the rain forest and didn't solve the land tenure problems; indeed, it only made things worse because the large landowners ended up with even more land.

Many more factors contributed to the environmental crisis. The military had done its share through a scorched earth campaign in the counterinsurgency zones. The army routinely set fire to forests where subversives were supposed to be hiding; in fact, a huge fire in the Petén that consumed several thousand square kilometers of rain forest in 1987 was apparently the result of army carelessness in a counter-insurgency campaign. Also, the seven lumber companies operating in Guatemala (four of them foreign-owned) routinely violated laws regulating the harvesting of mahogany and cypress. The export of wood products was increasing dramatically every year (by 142 percent from 1986 to 1987, for example). Guatemala had become the second largest supplier of windowsills, doors, and wood planking to the United States, and the Guatemalan government, desperate for foreign exchange to help repay a massive foreign debt that already consumed more than 40 percent of Guatemala's export earnings, chose to look the other way when the lumber companies flouted environmental laws, such as they were. And it was the need to increase Guatemala's export earnings that led USAID to promote nontraditional crops such as snow peas and broccoli—crops that required tremendous amounts of pesticides and further stressed the land by actually decreasing ecological diversity. Guatemala's environmental picture was a convoluted mess in more ways than one.

At the boundary between El Quiché and Verapaz, the road descended into an immense canyon and recrossed the Chixoy River. A little way upriver I found a good example of the perplexities of Guatemala's ecological morass: the Chixoy Dam and hydroelectric plant, one of the many environmental disasters financed by the World Bank. Because electricity was too expensive, too scarce, and too unevenly distributed in Guatemala, a huge portion of the population burned wood for its energy—with obvious consequences for the forests. To alleviate this problem, Guatemala borrowed money for the construction of Chixoy Dam, the largest hydroelectric plant in Central America. However, extensive and unchecked deforestation in the region of the dam reduced and continued to reduce the effective life of the power plant because accelerated erosion brought sedimentation to the reservoir and clogged it (this deforestation resulted from harvesting for a papermaking plant and from firewood grazing). The sedimentation of the reservoir inevitably meant that prices for electricity remained high, thus increasing campesino dependence on wood, thus furthering the deforestation, thus speeding up the erosion and the sedimentation . . . and so on. On top of all this, since Chixoy now accounted for 50 percent of Guatemala's foreign debt, there was an even greater need to increase export earnings . . . and so more timber was cut and more fields were planted in nontraditional crops at the further expense of the environment.

On the hopeful side, the concept of conservation had gained some currency in Guatemala. Several *biotopos*—nature preserves—had been established around the country in an effort to preserve the natural habitat of some endangered species, such as the manatee, the ocellated turkey, and the quetzal.

The Biotopo del Quetzal is located high in the Chuacus Mountains in the department of Baja Verapaz, close to the coffee town of Cobán. Either approach to the Biotopo, eastern or western, involves passing through an extensive dry region of scrub vegetation and cactus. Then, as the road climbs higher and higher, the landscape changes suddenly from desert to cloud forest, from sere brown to the intensest, lushest green imaginable. A heavy mist contributes to the drama of the change, a mist that swirls and boils and pours thickly through branches, vines, and ferns—the matted verdant foliage of the cloud forest. Everything dampens and chills in the heavy mist. The local people call it the *chipi-chipi*, a nearly constant light drizzle that keeps the forest fecund and dank. Now and again the light drizzle turns heavy, a momentary cascading of waters that drenches the land. It seemed to me impossible to keep clothing, especially footwear, dry.

We needed the headlamps to see, and even then not much was visible other than the wall of mist. We were now in the region of the Kekchí people. Ghostly forms loomed into the frail light of the beams: shepherds with their flocks, the sheep barely distinguishable from the fog, and scores of women carrying firewood in bundles on their backs. Once, as if in a dream where stark but inexplicable images flash in the mind, the white curtain of mist parted to reveal a roadside procession, fifty people or more, heads covered and bowed, following two men who bore a tiny coffin.

The entrance to the Biotopo was a short, steep driveway marked by a simple rustic sign. We arrived late on a gloomy afternoon when the rain and mist were heavier than usual. The Biotopo was already closed, a log gate barring the entrance. But a middle-aged man appeared out of the mist—campesino hat, machete, faded Stanford sweatshirt—and, learning that we had hoped to camp, opened the gate for us. No doubt the sight of three children in the car helped decide the guard in our favor. Guatemalans adore children; again and again during our stay there, extra consideration was extended to us because of the kids.

We parked just inside the gate and the guard helped us carry our gear up the path to the visitor's center, got us registered, and then walked us over to the campsites. We were the only campers that night, and I think he was amused that a family of gringos had appeared out of the mist to share the preserve with him. Grandfather-aged, he was rather pleased to have children about; he showed them pictures of the *quetzalitos*, and pointed out the long, pretty tail feathers. In the morning, he said, we could see a couple of the birds down by the highway. They were hard to find, but he would point them out to us.

The evening was gloomy. The rain never let up—drizzle, drizzle, downpour, drizzle. We were soaked through and through and the tent sagged, but I couldn't have been happier. The air was redolent, the silence therapeutic, and the campsite good: well arranged and cared for, clean, yet still simple. Just what a camper wanted—and not an RV hookup for a thousand miles.

The guard had pointed out the path to the only *comedor* in the area. At dusk, we donned our rain gear, though the penetrating mist rendered it ineffectual, and pushed through a path of wet ferns toward the highway. A few hundred meters up the road we came to the *comedor*, a small adobe *rancho* roofed with tin sheets. As was common in the Verapaces (the two adjoining departments of Alta Verapaz and Baja Verapaz, so named by Fray Bartolomé de las Casas, because he thought "true peace" would Christianize the Indians more effectively than violence), a long porch fronted the *rancho*. It was dark. Some men sat under the porch on piles of firewood. They smoked and talked in low voices, pausing to wish a hushed "Buenas noches" as we passed inside.

A half dozen tables were arranged around a cluttered, narrow room. The only light was provided by lit wicks stuck in tins filled with oil. We occupied a table in the back, next to where two girls sorted through a pile of beans. They whispered in Kekchí, a poetic-sounding language, somewhat oriental in its combination of gutturals and sibilants. The rain, tapping on the tin roof and dripping through the pine trees, contributed similar sounds, as though it were part of the human conversation.

We ordered the only food available: beans, eggs, and tortillas, standard fare for centuries in the highlands. Most travelers to Central America, at least those who have written about their journeys, have disliked this food; disparagement of the "cuisine" is a common motif in travel books on Central America. In 1875, for example, British writer J. W. Boddam Whetham wrote that Guatemalan tortillas (or "maize-flour fritters," as he called them) were "the most detestable things I had ever tasted" (*Across Central America*). Well, it wasn't five-star food, of course, but on that night of rain it tasted just fine, especially with a few bottles of beer to wash it down. And to me, anyway, the tortillas were exceptional. From the kitchen came the pit-pat of the women working the dough back and forth in their palms, flattening it into a patty. The author of a travel book on Guatemala, observing this time-consuming, manual procedure in a *comedor*, decided that the cooks were "too poor to own a hand-stone and quern, let alone the comparatively high-tech manual tortilla press so common in Mexico" (Maslow, *Bird of Life*). This conclusion was unwarranted and revealed a typical gringo bias. Guatemalans of all income levels disdain tortillas made by contraptions; even in the capital's finest restaurants, tortillas are patted out by hand, usually in a location visible to the patrons—right in the dining room, or in a chickee just off to the side—so that they may see for themselves that the restaurant is using only the freshest, finest tortillas. Any restaurant using a tortilla press or any other kind of "advanced" technology would soon lose business.

The travel writer had made a casual and simple mistake—the kind that fill travel books, especially those relying on superficial journeys of a month or two. But the simple mistake also suggested something about our Anglo values. So often we assume that technology, or anything that simplifies and makes production more efficient, is an obvious good: if you could afford a tortilla press you would buy one because it would make your life easier. Too often we choose on the basis of ease, not on what makes better food. No wonder mass-produced bread in the States is so awful.

While we were eating, some gringo backpackers arrived, laughing and loudly proclaiming "Buenas noches" as they entered. The Kekchí girls behind us whispered something and giggled. The three gringos were large, and their heavy frames filled the tiny chairs. Their bearded faces were only partly visible in the limited glow of the candles. They talked at length about a place called Poptún, a popular way station for bohemian travelers on the road to Tikal. Their accents suggested that one of the speakers was Australian, one northern European, possibly Swedish, and one an American. The Australian and the Swede were describing Poptún, and the enthusiastic young American asked questions about getting to this bohemian Shangri-La.

The loud English, the soft Kekchí, and the now frenetic Morse code of the rain conducted their separate conversations in the dark dining room. I drank a beer and then another and chewed slowly through the tortillas. This, I decided, was what travel in Central America was all about, a scene just like this. This was the moment I had been waiting for, and I was happy.

It rained and rained that whole damned night, and at dawn it was still drizzling. I emerged from the damp tent in the first moments of dawn and saw the guard by the visitor's center. He waved me over. Somehow he'd gotten a fire going in this dampness—a skill one had better develop in the land of the *chipi-chipi*—and had boiled some coffee.

While we drank the overly sweet coffee, the guard explained how to go about spotting a quetzal. It wasn't easy. Members of the trogon family, quetzals were shy and rare. Over the centuries the males had been prized and hunted for their incredibly long and beautiful tail feathers. More damaging than human predation, however, was the destruction of their habitat, the cloud forest of the Central American mountains. The destruction of these forests had helped bring the quetzal to the brink of extinction. And since the birds could not survive in captivity, there was no hope of breeding them. The Biotopo was an attempt to preserve a small part of the cloud forest (a mere 2,850 acres) in the hopes that the quetzal could survive a little longer, but most environmentalists were pessimistic. Many predicted that the quetzal would not survive past the first decade of the twenty-first century.

The guard pointed out the trees that the quetzals favored, in particular a broad-leafed tree called the *aguacatillo*, which produced the quetzal's preferred food, a small avocadolike fruit. Of late, a pair of quetzals had been feeding off the *aguacatillos* down by the highway. But since it was not the mating season, we would not see the bird's most distinguishing characteristic, the long tail feathers of the male. Therefore, the guard said, we should look for the bright red patch on the breast. But we would have to look closely; quetzals were small and they could sit for a long time without moving. If, however, one took flight we could identify it by its unique way of flying, which he demonstrated with his hand: an up and down bobbing flight, like a boat going over waves. Listen carefully for the distinct call of the quetzal, the guard said. He made two high-pitched, hollow whoops; that call would direct us to the tree in which the bird was perched.

It was still early when we all trooped down to the highway and took up a position near an *aguacatillo* tree. Fog completely concealed the mountains and rolled through the trees, now and then exposing clumps of green, like broccoli boiling in milk. A few minutes later, the Swede and the Australian we had seen the night before joined us, and for the next hour we all stood in the road craning our necks. Once a man came out of a *rancho* and shouted, "¡Un quetzal!" and when we all looked his way he waved a one-quetzal bank note in the air. Then he disappeared into the *rancho*, guffawing either at the cleverness of his joke, or at the gullibility of the gringos. It was so funny that he repeated the joke four or five times as he went about his daily chores.

While we awaited the quetzal's appearance, I thought about another bird, a little parrot that I had bought in the capital. One day, while driving in Zona 10, I saw a man standing in the middle of the road, as vendors were wont to do in Guatemala. He had a stick on which perched two little parrots. I bought the birds for my children. After a few days, however, one acted lethargic and wouldn't eat. By evening something was evidently wrong, so I bundled the bird in a tortilla basket and walked a few blocks over to a veterinarian's office. It was after hours, but I explained the emergency and the maid went off to inform the doctor. I was admitted into a bare concrete office. The doctor took up the little bird.

"But he's just a baby," the doctor said. There was so much sorrow in his voice, my stomach tightened. While the doctor gently fingered the bird, then injected it with antibiotics, he lectured me: "How could you buy a little bird like this? It's too little—just a baby. He belongs in the nest still." I explained the circumstances of the purchase, and the doctor sighed. "The poor people in the *campo*, they rob the nests. They take the babies, but they don't know how to care for them, they don't know the first thing about it. How could you buy a *chiquitito*?" He was obviously disappointed with me, and heartbroken about the bird. I felt terrible.

He shrugged. "Well, what more can I do? I have done all I can do. If he is a strong one, he pulls through. But I have doubt. Look—he's no strong one, *pobrecito*. Now take him home and give him water. And please do not buy anymore *pajaritos*. At least you brought him here. He would have died out on the street. The *indito* is happy, though. He has his money. He doesn't care now. He will go steal more babies from the nest. For this reason, you should not buy."

The incident was a small example of the big environmental issues that confronted Guatemala. The basic issue would not go away: the poverty of vast numbers of human beings versus an environment that could not tolerate the kind of exploitation Guatemala's social pressures exerted upon it. Nests would be robbed as long as some pittance could be gotten out of doing so. Forests would be burned. The Biotopo was but a small, ineffectual attempt to preserve the cloud forest, the conservational equivalent of the shot the veterinarian gave my little bird. The damage was already too extensive to reverse. Was there any hope for a bird as delicate as the quetzal?

Many ecologists say no. If this prediction comes true, I am glad I got a chance to see them. The pair passed right over our heads while our attention was momentarily diverted by two squabbling turkeys in the *rancho* across the road. We caught only a fleeting glimpse as they passed, but the strange bobbing flight left no doubt. The birds settled in a tree about thirty-five yards from the road. The Swede had binoculars, and we all got a look, just clear enough to see the red patch on the breast.

The quetzal is surely an apt national symbol for Guatemala: a bird that will not tolerate captivity, that will die if deprived of its freedom—the poetasters of patriotism have worked over that symbolism ad nauseam. But more and more Guatemalans understand that the quetzal is symbolic in other ways as well, for the bird is nearly extinct, a victim of people's encroachment upon and destruction of the environment. The death of the last quetzal will be a harbinger for the death of Guatemala's entire ecosystem.

An hour or so behind everyone else, the California college student, sleepy-eyed and wild-haired, came out to the highway. For several minutes, we entertained ourselves trying to point out the stationary quetzal, but the student just couldn't detect it in the thicket of green.

The quetzals fed at dawn and at dusk, and in between they retired into the cloud forest, where humans couldn't go unless they chopped it down. Two trails, however, had been cut into the Biotopo, and for the rest of the day we hiked along these trails and read from a trail guide about the amazing flora—trees, vines, epiphytes, ferns, flowers, mosses, lichens, mushrooms, all in various stages of growth and decay. It was a green, watery world. The rain poured down, dripped through the trees, and soaked us to the skin. We hiked to a waterfall and crossed rushing streams. We sat on a bench and listened to the ruckus of some unseen monkeys high in the canopy. We couldn't see them, but they saw us—sticks and broken branches, thrown down as warnings, fell all around us.

Somehow, the California college student ended up making the hike with us, and he managed to ruin the beauty of the cloud forest with his nonstop chatter, a long-winded monologue about his life story, which in truth was as bland and uninteresting as a mall. Even the part about his conversion to Hinduism was somehow insipid and unoriginal: seeing the light during a cathartic out-of-body experience, and so on. That was really the start of it—just after he'd given up trying to discern the quetzal, he'd blurted right out that he was a vegetarian and a follower of a certain Hindu holy man. We made the mistake of feigning interest, and he launched right into the story of his spiritual awakening, following us up the trail. Despite his renewed spirituality, the college student couldn't recognize that his tedious tale paled in comparison to the beauty around us. He barely noted the phosphorescent ferns, the luminous mosses, the shimmering epiphytes, the sparkling spider webs. Only once did he pause to comment on nature—a speculation on the psilocybin possibilities of the mushrooms. "Go ahead, try one," I muttered to myself.

At the end of the trail, back near the campground, the streams that ran down the mountain fed several pools. We took off our shoes, rolled up our pants, and waded into the cool water. The college student then stripped in front of us and dove in. When he emerged he went on with his story. The central revelation of his sophomore year in college, he said, was that "meat is murder," and he began casting around for some philosophy that would accommodate this insight. A chance encounter in an airport, where he was given a copy of the writings of a Hindu holy man, changed his life and led him to convert. To this day he's the only person I've ever met who actually paid attention to those airport mountebanks.

The Road to El Estor

NEAR THE BIOTOPO, just outside a town called Tactic, was the turnoff for one of the world's great roads, the road to El Estor. Its 120 kilometers were in poor condition, but this is a prerequisite for any great road: it cannot be built for speed. Speed contributes to urgency and anxiety, the need to actually arrive somewhere; and I think we all know by now that the best journeys, the true journeys, have no destination to speak of. El Estor, Guatemala, was certainly no destination to speak of, and that fact alone made the journey there too tantalizing to pass up. Paused at this road's junction with the paved highway that took one from Cobán back to Guatemala City, I sized up the possible directions. One road was smooth and easy and led eventually to a large modern city with all the conveniences that made life simple. The other was rough and rutted and led to the very epitome of a backwater boondocks. The choice was easy. I turned toward the rutted unknown, stopped at a junction hamlet called San Julián for gasoline, fruit, bread, and drinks, and prepared for a drive on a true road to nowhere.

Actually, I did have a reason for taking this road: there were two places along its route that I wanted to visit, if for no other reason than to say that I had been there. The first was Panzós, where an infamous massacre had occurred a dozen years previously. The second was El Estor, the end of the road, where an American nickel mining operation had started and failed in the 1970s.

In its first twenty-five kilometers, the road followed a stream and a broad canyon whose steep slopes were planted in coffee. Two small towns in this canyon, Tamahú and Tucurú, were home to the Pokomchí Indians, yet another of Guatemala's many distinct tribes. A profusion of banana and orange trees around the towns hinted at the fertility of the region. After Tucurú, the road dropped dramatically, three thousand feet in thirty miles. The canyon opened up into a broad, steamy lowland valley, and the stream widened into a river, the Polochic.

By the time the road leveled out at Panzós, near sea level, an intense, humid heat pervaded the car. The land turned swampy, the swamps watched over by solitary *corozo* palms and an occasional wattled hut. This was the only place in Guatemala where I saw rice paddies. Near Panzós, the jungle took over. Huge trees, thick with vines and long lianas signaled my arrival in Conrad country.

Panzós was a boondocks town, notorious for malaria and massacres. Once boats had docked there to take on coffee bound for the big ships at Puerto Barrios. But the old narrow-gauge railroad that used to connect Panzós to Cobán had long since vanished in the jungle, and now the riverside wharves had nearly collapsed with desuetude. The town smelled of mildew and mold. Mosquito hordes swarmed in the evening air, unleashing a fierce malarial attack. Fireflies flared in the trees. Frogs argued in the river. Rain seemed ever imminent. All that was needed to make this place truly worthy of Conrad was some history of slaughter. The Guatemalan army obliged.

Apparently there was no place in this country so small, so removed, or so unimportant that the army would not stage a massacre. In 1978, the soldiers swarmed into Panzós and killed more than one hundred peasants in one of the earliest, bloodiest, and most senseless of Guatemala's many massacres. Panzós was the harbinger of the policies of the Lucas García regime. The murdered peasants were part of a group of some seven hundred Kekchí Indians who had marched to Panzós to protest land seizures. In response, the army deployed troops there. Soldiers dug mass graves outside of town before the protesters ever arrived. General Lucas García apparently wanted to send a message that would more effectively terrorize the population than the mere kidnapping, torture, and assassination of a few leaders. The general also had a personal interest in Panzós: he owned seventy-eight thousand acres in the area, most of it cattle pasture, and beef was a huge earner of export dollars.

In one sense, the massacre at Panzós backfired. Along with the Spanish embassy massacre a year and a half later, it galvanized opposition to the government and the military and brought more of the indigenous population into open resistance. Furthermore, the Panzós massacre became an international news story and brought upon Guatemala the scrutiny that it had hitherto avoided. After Panzós, it was clear that the army was at war with the indigenous population. Massacre became a standard policy for the next seven years.

Panzós was not too small for the attention of the Guatemalan army and it was not too small for the Mormon Church. I was outside a refreshment kiosk, drinking a Coca-Cola, of all things, when two affable louts came strolling up: blonde, tall and broad as middle linebackers, neatly dressed in white shirts with black ties and black pants, they grinned down at me.

"American?" the tallest one asked. The nameplate on his shirt pocket announced that he was Elder J. Young.

I nodded.

"Hey, great. Isn't it great, Steve? A fellow American."

We stared at each other.

Steve (his nameplate read "Elder Thompson") ordered two orange sodas.

"Don't see many Americans around here," Elder Young said. Then he frowned: "You aren't one of those Catholics, are you?"

"What Catholics?"

"Liberation theorists. They go to all the poor places."

"No," I said. "But what about you. This is a pretty small place for missionaries."

Elders Young and Thompson took this as an invitation. They launched into a lengthy explanation of Mormon missions in Central America. Tens of thousands were converting, they said. Dozens of missionaries were spreading the Mormonite gospel in Guatemala. They learned Indian languages and traveled all over the country.

But why Central America?

Because, Elder Young explained, the Central American Indians were once the Lamamites.

"The Lamamites?"

"Right. They're descendants of Lehi's race. Lehi voyaged to the Americas from the Holy Land. It's all in here." He tapped a scarlet-covered Book of Mormon. "The Indians here in Guatemala are descendants of the Lamamites. We're bringing them the word of God that they lost centuries ago. They're happy for that. They thank God for bringing us to them."

My face must have shown my disbelief.

"It's true," Elder Thompson protested. "Let me tell you about a man I know in an Indian village up in the mountains. God came to him in a dream to tell him that the Mormon Church is the true church. He's converted and all his family, and let me tell you these Indians have big families."

"What did God look like? In his dream, I mean."

"Well, here's the fascinating part. It turned out not to be God Himself, but His prophet Spencer W. Kimball of the Council of the Twelve! Kimball spoke to the man in a dream and told him to convert. Now he's a great leader in his village."

"How did he know it was Kimball?"

"Later we showed him pictures of the church leaders. He recognized Kimball from the dream."

I was saved at last when the two linebackers spotted a man crossing the plaza. "Gotta go," Elder Young said. "There's our contact." They called out and jogged over to the man, a hunched-over peasant carrying a huge bundle. He flinched when he saw them bearing down on him.

Beyond Panzós, the road cut through delta and swamp for fifty kilometers until it reached Izabal, the largest lake in Guatemala. The country was as feral and extravagant as any I had ever seen, including Amazonia. The road ended at a place called El Estor, the odd name apparently being a corruption of the English word "store." For some inexplicable reason, a United Fruit Company provisions outpost once guarded this isolated shore of the lake, but all that now remained were some structures of crumbling concrete and rotting planks. A sign near the decayed docks summarized life in El Estor: the average temperature in town, the sign informed anyone who cared, was 39 degrees Celsius, or 102 degrees Fahrenheit. I suspected this was an understatement. Ever since Panzós, I'd been suffering from a nervous tingling feeling, like something creeping all over my skin. There were small red bite marks on my waist and under my arms. I remembered that one hundred years earlier a young woman, Helen Sanborn, had journeyed through this hot fen and reported experiencing eerie sensations:

> I wondered if I were in fairy-land; but then there were no fairies, for the inhabitants of this land dwelt in mud huts and were dark enough to be goblins. I felt like pinching myself to see if I were awake or dreaming, and said to myself, "Who am I?" "Where am I?" "Can this be a part of the same earth on which I dwell?" Every moment now was bringing us to stranger and stranger sights, and I wondered with something of apprehension as to what lay before

us, and how we should fare when we came to penetrate into this land and mingle with this uncivilized people.

A WINTER IN CENTRAL AMERICA AND MEXICO

Somehow, five thousand people, mostly Kekchí Indians—the "uncivilized people" whom Sanborn feared—endured the heat, the humidity, and the insects and made a life for themselves in El Estor. They must have been of a hardier stock than the occasional gringos who had ventured into the region, hoped to profit from the spoils of the earth, and failed. The pluck of the Kekchí was evident in their buildings, whose well-kept appearance contrasted with the ruins left behind by the foreigners. The United Fruit Company store was not the only enterprise that strangers had abandoned on the western shore of Izabal: on the outskirts of town were the sprawling remnants of a nickel mining operation that went under the name of Empresa Exploraciones y Explotaciones Mineras de Izabal (Exmibal). Exmibal's parent company was the Canadian-based, US-controlled International Nickel Company (INCO).

The whole business began in the 1950s, when an Izabal landowner had some soil analyzed, and a high concentration of nickel was revealed. For the next decade, the International Nickel Company negotiated with Guatemala for the rights to mine the nickel. The negotiations went through several stages. Various interest groups in Guatemala were divided over what should be considered acceptable terms for a contract with INCO. Experience with the foreign exploitation of other natural resources in the region had taught Guatemalans to be wary of entering into deals with corporations like INCO, which demanded privileges such as exemptions from taxes and import duties and exemptions from a law requiring that 90 percent of employees must be Guatemalan. INCO also wanted to keep its dollar earnings in foreign banks rather than in Guatemalan banks. There were plenty of Guatemalans, especially powerful ones, who were willing to accede to these neocolonial demands. But this time members of the university and other progressives campaigned for a fairer contract; many of these progressives suffered for it, and some were even assassinated, early victims of the death squads.

In 1971, a contract was signed. But world market conditions had changed, and INCO soon lost enthusiasm for the project. The first load of nickel was not shipped out until 1978, and after only three years of supposedly marginal profits, INCO shut down the Exmibal project and abandoned the Izabal site. What was once expected to be the largest bonanza in Guatemalan history proved to be a bust.

I saw many ruins in Guatemala—Antigua, Iximché, Utatlán, the great Maya ruins of the Petén—but none struck me in quite the same way as the Exmibal ruins. It is one thing to ponder the ruins of some long-gone civilization. It is quite another to visit a ruin of your own. Visiting the Exmibal remains was like seeing the ruined future of western civilization. The identical concrete block houses placed in perfect rows along asphalted streets composed a suburban ghost town; weeds, vines, and ferns had rioted against the manicured lawns that had once hosted picnics, barbecues, and evening games of croquet. The abandoned tennis courts, nets long rotted away, were nothing but mysteriously marked rectangular plots left for some future archaeologist to puzzle over, to measure, to diagram, to speculate on their relationship to certain astronomical coordinates . . . Exmibal revealed how paltry our enterprises have been.

The hills above this ghost town were mostly green with trees and pasture, except in a few places, where they were carved up and gouged like an Aztec victim's chest. These wounds, the results of the nickel company's exploitation, were the last thing I saw of El Estor, for I had to return the way I came. A ferry crossed Lake Izabal from El Estor to Mariscos, but it did not carry cars. There was no other way out of town except by the road that had brought me here. And so I had to return over the ruts through Panzós and Tamahú and Tucurú; through Kekchí country and Pokomchí country; through river delta and jungle and canyon, 130 more kilometers of bouncing and swerving. I didn't mind.

The Oriente

THE HIGHWAY FROM COBÁN to Guatemala's Oriente was relatively smooth and easy. It came down out of the Sierra de las Minas into the dry valley of the Motagua River and ended at the river, where it junctioned with the highway to the Atlantic near the town of El Progreso. Because of the irony implicit in its name, El Progreso, a hot dusty town, had achieved some small notoriety in the travel books of famed writers like Paul Theroux and Aldous Huxley.

When I was there, the town was notorious for a different reason: UFOs. For several weeks, the newspapers ran daily stories about strange lights and other unusual sightings that were supposedly concentrated in the immediate vicinity of a large concrete factory just outside of Progreso. Some members of Congress even undertook a fact-finding junket and drove out to El Progreso in their Mercedes-Benzes. They spent the night on a hillside above the cement factory.

Their account was headline news the next day: yes, they saw the darting lights, and they were at a loss for some rational explanation.

I soon found, at work and at parties, that most people were not at a loss for an explanation. My students had numerous elaborate theories, which they propounded to me at length. Some said aliens had established a base in El Progreso; some said that a kind of harmonic convergence was going on; others posited that the US government was conducting top secret experiments—a new weapon that destroyed merely by passing a beam over the target. The stories ran for about two weeks until a sort of UFO hysteria broke out, and then the stories vanished as mysteriously as the lights around El Progreso. What had it all been about? My colleagues speculated that it had been a diversionary tactic devised by the government to draw attention away from something else, some graft or scandal most likely. The prominent attention given to the congressional junket supported this theory—and the members of Congress had certainly done their best to fan the flames of hysteria. People in Guatemala have a predilection for the supernatural anyway. I had heard discourses on everything from reincarnation to harmonic convergences and the power of pyramids, and so the possibility that Guatemala had been singled out as a site for alien visitations was a story of great moment in the faculty lounge and in the hallways at the university. Perhaps the UFO reports were a government ploy to distract the public, or perhaps the reports were simply intended to increase newspaper sales. Who could say? Whatever, the need for the diversion soon passed; after a couple of weeks there were no more reports of UFOs buzzing about the countryside.

Not far from El Progreso, about 140 kilometers toward the Honduran border, was the site of a more established, more respectable supernatural phenomenon: Esquipulas, home of a shrine dedicated to the miraculous Black Christ. The town's huge basilica was visited by pilgrims from all over Central America, especially during Holy Week and on January 15, the shrine's holiest day. The story of the Black Christ is similar to that of the Virgin of Guadalupe in Mexico. Sometime near the end of the sixteenth century an Indian of that desert region supposedly had a vision of Christ. To honor the miracle of this theophany, local people hired a sculptor to make a statue of Christ. Whether by chance or on purpose, the sculptor chose to carve the statue from dark wood—and the statue immediately became a special object of veneration for the Indians. Their devotion to the Black Christ probably had pre-Columbian origins: blackened representations of deities were apparently common in Maya religions.

For years the statue was kept in a small chapel. From the beginning, reports of its ability to cure illnesses attracted pilgrims, including in the mid-eighteenth century an archbishop who, convinced of the statue's powers, ordered the construction of a large basilica. For the last two hundred years, the Black Christ has been guarded in this basilica, gazed upon by hundreds of pilgrims every day.

I went to Esquipulas after spending a few days in Chiquimula, a hot town fifty kilometers away, where there was a branch campus of the national university. I led a seminar for teachers of English—two days in an airless concrete room with forty people while the outside temperature climbed to 110 degrees. It was April, the hottest month of the year in Guatemala, and Chiquimula is in the country's hottest region. It was impossible to drink enough. Simple acts, like inhaling the hot air, required a concerted effort and caused anguish in the head. At the end of the seminar, I was ready for some cooler place, and nearby Esquipulas, about eighteen hundred feet higher in the mountains, beckoned.

I first saw the basilica from the mountain road above the town—an impressive sight because the huge basilica was truly in the middle of nowhere, all alone on the desert plateau. Humankind seems to prefer building its most monumental works in austere places where nature is unimpressive. Hence ziggurats and pyramids in deserts, skyscrapers on Manhattan Island, basilicas in the scrub plains. Nothing remarkable has ever been constructed near Niagara Falls or Iguaçú or the Grand Canyon. In Guatemala, the basilica of the Black Christ was not on the shore of Lake Atitlán or at the foot of Agua; it stood isolated in a dry mountain valley, where the eye was immediately drawn to it, startled by it. One had to exclaim upon seeing it.

Esquipulas itself was like most shrine towns the world over: one part spiritual and four parts commercial. There is something about holiness that brings out the most meretricious side of humans—well, Christians, anyway. Chartres, Guadalupe, Compostela, Jerusalem, Esquipulas, in all these places entire economies have developed around the pilgrimage. The mercantile crowds out the spiritual. Vendors prey on the crowds, pushing gaudy trinkets as holy relics, pandering to pilgrims and tourists, hawking and cheating in the name of the sanctified site.

Frederick Catherwood, the English artist who accompanied John Lloyd Stephens on his unprecedented journey through Central America in 1840, sketched the mile-long main street in Esquipulas for Stephens' great book. The basilica is a squat and heavy building, but Catherwood gave it a light, almost floating appearance. In his drawing, the basilica seems to hover in the distance like something that has ripped itself from the gravity of the earth and has begun its ascension to heaven. This effect, I later discovered, was quite realistic: late in the day, the shadows fell in such a way that the great platform upon which the basilica rested was obscured, and the light of the setting sun transformed the appearance of the basilica itself, heightened its whiteness until, shimmering, it seemed as elusive and airy as a vision. The late light of the sun broke down the heaviness of the church's thick walls (so sturdy they had withstood centuries of earthquakes) and changed them into, as Stephens remarked, "a work of enchantment." The shadows in Catherwood's drawing indicate that he did indeed draw it late in the day.

The scene that Catherwood captured in 1839 also shows the town's one street lined by thatched stalls—evidence that a certain commercialism has long been a part of the pilgrimage to the Black Christ. On the day I visited, the greatest activity was in fact outside on the sidewalks and in the street, where people were bargaining for straw hats (an important emblem of the pilgrimage), for candles, and for blocks of a pasty, sickly sweet candy that was piled in purple and brown mounds on tables near the steps of the basilica. A few harridans switched the flies away from the candy. Also for sale were the long, colorful ribbons with which wealthier pilgrims decorated their cars—evidence that they had made the pilgrimage. Many vendors offered a variety of placebos promising to effect miraculous cures. Especially popular were packets of a whitish clay, which was supposed to be holy earth and thus a great curative when consumed.

But this crass commercialism did not intrude upon the sanctity of the basilica itself. Inside, the church maintained an aura of holiness: people crawled on their knees down the aisles toward the altar, sobbing, chanting, murmuring prayers; candles and incense burned all around, filling the dim nave with smoke; and the Black Christ agonized over it all. To a visitor from a Protestant background, for whom religion was something reserved, something dour and unadorned, these displays of abject religiosity were shocking, almost frightening. In general, American travelers find Guatemalans too extreme in their religious lives. The Catholics are regarded as morbid, vulgar, and primitive, a little too heathenish to be good Christians. And more recently, the evangelical Protestants are considered too enthusiastic for the tastes of somber northern Protestants. Americans tend to react with a smirk or a frown to the various displays of Guatemalan spirituality, whether it is the plastic doll of the Virgin Mary on a bus dashboard, or the gaudy processions through city streets with a bloodied Christ on a platform riding the shoulders of purple-robed penitents, or the tormented wails of fervent women falling on their faces and tearing at their hair during an evangelical revival. Most

Americans think these displays ridiculous or even disgusting, and travel writers in particular have caviled on the matter—either reproving the Guatemalans for excessive enthusiasm or scoffing at them and finding the whole show just too damned weird. John Lloyd Stephens, a good, rational-minded nineteenth-century Protestant, was taken aback at the open demonstrations of fervor and idolatry he saw in 1839: "The feelings of the women burst forth in tears, sobs, groans, and shrieks of lamentation, so loud and deep, that, coming upon us unexpectedly, our feelings were disturbed, and even with sane men the empire of reason tottered. Such screams of anguish I never heard called out by mortal suffering."

On some occasions in his travels, Stephens deliberately avoided witnessing processions, finding them a bit too indecorous for his sensibilities. Latter-day tourists were not so stern or squeamish, and indeed by the middle of the twentieth century processions had become popular tourist attractions, especially the processions during Holy Week, when the streets were decorated with beautiful carpets of colored sawdust. Stunning examples of ephemeral art, these carpets were the product of weeks of work. The colored sawdust was laid in intricate designs on the streets. Then the block-long carpets were destroyed as the processions passed over them. Tourists had become such a familiar part of the procession tableau that artisan shops in Antigua now included figurines of camera-toting tourists in the clay-model sets of Holy Week processions. But there is a connection, I believe, between Stephens and the latter-day tourists, for most of the tourists do not photograph the processions solely for their beauty, their pageantry, or their splendor. Most photograph the processions for their shock value—to show friends and neighbors back home what a wild and grotesque place they've been to. The cameras click like crazy whenever a particularly gory statue sways past—Mary with a sword stuck in her side, for example, or a cross-carrying Jesus purpled with blood and gaping wounds. I remember one such procession in Quetzaltenango, when a young American tourist next to me groaned "Oh, how gross!" as the bloody Christ approached. She snapped nearly a dozen photos.

Esquipulas, because of its isolation and its intense religiosity, is not frequented by tourists. It is, perhaps, the most unadulterated place in Central America, the one place where you can see Central Americans exactly as they are (the basilica is the most important shrine for all of Central America, not just Guatemala); and for this reason, Esquipulas was, symbolically, the ideal place for the Central American peace talks held there in the late 1980s and early 1990s. The peace talks and the accords resulting from them were the product of Central American initiative, not outside interference (in fact, the Reagan administration refused to participate and rejected the legitimacy of the accords—largely because the Central Americans had accomplished them on their own, without Washington's "help"). Esquipulas was thus the ideal location for the talks, not only because it was a holy site, but also because it was a purely Central American site.

Most of the Oriente, Guatemala's eastern region, where the towns of El Progreso, Chiquimula, and Zacapa are situated, is dry, hot, conservative country. Predominantly ladino, the people of the Oriente are supposed to be hard-working, hot-tempered, and stingy. They favor cowboy apparel and settle disputes with guns and machetes. Guatemala's East is, in fact, similar to the American West. Much of the Oriente is scrubland where only cactus and other xerophytes grow, but the irrigated river valleys, especially along the Motagua River, support tobacco and melon plantations. The highway to the Atlantic, which connects Guatemala City with Puerto Barrios, bypasses the fruit fields and tobacco farms as it parallels the river.

Just before the Caribbean, the land turns green and lush again, and the highway cuts through the vast banana plantations of Del Monte. This banana belt has figured prominently in Guatemala's political history, for the plantations once belonged to the United Fruit Company, the US corporation whose meddling in the politics of the Central American countries—and particularly its unflagging support of corrupt dictators—has given currency to the epithet "Banana Republic." In Guatemala, that meddling led to one of the fruit company's more conspicuous and egregious actions—support for a CIA-engineered overthrow of the constitutionally elected government of Jacobo Arbenz in 1954. The meddling in this case was egregious because it helped put an end to Guatemala's only period of social reform, the ten years between 1944 and 1954, sometimes referred to as the Guatemalan Revolution.

In the first half of the twentieth century, the United Fruit Company dominated Guatemala's economy even though bananas were not nearly so important a cash crop as coffee. Bananas were a lucrative crop, to be sure, but the key to United Fruit's power was its virtual monopoly of Guatemala's transportation infrastructure. United Fruit accomplished something no Guatemalan government had been able to do for twenty years—complete a railway line from Puerto Barrios on the Caribbean coast to Guatemala City. In 1904, the government of Guatemala contracted with a man named Minor Keith—the driving force behind United Fruit—to finish the remaining sixty miles of track. Keith was an experienced railroad builder—he had built Costa Rica's railroad in the 1880s—and he was also experienced at driving a hard bargain. Through his company, International Railways of Central America (IRCA), a subsidiary of United Fruit, he brought in the necessary capital and expertise to get Guatemala's railroad up and running. In return, the Guatemalan government granted generous concessions, including control of all track already laid in the country, control of the port at Puerto Barrios, extensive land alongside the railway, and exemptions from taxes. United Fruit took advantage of its control of the port by setting up the United Fruit Steamship Company, the so-called Great White Fleet, which carried *all* of Guatemala's overseas trade. With a monopoly on all commercial transport in and out of Guatemala and control of Guatemala's electric company, United Fruit made enormous profits and exerted its will on the country's government. Guatemala saw precious little of the profits but the country's politicians did nothing about it. They knew that by currying favor with the company they were smoothing their own paths to power, and enriching themselves to boot. For nearly half a century this system worked well for United Fruit and for the dictators like Jorge Ubico, who maintained power with the help of United Fruit and the US government.

All that changed in 1944. A coalition of students, business professionals, and reform-minded military officers led a series of protests that toppled Ubico. The fairest elections ever held in Guatemala brought a teacher of philosophy, Juan José Arévalo, to the presidency, and Arévalo immediately instituted reforms that promoted popular democracy and economic modernization. The Fruit Company opposed Arévalo's reforms, especially any suggestion of land reform. United Fruit had vast holdings in the banana belt, the majority of which were not under cultivation. When proposed land reform legislation targeted some of United Fruit's fallow land, neither the company nor the US government was going to sit idly by.

Nineteen fifty-two was a decisive year. In Guatemala, the administration of Jacobo Arbenz, Arévalo's elected successor, passed an agrarian reform law; and in the United States the probusiness Eisenhower was elected president. A showdown was inevitable. Arbenz, a military man and a landowner, promoted a just economic system in Guatemala, one that would remove the country from its semicolonial dependency on the United States and would allow the lower classes to advance, through their own initiatives, to the middle class. He decided that this could happen only if land were more evenly distributed and if the country's infrastructure were not monopolized by foreign companies. Guillermo Toriello Garrido, Guatemala's delegate to a meeting of the Organization of American States (OAS) in 1954, explained the position of the Arbenz government. Foreign investment, he said, was not always "a panacea to cure the ills of those countries that have fallen behind. . . . [F]requently one forgets that some investments are the principal cause of that backwardness one encounters in some countries. Investments of the monopolistic type in many cases have asphyxiated development."

United Fruit, already displeased by the labor reforms under Arévalo, was further incensed by Arbenz's proposed land reform—which targeted a total of 372,000 of the company's fallow acres (out of the 550 million acres owned by the company, less than 15 percent of which was under cultivation)—and by his efforts to break the company's monopolies on transportation and electricity.

Fortunately for United Fruit, the Eisenhower administration took control of US foreign policy in 1953, and immediately began to harass the Guatemalan government about the land reform measures and other "communistic" acts. John Foster Dulles, Eisenhower's secretary of state, and his brother Allen Dulles, director of the CIA, coordinated the campaign of harassment. Both had worked as lawyers for United Fruit, and both owned stock in the company. The first stage of the campaign was an attempt to sow discord in the Guatemalan army, apply psychological pressure to the Guatemalan government, and create tension and alarm in the society in general—the paradigm of "destabilization" that the CIA worked to such great effect all over the world during the cold war.

John Peurifoy, the new ambassador to Guatemala, was hardly ambassadorial. Winston Churchill called this belligerent man "a bull who carries his china shop with him." Peurifoy pressured the government by arguing the fruit company's case and threatening to isolate Guatemala and undermine its economy. He also recruited disaffected military leaders. The CIA set up a clandestine radio station that broadcast propaganda against Arbenz. And E. Howard Hunt got his career going by putting together a potential invasion force—or, to use the more sophisticated vocabulary of later years, a cadre of freedom fighters. The campaign was soon organized enough to merit a name: Operation Success.

The US government was primarily interested in protecting the property and interests of United Fruit. Even in the 1950s, however, such blatant subterfuge on behalf of a multinational corporation was recognized as impolitic. Secretary of State Dulles, therefore, tried to argue that Guatemala was a communist country under the influence of Moscow, a claim that has been exposed over the years as just plain silly. Some of Arbenz's political and economic philosophy was influenced by socialism, but then so was Franklin Roosevelt's. And for that matter, the reformation of social welfare structures in England and other European countries in the 1950s was far closer to socialism than anything going on in Guatemala. But Arbenz refused to outlaw the Communist Party; indeed, he was even so bold as to actually seek the advice of Communist leaders on certain issues. Ambassador Peurifoy and Secretary Dulles knew a red duck when they saw one, and soon they were telling anyone who would listen that Guatemala had gone red.

They found a willing audience. Nicaraguan strongman Anastasio Somoza and the other client caudillos of Central America offered support. Somoza told Dulles to give him the guns and he'd clean up Guatemala in no time. Meanwhile, in the United States, Dulles needed to build public support for Operation Success and the overthrow of Arbenz. In the age of McCarthy, the public was easily duped. United Fruit paid for US journalists to visit the banana plantations, where they were given "proof" of the company's benevolence and the Guatemalan government's totalitarian leanings. Eager reporters decried "the first American satellite of Moscow" and speculated on the inevitable tumbling of numerous Latin American dominoes. Guillermo Toriello, speaking before the OAS, called the US actions "the internationalization of McCarthyism." To the American press, such a complaint was all the more proof of Guatemala's Communist connection. The *St. Louis Dispatch*, for example, cried that "a close study of the words spoken by Toriello certainly leads to the conclusion that he spoke there as the voice of Moscow."

In two years, the CIA created a climate of uncertainty within Guatemala and fostered suspicion and hostility toward the country back in the United States. After this, the actual overthrow of Arbenz proved quite easy. In June 1954, a small force of disgruntled exiles, led by a man named Castillo Armas (and supported by a band of mercenaries and CIA operatives) found it all too easy to invade from Honduras. Arbenz panicked and fled the country, and, just like that, the social renovation that occurred under Arévalo and Arbenz was scuttled, Guatemala was saved from communism, and United Fruit was saved from land reform.

For more than half a century, the banana company ruled the region by deciding who could rise and who could fall. Given this history of intrigue, it was surprising to find that United Fruit was no longer a presence in Guatemala. I turned off the main highway and followed a horribly rutted road to Bananera, the former headquarters town of United Fruit. In the early 1970s, only twenty years after dismantling Guatemala's social revolution and democracy, United Fruit sold its

Guatemalan holdings to Del Monte and abandoned the country altogether. Still, I expected some evidence of grandeur, some signs that
these hot lowlands once were the home of kingmakers, intriguers, and
wily operatives. Hundreds of Americans—managers, agronomists,
doctors—used to live here in neat bungalows, with a bridge club for
the wives and a golf course for the men. But in Bananera little remained: a few run-down buildings, the railroad track that once gave
United Fruit a monopoly on transportation, and the now burned-out
golf course—one sad hole in the middle of the town. Even United
Fruit's doggerel name was gone. The Guatemalans now called the
town Morales.

Shelley's words could well describe what was left of the mighty
United Fruit in Guatemala:

> Look on my works, ye mighty and despair!
> Nothing beside remains. Round the decay
> Of that colossal wreck, boundless and bare
> The lone and level sands stretch far away.
>
> "OZYMANDIAS"

Operation Success is but a small, and now largely forgotten, episode
in US history. The principal players are long gone, and they are remembered more for other actions on the grander stage of Europe.
Twenty, thirty, forty years have passed, time has made the events of
those days inconsequential, and we look back on them with curiosity
and mild amusement: Did they really treat these nations as their
toys? It is obvious that the Americans were deluded in those incipi-
ent days of the cold war. They saw red everywhere and charged like
bulls, trampling and goring the small countries unlucky enough to
be caught in the ring. It is even more obvious that fruit company
profits were the real bottom-line motivation for the whole episode.
To Americans, the Arbenz overthrow might seem like a silly blun-
der, a peccadillo in our history for which we are apologetic but not
really tortured with guilt. It's over and done with, and anyway we've
learned a lot since then, matured as a superpower. We know we can't
do things that way anymore.

In Guatemala, however, the long-term effects have been devastating. Operation Success radically altered Guatemalan history, and it
is even possible to argue that the country never really recovered from
it. For thirty years after the CIA intervention, the military ruled Guatemala; even during the brief periods when a civilian won an election
and actually took office, the military made sure that the civilian did

things its way. Most observers doubt there was any real change even after *la democracia* was established in 1985, when Cerezo took over. The military will long remain the fourth branch of government in Guatemala, and easily the strongest branch.

Six years after the overthrow of Arbenz, the first guerrilla groups took up arms. More than thirty years of civil war and 100,000 political killings have followed. While it is too facile to say that the events of 1954 caused all subsequent problems in Guatemala, I believe that if the social program of the Arévalo and Arbenz administrations had been allowed to continue, much of the violence and repression that Guatemala saw in the decades after the coup would have been stemmed. A mild land reform program, such as the one Arbenz promoted, the continuation of social welfare programs begun under Arévalo, and regularly held elections for legislative and executive offices . . . had all these aspects of the Guatemalan "revolution" been allowed to evolve, the civil war and all those deaths might have been averted. Consider Mexico, Guatemala's neighbor. A revolution there led to land reform, social welfare, and democracy. And while Mexican land reform has proven faulty and Mexican democracy has offered voters little real choice, the mere *possibility* of some redressing of social inequities has helped Mexico avoid the kind of social upheaval that Guatemala experienced (except in the border state of Chiapas, where Guatemala-like conditions obtain). But since 1954, in Guatemala the possibility of redress has been all but nonexistent, and violence has filled the void.

When I lived in the country, I came to understand that the "internationalization of McCarthyism" that Toriello warned about in 1954 was still very much a problem in Guatemala. It was as if Guatemala had gotten stuck in the 1950s. Crude cold war rhetoric still had currency. Communist conspiracies were perceived everywhere. Anything mildly liberal was despised, feared, thwarted. The United States had instructed Guatemala's rulers in McCarthy-era ideology but had forgotten to update them on revisions as the ideology became more sophisticated and more tolerant. Even in the late 1980s, Guatemala still did not have diplomatic relations with the Soviet Union, Cuba, or any other Communist country. Just before I arrived, the Bolshoi Ballet canceled a performance in Guatemala because the Russians had received death threats warning them against appearing in the country. Like loud macaws, the army had learned to squawk in imitation of the Dulles brothers—and they were going to squawk, squawk, squawk the same phrases over and over long after their trainers were gone—no matter how tiresome the noise became.

One night at a party I was talking to a Guatemalan who was born in 1952. His father was an activist in Arbenz's party; consequently, the entire family fled to Mexico in 1954—as did Arbenz—when Castillo Armas' "forces" took Guatemala City. The son eventually came back to Guatemala to live with relatives; the father stayed in Mexico the rest of his life. My acquaintance turned somber as he told me all this. He'd had too much to drink, and now his eyes were watery and red. "How could you do this to us?" he asked me. "What was the purpose? For you it was a weekend, nothing more. For us, it has been a lifetime—the lifetimes of two, three generations and how many more? Why do you gringos think, 'It's only little Guatemala, we can do what we want'? Why?"

His voice was more pained than angry. His eyes filled with tears, and he came close to breaking down altogether. A friend came over and patted him on the back, held him.

"His father never recovered from the defeat of Arbenz," the friend explained. "He committed suicide in Mexico, the poor man."

It was not an isolated case. Many Guatemalans were still bitter about the 1954 intervention, and for many it was a national trauma with psychological consequences. When the man spoke of the gringos' "weekend in Guatemala" he was alluding to a short story by the Nobel laureate Miguel Angel Asturias, whose fiction severely criticized the fruit company and the CIA for the overthrow of Arbenz. It was hard to deny that for the United States the events of 1954 were trifling, hardly worth the memory. But for Guatemalans, even those born long after 1954, the affair was devastating, like a disease that had become congenital, passed on from generation to generation. For many Guatemalans, the Good Neighbor stood next to Pedro de Alvarado as the great villains of Guatemalan history.

Near Morales, I turned off the Atlantic Highway onto a newly paved road that headed north to the Petén, Guatemala's jungle hinterland. The landscape was prehistoric tropical—huge drooping ferns and curling fronds. It was like driving into the Mesozoic diorama in a museum of natural history. I expected to see cavemen, dinosaurs maybe.

Instead I came to a bridge, a huge modern bridge, newly built to carry the Petén traffic across the Dulce River. On one side stretched the wide sheet of Lake Izabal. On the other side, the Dulce River began its short, dramatic run from the lake to the sea. On the lake side of the bridge was a stone fort built by the Spanish in the seventeenth century to protect the lake and the coast from marauding English pirates. Just downriver were several small islands where tourist hotels were sited.

I planned to spend a few days at one of these hotels, resting up for the rugged drive into the Petén. Down on the banks, I contracted a man to take me by motorized canoe downriver a few kilometers to the Hotel Catamarán.

On the island, a number of pleasure crafts were docked at the small marina, English names painted on their sterns: *Lady Lu, Kiss Me Kate, Liquid Assets.* The hotel was really nothing more than a collection of cabins on stilts. But there was a waterfront terrace where you could order beer or rum and watch the macaws twist their peculiar heads as they screeched and squawked.

At the next table sat a group of fishermen from Texas, middle-aged men on a holiday from winter.

"The president has a yacht out here," one said. He wore a baseball hat that had the word "Evinrude" scripted across it.

"What president?"

"President of here, Guaddymala."

"Who told you?"

"Bartender. He speaks English real good, that boy, but he can't add a bill up right," Evinrude said.

I went for a walk around the island to look at the various tropical birds whose clipped wings kept them imprisoned on the island. They had domesticated in their imprisonment, squawking and doing antics when I passed in hopes of getting some morsel from me. When I came back to the terrace in the gloaming, the fishermen were still there, a bottle of rum resting in a bucket of ice on the table between them. Their voices boomed in the tropic night.

"And they were all dead?"

"Every last one of them. Lying in the canoes, face up, picked clean by the vultures."

"I heard vultures go for the soft tissue first—eyes and genitalia."

"Ain't nothing soft about my genny-tail-ya, Roger."

Their bursts of laughter provoked excited squawks from the macaws; long after I retired to my cabin I lay listening to these distant peals and squawks, the feral cries of the jungle in darkness.

At dawn, the Texans and their pleasure craft were gone. As arranged, my man in the *cayuco* was waiting at the dock to take me down the Dulce River to the Carib town of Livingston. While I was drinking coffee on the terrace, an American couple came up the path to the dock. They wanted to go to Livingston, too, so we agreed to split the cost. The *cayuco* man revved the engine, and his son steadied the boat while we climbed in.

The Americans were young, good-looking, and smartly dressed. The woman, blonde and tanned, wore a khaki jumpsuit ordered from a safari outfitters catalogue. The man had on a photographer's vest, and two cameras dangled from his neck. The pockets of the vest were stuffed with plastic film canisters. I asked him if he were a photographer.

"Amateur," he shouted above the motor's roar. "Hobby of mine." He went back to polishing lenses, which preoccupied his attention most of the trip. Now and then he glanced up, selected something in the scene, and raised a camera to his eye. Occasionally, the woman tapped his shoulder and pointed to something on the shore or on the cliffs above. Squinting, frowning, the photographer considered the indicated subject, then shook his head. With each rejection, the woman pouted ever so slightly, but the photographer was too busy with lenses and filters to notice.

We were going too fast to enjoy the scenery. The Dulce River is renowned for the beauty of its twenty-five-kilometer run from lake to sea. It passes through a green-cliffed gorge, the sheer sides of which sprout a dense foliage. Trees grow from the cliffs. Vines and bromeliads dangle to the river's surface. There are birds everywhere—large seabirds resting on the islets and colorful tropical birds darting from one cliff to the other. Long trogon nests hang like slings from the branches overhead.

The woman, ignored by the photographer, undid the top of her pantsuit to reveal a mauve bikini top. She put on sunglasses and leaned back as best she could in the narrow boat. The driver and his teenaged son took turns stealing glances at this unexpected revelation, but there was more astonishment than lust in their eyes.

We arrived in Livingston at midmorning. Situated on a little bluff above where the Dulce River debouches into the Caribbean, the town is unique in Guatemala. Isolated from the rest of the country, accessible only by boat, Livingston belongs geographically and culturally more to Belize and the Caribbean islands. The people, descended from African slaves who intermarried with native islanders, are called the Garifuna. Their culture has almost no taint of Spanish influence (with the exception of Catholicism). In fact, the English, whose pirates and mahogany traders had long been active on the Caribbean coast of Central America, had contributed much more to Garifuna culture than the Spanish or Indians did. Many Garifuna speak a Belizean-accented English.

Life on the coast is decidedly more lax than in the rest of the country. The tensions of Guatemalan politics are almost never felt in Livingston. Indeed, there are few signs of authority, civil or military, in the town. Social mores are far less rigid; you can even smoke marijuana more or less openly. The residents of the town, and an increasing number of foreigners, relish the anarchical bliss of life in a place where laws are relative and the most ambitious thing to do is to fish. In this context, it is ironic that the town's name honors the Louisiana judge who drew up the criminal code used in Guatemala early in the nineteenth century.

Such a carefree place was bound to attract drifters and seekers. Livingston had the same communities of roaming merchants that you could find in many of the world's torrid outposts—Lebanese, East Indian, Chinese. Along with the ladinos and Maya who had moved to the coast, perhaps to escape the tensions and hassles of the interior, Livingston had the feel of a world village—or a pan-equatorial village at any rate. More and more young First World drifters were arriving as well, just to hang out, get high, and listen to Belizean reggae.

There was a lot of reggae to choose from. Every night, the dance music was pounding at the Disco Raymundo down by the docks and at the little shacks strung out along the shore. The foreigners went from one shack to another—wherever the jukebox was loud and the beer cold. Plenty of local girls were available for dancing, and some local boys, too. The local girls waited inside by the jukebox. The boys stood out on the docks, smoking marijuana and saying to each other, "Thas right, thas right, mon" whenever a pretty foreign girl came along. As night fell and lightning jolted the sky out over the Caribbean, I crossed from my hotel to the Disco Raymundo. A Bob Marley tape played, and the dancers were singing along: "Don't worry, 'bout a ting . . . " I bought a beer and went out to the docks to watch the distant storm. Huge bruise-colored clouds roiled on the horizon, and every few seconds a streak of lightning lit up and shivered the cumulonimbus mass. The photographer and his companion passed on the street above. They paused, peered down to the docks and the disco, seemed to consider coming down, and then passed on to the large hotel. "Thas right, mon," the Garifuna men murmured.

A man emerged out of the shadows and staggered down the dock toward me. I saw in a flash of lightning that he was an American. He pointed a finger at me and drew near.

"God, god, goddamn it!"

I looked for an escape route.

"I'm telling you there's money to be made in that shit. Talking about birdshit."

"Birdshit?"

"That's right, you got it. Bird, bird, bird SHIT!"

I nodded.

"You see, man, there's this group of islands out there some-

where"—he waved at the sea—"where all the seabirds go. I don't
know what kind of birds, man, but big birds, big fucking birds, and
they shit like crazy. *Huge* droppings. Tremendous turds. All day long
they flap and squawk and shit all over the rocks—yes, just like I'm
telling you. I seen it. Been out with the *tiburón* [shark] fishers and I
seen it. Man, you scrape that shit off the rocks and it's like pure, the
purest shit you can imagine. Best fertilizer in the world. It's worth
like a fortune and I just need to find a boat and start mining it. You
like that? Mining birdshit! You got a boat?"

"Sorry, boatless at the moment."

He frowned and pointed out to the pier where a power boat with a
tall tuna tower was tied up. "That ain't your boat?"

"No."

He swore and staggered off. As he passed the Garifuna men, he
mumbled, "Bird, bird, bird SHIT!" The Garifuna, watching him carefully, chorused, "Thas right, unh huh, mon."

Late that night, I went to the African Place, a restaurant done up
as a Moorish palace. The owner, an eccentric Spaniard, had spent
years decorating the walls with arcane symbols and mysterious tal-
ismans. No one could say why he did it, or why he chose to locate
his fantastic replica in so obscure a place as Livingston. But then the
Caribbean coast of Central America fostered numerous fantasies and
delusions. Foreigners were hatching get-rich schemes as early as the
1820s, when some confidence men, representing a fictitious Central
American country called the Kingdom of Poyais, sold a half million
dollars' worth of bonds to gullible investors. Gringos and other foreigners had been working the coast ever since in a variety of illicit
occupations from piracy to gun- and drug-running. A few, like the
filibuster William Walker, had died during their escapades. And a
few, like United Fruit's Minor Keith and Sam "the banana man" Ze-
murray, had struck a bonanza. In between there were hundreds of
small-time operators, such as those O. Henry wrote about in his
novel of Honduras, *Cabbages and Kings*. The contemporary versions
of these speculators were called Caribbean cowboys.

Livingston was a hot spot for the cowboys. I happened to meet
one in the African Place. He called himself a "wave consultant." A
blonde-haired California boy who shunned shirts and shoes, he had
been traveling up and down the coast looking for places to open up
skin diving and surfing stores. Around Belize and Livingston the diving was good, but there was no surf. For surfing, he said, Puerto Li-
món down in Costa Rica was the best. He went into rapture speaking
about it: "The place is unreal. It's a dream point. I'm talking about
beautiful lefts with jetty breaks up on Pico Mortal, twelve feet plus,

and I'm not shitting you. It's not for beginners, that's for goddamn sure. Curls like God gone crazy. The breaks come off a coral bottom, very tubular and powerful, man. And Salsa Beach—Jesus, it's dream surf. Shred a fifteen footer that's peeling perfect to the left and right and you'll know the *pura vida*, man. Your occasional closeout set and grinding barrels. Jesus God! It's a surrealistic arena, no shit! You can't lose with a surf shop there, you just can't lose."

And then back at one of the disco shacks there was a man who said he was "working the war" over in Salvador. He was up in Guate for a vacation, but was thinking of staying because he'd heard rumors of jungle treasure. Seems there was a gringo—no one knew if he was American, Canadian, British, or what, but he spoke English, anyway—who appeared in the capital three consecutive years at the beginning of the dry season. Each year, he hired a helicopter to fly him out to the *altiplano*, high in the mountains where there were no roads or towns, a place riddled with stupendous, impenetrable gorges, sheer cliffs, and riotous growth. He was let down at a certain spot, and then he would vanish for the months of the dry season, having arranged to be retrieved at the same spot on a certain day. He always went in with empty crates and returned with heavy, sealed crates. He would immediately leave the country with the crates, having bribed the authorities not to open them. Only after the third year did this unusual activity attract attention. The helicopter pilot spread the story, and the authorities began to think they might get more money out of the gringo than they had so far extracted. They wanted to know what he was up to, but they had nothing to go on. No one even knew the stranger's nationality. Had he discovered something? A lost city of Maya treasures? Spanish gold lost to the pirates? The mystery awoke curiosity and greed in many people, and they anxiously awaited the return of the inscrutable gringo.

He never came back. Perhaps he had already gotten everything out. But that was not what people chose to believe. They chose to believe that he was exceptionally astute, this gringo, knew that he would be a marked man after the inevitable arousal of curiosity, and so had quit while ahead. Way ahead, they assumed, because he had spent quite a pile in hiring the copter and in paying bribes. There was general agreement: the treasure must be fabulous.

The pilot swore he could get people to the mystery man's drop site—for a good fee, "claro que sí"—and there were takers. Maybe a dozen people had been left out there in successive dry seasons. Most came back quite empty, swearing there was nothing up there but wild forest. Some two or three never came back.

"Now wait a minute," I said. "Do you believe all this?"

The mercenary confessed that he did. "You have to believe the guy got onto something. So many witnesses to the external clues. But what it is, God knows. And then there's the map."

He produced a map of the area, supposedly a copy of the mystery gringo's map, that was being sold for twenty dollars. The mercenary had bought into it. "I had it checked out by a friend at the Geographical Survey, over at the embassy. He says it's legit, topography-wise. Those boys do flyovers of the whole area, and their line is, forget it. The site is as unapproachable as Antarctica in winter. They don't know what to make of the story. But I figure it might be worth a try, what with my jungle training and survival skills. All I need is some investors with balls enough to take a little risk."

He glanced sidelong at me. I didn't believe the "mercenary" about the treasure, and I suspected he was also lying about El Salvador. He didn't look like a soldier. Bald, potbellied, and pale—his whole appearance belied his "jungle training." But, then again, in the atmosphere of the Caribbean coast, especially in a Livingston disco, almost any fantasy sounded plausible enough.

The locals tried to get in on the game, too. I was walking back to my hotel late at night when, on a lonely side street, I passed a wheelbarrow (in Livingston, a town without cars, wheelbarrows were used for hauling goods.) Something stirred. I turned to see a boy clad only in underwear climb down from the wheelbarrow and run up to me. He was clutching something bulky. I peered, and he waved it in front of me. "Hey, buy me dah munkey, mistahs." The monkey rolled its sedated eyes up to me and seemed on the point of losing consciousness. The boy followed me all the way to the hotel, and when I glanced back before going in, he held up the heavy-headed monkey again, as though one more look would convince me to buy.

The Last Road

I HAD BEEN LOOKING FORWARD to driving the Petén highway for so long that when I finally got to it, the route inevitably proved disappointing. After the bridge over the Río Dulce, the road remained paved another thirty kilometers to the town of Modesto Méndez, where you could see Belize just down the Sarstún River. For the next 170 kilometers, the car slogged through mud, hopped ruts, and scraped ridges. It was a wild ride, and yet very dull. The jungle was already gone. Trucks and tractors had followed the road in and destroyed the thick stands of zapotes, cedars, ceibas, and mahoganies. Now there were weed-infested cornfields, in which the uprooted stumps of the old trees—blackened from burnings—lay like the victims of a fire bombing. Smoke from the ongoing fires hung in the humid air and closed off the horizon. Out there somewhere in the last shrunken remnants of rain forest were rare animals like the peccary, the ocelot, the coatimundi. But they kept far from the fields and roads, and I saw no sign of life except machete-bearing men and their smoke-spewing machines.

I bought gas in Poptún and the attendant—touching his eye, a Spanish warning—told me to be careful. The American owner of a nearby *finca* had been murdered recently. There were no suspects, no motives, no leads, but the attendant thought that the local army commander disliked foreigners. Go straight to Tikal, he said, and be especially careful at any military roadblocks.

But there were no roadblocks. One hundred more kilometers of burned-out rain forest brought me to Flores, an island city in Lake Petén–Itza. Cortés had once been here, during a quixotic and disastrous journey to Honduras by way of the swampy Mesoamerican lowlands. Bernal Díaz, chronicler of Cortés' enterprises, wrote that the city then on the island had "lofty *teocallis* [pyramids] glistening in the sun." Cortés was received warmly enough by the natives, who were descendants of the Maya; nevertheless, he forced them at swordpoint to break up their idols and accept Christianity. What the natives thought of the crucified Christ is unknown, but they took a great interest in a lame horse (a creature previously unknown to them) that Cortés apparently left behind him. When the conqueror was gone, they abruptly ignored the man on the cross and deified the horse. Spanish priests visiting the place more than a century later found equine idols being worshiped as the god of storms.

The great Maya ruins of Tikal lay sixty-five kilometers from Flores by a newly paved road. Tikal was now easy to get to. Most tourists came by airplane to Flores, and then bused to Tikal. The number of sleek air-conditioned tour buses hogging the road to the ruins was a portent but, happy to hear the tires hum on smooth asphalt, I paid no mind.

When, however, I arrived at Tikal National Park and entered the lobby of the tourist hotel—ludicrously named the Jungle Lodge— I realized how deluded I had been in thinking that I was on some archaeological adventure into the primitive wilds. All around me moiled another hundred or so adventurers, and they all wore pink baseball hats that read "Globe Gleaners." It was like walking into an Assembly of God picnic. The Globe Gleaners were mostly middle-aged Americans from somewhere in the Midwest. Their matching luggage lay scattered about the lobby and prevented access to the front desk, where their cicerone was arguing with the clerk.

I bypassed the lobby and went into the bar to wait out the Globe Gleaners' registration. The bar was done up in jungle decor. Samples of the Petén's fauna were tacked to the wall, the taxidermy so carelessly done that the carcasses looked like road kill. I was drinking a lukewarm Gallo when a hand fell on my shoulder and dug into my skin.

"Hola, hombre, what d'you say?"

I looked up into a splotchy red face shaded by a Panama hat. The man wore a smart khaki jacket and a shirt printed with blue parrots.

"Mind if I join you, what d'you say?"

I said nothing, and he sat down. He held a sweaty glass of rum and Coke. "What brings you here?" he asked.

"The golf," I said.

"There's a golf course here?" he said, turning around as though it might be in the bar somewhere.

"Sure. The Mayans loved the game."

"Oh, I get it. That's funny, very funny. Know what brings me here? I'm working, that's what."

He took out a notebook and wrote something. He sucked on his pen, and then flipped shut the pad. A sip from his drink, a scowl at the nearly empty glass, a snap of his fingers: he was engaged in an elaborate, self-conscious pantomime. "Otro, otro," he called when he had the barkeeper's attention. He turned back to me. "How do you say, 'No ice'? Ice is bad, you know. Frozen water, that's all it is, you know, and that means amoebas, dysentery. Just a traveler's tip, me to you. I'll bet you paid to come here, didn't you? Me, I've been all over the globe and never paid a red cent moneywise. You want to know how, do you?"

The rum and Coke appeared. He leaned forward and huddled over it, as if I had threatened to steal it. "Do you?"

"I can't imagine," I said.

"Hah!" His face showed triumph. He tapped the notebook. "Expense account. I write, that's what I do. And newspapers pay me to go. Expense account, you see."

"You're a writer?"

"Indeed I am. Freelance correspondent. I sold seven articles last year, cleared twenty-five hundred bucks, not including the free travel and the expense account."

"What do you write?"

"Articles, hombre, articles. Sunday travel sections, features, the whole nine yards. I sell to newspapers all over the South. I can sell anything I write."

"Anything?"

He turned solemn. "It's the secret of my craft," he said. "You have to know what an editor wants. You think he cares what you think? No! Of course not. He doesn't give a hoot about your big ideas. He wants to sell papers. There's no room for ego, believe you me. You give them what they want."

"And what do they want?"

"Local color."

"Local color?"

"Local color."

We pondered this revelation.

"You mean like 'redolent markets and ancient mysteries'?" I asked.

He pointed his Parker at me. "There you go, you got it. Redolent markets, that's good." The notepad flipped open again and he wrote.

Then, abruptly, the freelance correspondent took his leave. "Remember," he said as he stood above me, shook my hand, and winked. "Remember, no one cares what you think. Call it my motto. Adiós, amigo."

He left me with his motto and a bill for three rum and Cokes, no ice.

When I finally got checked into the Jungle Lodge, it was too late to walk out to the Acropolis and see the pyramids. I looked into the dining room, but it was already full of Gleaners poking their plates and making noises. I went out into the hot, insect-loud evening. There were some eating shacks over by the entrance to the park. I chose one with a screened-in porch and sat at a table covered by a blue-checkered plastic spread. The humidity had balled up the salt in the shaker and a trail of ants crossed the plastic spread to the bowl of sugar. Just off the porch was a tin-roofed shelter, no walls, under which a beaming, buxom woman labored over an adobe stove. "Eh, joven," she called through the screen. "What would you like? I have chicken, pig, rice, beans, plantains."

I ordered the rice and beans and another lukewarm beer. "Is business good?" I asked her when she brought the food.

"Oh, yes, very good."

"Many tourists?"

"Ay, no, the tourists do not come here," she said. Only the park workers and the "hippies" came to her little *comedor*, she explained.

"The hippies? What hippies?"

She pointed to a grassy area near the parking lot. "Those who stay over there."

Thus I found out that camping was allowed at Tikal. There were some shelters where, for a few dollars, you could string up a hammock. After a few beers, I took a fancy to the idea of sleeping outside—it would beat passing the night in the Jungle Lodge with the gabby Gleaners, even if I lost my money.

I claimed a shelter and strung up my hammock—a tourist purchase that had finally come in handy. Sure enough, I could just make out the dark form of a pop-top camper in the moonlight. Jethro Tull's "Thick As a Brick" pounded in the night above the insect chirrups, and an incense I associated with college dorms came drifting on the scant breeze, competing with the dominant smell of mold and decay. I coated myself with repellent, climbed into the hammock, and stared up at the night sky, where Scorpio was making its slow crawl across the Milky Way, until I fell asleep.

At dawn I hiked to the ruins, about a twenty-minute walk from the hotels to the main plaza, where the highest pyramids rose above the jungle. The first two hours, when I was alone in the park, were tremendous. Wild turkeys dashed across the plastered roads the Maya had built. Spider monkeys swung in the branches overhead and toucans pecked at berries and fruit. A national park, the rain forest around Tikal remained pristine; in early morning and in the evening, the animals emerged to hunt and to forage. The trees, tall and overarching, provided the canopy that would sustain the prolificacy of a tropical forest.

In the main plaza, a mist hung in the treetops and on the pyramids. It was ghostly and still, and I tried to imagine what this might have looked like as a teeming city. The great mystery of the Maya—Why did they abandon their huge cities at the height of their accomplishments?—has never been satisfactorily answered. Archaeologists call it the collapse of the Classic Maya civilization. The Maya lived on after the collapse, of course; they live on today. But suddenly in about the tenth century AD they stopped building the huge structures they had been constructing for several centuries. They stopped carving stelae and recording dates. They didn't disappear, as many people think, but they did stop practicing their culture, and they abandoned their principal cities to the jungle, a jungle so dense that more than seven hundred years passed before the ruins were revealed.

But the real mystery of the Maya concerns their Weltanschauung. You look at the massive architecture; you study the stelae carved over with fantastic dates and berserk calculations (one carving, for example, commemorates a date older than the universe); you gaze at depictions of vision serpents and cosmic monsters and world trees as they file along a frieze, and you ask yourself: What mad dreams drove these people? Dogs beating drums; grotesques guiding canoes, their wrists bent to their foreheads in a gesture of death; kings exacting blood from their penises, and queens drawing thorny cords through their pierced tongues. What was it all about? What were they thinking?

I was standing atop Temple I (145 feet high) when the hordes arrived. I watched and heard them come up the causeway, roaming bands of tourists, louder than howler monkeys, led by the pink-hatted Gleaners. They reached the Great Plaza and swarmed over the ancient stones. Cameras clicked. Video cams whirred. "The first thing we see as we travel around the world," Claude Lévi-Strauss wrote in *Tristes Tropiques*, "is our own filth thrown into the face of mankind." My own experience confirmed this rather drastic statement.

In the North Acropolis, a sudden shower sent everyone scurrying for shelter. A gush of rain, flashes of lightning, reports of thunder: some of the tourists sent up wails and waddled in circles until they found safety under a wattled structure. Huffing and wheezing noises mixed with the delighted chortles of the more good-natured tourists, who wanted excitement and adventure to relate to the folks back home.

"Wait till I tell Mrs. Hardy about this!"

"She won't believe a word of it!"

A cicerone in a soaked pink camp shirt ran up to the shelter. "Gleaners? Any Globe Gleaners here?"

No one answered him. "Oh, where in hell—" he swore and then dashed off into the downpour.

"He's not as pleasant as our guide," someone said.

"Pleasanter'n ours. We got us a regular Atiller leading us. Kind of cute, though."

When the rain diminished, I walked off into the drizzle. Near the periphery of the lost city, where branch trails dove into the jungle toward less accessible ruins, a boy came up to me: one of the many locals hawking trinkets to the tourists.

"I'm not buying," I told him. He stared up at me and said nothing for a moment. When I started walking off, he followed.

"I'm not buying," I said again.

"Well, I'm not selling," he said.

This caught my attention. "What do you want, then?" I asked.

"I am a guide," he said, with great dignity. "I thought maybe you want to see the idol."

"Idol? What idol?"

He waved to the trees beyond the path.

"How much?" I asked.

He shrugged, as though the question pained him. "What does it matter?" he said.

I liked his nonchalance, so I agreed to hire him. We climbed over a few ruined walls, and then took a path into the forest. Before long, we reached a giant tree with spikes on its trunk and lianas drooping from the branches—a ceiba, the sacred tree of the Maya. The boy pointed. A little stone image had been placed at the base of the tree. Some incense was burning, two coils of smoke rising in the air.

"What is it?"

"The idol."

"What kind of idol?"

The boy shrugged again. It looked fake to me.

"It's not authentic," I said.

The boy sighed. "No, it's not authentic."

"Then why do you show it to me?"

He shrugged.

"Who put it there?"

"My grandparents." He pointed, and through the trees I saw a dilapidated shelter. Some children stood silent outside it, watching us.

"Do they put it here for the tourists, or do they pray to it also?"

The boy shrugged again. "What does it matter? They are ignorants."

He didn't say anything else, but his tone spoke volumes. I could imagine him saying, "What made you think there would be authenticity, gringo? You didn't pay so much money and come so far for 'the authentic.' It was fantasy and exotica that you wanted all along. I'd show you 'the authentic,' but you could not bear it if you saw it."

I gave him his money.

After two days of sightseeing the ruins in the company of my compatriots, I had had enough. My map showed one last road. It ran from Tikal to another ruin, Uaxactún: twenty-five kilometers traversible only in dry season. No buses. No tourists. It began in the parking lot of the Jungle Lodge and ran due north, where it quickly got lost in the towering trees of the virgin jungle. I asked about road conditions, got conflicting reports from the park workers and an incredulous stare from the factotum of the Jungle Lodge.

"But, señor, why go there? There's nothing to see."

I did not need further encouragement.

The road turned out to be in fairly good condition. Because it did not carry much traffic, it had not deteriorated in the way the Petén highway had. There were places where it narrowed to the size of a track, and there were several gullies and washes where I had to inch the car forward, expecting at any moment to puncture the oil pan. Once I came upon a two hundred–foot trench of mud, and I had to get out of the car and look for a way around it. Now and then there were pole and thatch houses, small *ranchos* with maize plots and fenced-in pales where chickens and children scratched at the soil. The kids ran out to see the passing car. I honked and waved; they stared at the unexpected apparition and slowly raised limp hands to salute it. A few energetic boys ran alongside the car as it bounced over the ruts.

In tiny Uaxactún, I drank several bottles of soda in the town's only store. I had come a long way, penetrated the most remote land I could imagine, but I had not succeeded in outrunning Coca-Cola. The store owner pointed me toward the airstrip, which cut right through the ruins of the Maya city. Followed by every dog and child in town, I walked over to see the temples and palaces, such as they were. Little excavation had been done in Uaxactún; the structures remained covered with humus and clotted with vegetation, almost exactly as they had been found by the great Mayanist Sylvanus Morley at the beginning of the century.

I sat on a stone and took out my map. The children peered over my shoulder, and we had a brief geography lesson. Here is Guatemala, I said. This is the capital, the oceans, and the mountains. All these words are the names of towns and cities. And these lines are roads. Up here is Tikal, and this dot is Uaxactún.

There were only a few scattered names in the Petén portion of the map, and a couple of dotted lines indicating unpaved roads. One of the older boys studied the map, compared the crowded southern part with the empty north, and said, "Aquí no hay nada." Here there is nothing. They all giggled.

Back at the store, I bought them Chiclets—an odd gift, perhaps, since chicle, the resin from which chewing gum was once made, came from the sapodilla trees found in the Petén. Once there was a pretty good chicle trade in these parts, and the *chicleros* could make money bleeding trees. But most chewing gum was now made with cheaper synthetics and only a few hardy men carried on the trade.

I met one of them on my way out of town. I had noticed a track leading away from the airstrip across the dry jungle savanna. I drove over to it, got out of the car, and stared down the narrow brown ruts that wound through the grassland. Far off, the giant hardwoods of the rain forest reached for a sky heavy with cumuli. What lay down this track, I wondered? What beautiful and implausible Nowhere did it lead to?

The man came up behind me, leading a mule. "Buenas," he said as he passed me by and started on the track.

"Excuse me," I said.

He turned and looked back at me. The mule paused, machete and saddlebags dangling on its flanks. The man was wizened and grisly. He grinned, and I saw he had but a few teeth. The brim of his white straw hat shadowed his face. Half of one ear was missing.

"Sí, extranjero?" he said. Yes, stranger?

"I only wanted to know—where does this trail go?"

"Ay, lejos—muy lejos." Far, very far. There was an encampment, he said, where the *chicleros* lived while they worked in the forest. No women. No families. Just men, mules, and the jungle. The camp was called Los Apóstoles.

I asked the *chiclero* his name.

He grinned. "Don Esteban, por el mártir" [after the martyr].

"That's a good name," I said. "Tell me, Don Esteban, can a vehicle travel on this trail?"

He looked with jovial derision at my car—a car built in the suburbs of Detroit, a place so fantastic and distant Don Esteban could not imagine it.

He looked me right in the eyes. "You'd never make it," he said. The mule snorted and Don Esteban turned back to the trail. "Adiós, extranjero," he shouted over his shoulder.

I was called many things in Guatemala, everything from "illustrious doctor" and "eminent critic" to "*gringo jodido*." But this last epithet, given to me by Don Esteban, seemed the most appropriate: *extranjero*. After two years in Guatemala I remained a stranger.

I watched Don Esteban walk away and I tried to imagine the lost world to which he went. My road led back to Tikal and the capital. On my desk in the rented house where I had lived for two years was an airplane ticket. In a week I would be back in the States.

A hot wind blew, the cicadas sang in the savanna, and the grumbling thunderheads that gathered on the horizon threatened to make my return difficult. But I lingered at the crossroads and watched the disappearing speck that was man and mule. Then I turned the car around. I had no choice.

Bibliography

Alvarado, Pedro de. 1924. *An Account of the Conquest of Yucatan in 1524*. Sedley J. Mackie, ed. New York: The Cortes Society.

Americas Watch. 1990. *Messengers of Death: Human Rights in Guatemala, Nov. 1988 to March 1990*. New York: Americas Watch.

Amnesty International. 1989. *Guatemala: Human Rights Violations under the Civilian Government*. New York: Amnesty International.

Barry, Tom. 1989. *Guatemala: A Country Guide*. Albuquerque: Inter-Hemispheric Education Resource Center.

Boddam-Whetham, J. W. 1877. *Across Central America*. London: Hurst and Blackett.

Bunzel, Ruth. 1959. *Chichicastenango: A Guatemalan Village*. Seattle: University of Washington Press.

Calvert, Peter. 1985. *Guatemala: A Nation in Turmoil*. Boulder, Colo.: Westview Press.

Carmack, Robert M., ed. 1988. *Harvest of Violence*. Norman: University of Oklahoma Press.

Díaz del Castillo, Bernal. 1965. *The Discovery and Conquest of Mexico*. New York: Noonday Press.

Gage, Thomas. 1648 (reprinted 1928). *The English-American, or A New Survey of the West Indies*. London: Routledge.

Galeano, Eduardo. 1969. *Guatemala: Occupied Country*. New York: Monthly Review.

Greene, Graham. 1939. *The Lawless Roads*. London: Wm. Heinemann.

Handy, Jim. 1984. *Gift of the Devil: A History of Guatemala*. Boston: South End Press.

Huxley, Aldous. 1934. *Beyond the Mexique Bay*. London: Chatto and Windus Ltd.

Immerman, Richard H. 1982. *The CIA in Guatemala*. Austin: University of Texas Press.

Jackson, Joseph Henry. 1937. *Notes on a Drum*. New York: Macmillan.

Jonas, Susanne. 1991. *The Battle for Guatemala: Rebels, Death Squads, and U.S. Power*. Boulder, Colo.: Westview.

LaFeber, Walter. 1984. *Inevitable Revolutions*. New York: Norton.

Lévi-Strauss, Claude. 1978. *Tristes Tropiques*. New York: Atheneum.

Macaulay, Rose. 1930. *Staying with Relations*. London: Collins, Ltd.

Martínez Peláez, Severo. 1985. *Motines de Indios*. Puebla, Mexico: Universidad Autónoma de Puebla.

Maslow, Jonathan Evan. 1986. *Bird of Life, Bird of Death*. New York: Laurel Trade, Dell Publishing.

Memmi, Albert. 1967. *The Colonizer and the Colonized*. Boston: Beacon.

Menchú, Rigoberta. 1984. *I, Rigoberta Menchú*. Elisabeth Burgos-Debray, ed. Ann Wright, trans. New York: Verso.

Montejo, Víctor. 1987. *Testimony: Death of a Guatemalan Village*. Willimantic, Conn.: Curbstone Press.

Recinos, Adrián, Delia Goetz, and Dionisio José Chonay, trans. 1953. *The Annals of the Cakchiquels*. Norman: University of Oklahoma Press.

Sanborn, Helen. 1886. *A Winter in Central America and Mexico*. Boston: Lee and Shepard.

Schlesinger, Stephen, and Stephen Kinzer. 1983. *Bitter Fruit*. New York: Doubleday and Anchor Books.

Schele, Linda, and David Freidel. 1990. *A Forest of Kings: The Untold Story of the Ancient Maya*. New York: William Morrow and Co.

Sexton, James D., ed. and trans. 1981. *Son of Tecún Umán: A Mayan Indian Tells His Life Story*. Tucson: University of Arizona Press.

————. 1992. *Mayan Folktales*. New York: Doubleday.

Simon, Jean-Marie. 1987. *Guatemala: Eternal Spring, Eternal Tyranny*. New York: Norton.

Smith, Carol A. 1990. *Guatemalan Indians and the State: 1540–1988*. Austin: University of Texas Press.

Stephens, John L. 1841 (reprint 1963). *Incidents of Travel in Central America, Chiapas, and Yucatan*. New York: Dover.

Tedlock, Dennis, trans. 1985. *Popol Vuh*. New York: Simon and Schuster.

Theroux, Paul. 1979. *The Old Patagonian Express*. New York: Houghton Mifflin.

Tisdel, Edine. 1910. "Guatemala: Country of the Future." *National Geographic* 21: 596–624.

Wright, Ronald. 1989. *Time among the Maya: Travels in Belize, Guatemala, and Mexico*. New York: Weidenfeld & Nicolson.

Index